Gunboat Diplomacy
in the Wilson Era

The U.S. Navy in Haiti, 1915-1916

DAVID HEALY

THE UNIVERSITY OF WISCONSIN PRESS

Published 1976
The University of Wisconsin Press
Box 1379, Madison, Wisconsin 53701

The University of Wisconsin Press, Ltd.
70 Great Russell Street, London

First printing

Printed in the United States of America

For LC CIP information see the colophon

ISBN 0-299-06980-X

This book is for

Matthew, Ellen, and Jonathan Healy,

with love

Contents

Acknowledgments

A NUMBER of people and institutions aided my work on this book. I located portions of its data with the help of Mr. Harry Schwartz of the Navy Department Branch, National Archives of the United States, and Lieutenant M. J. Collet of the United States Naval Historical Foundation, both in Washington, D.C. The Frères de l'Instruction Chrétienne in Port-au-Prince, Haiti, generously made available their fine library of Haitian materials, while Brother Ernest Even spared no effort to see that I received the maximum benefit from its use. My research in Haiti was made possible by grants from the American Council of Learned Societies and the Graduate School of the University of Wisconsin–Milwaukee. Of my colleagues at that university who have cheerfully shared their knowledge and insights upon request, I especially thank Professors Keith Bryant, Bruce Fetter, Frederick Harrod, Reginald Horsman, and Walter Weare. Edward L. Beach, Jr., kindly supplied the photograph of his father, Captain Edward L. Beach. My wife, Ann Erickson Healy, an accomplished critic and historian, has as usual been the greatest help of all.

GUNBOAT DIPLOMACY IN THE WILSON ERA

The U.S. Navy in Haiti, 1915-1916

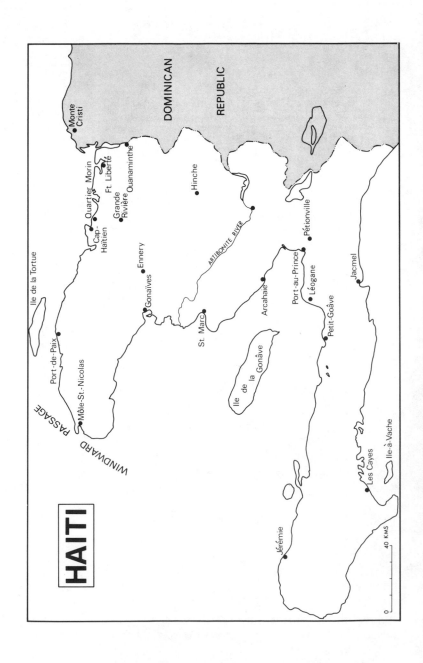

Introduction

WHEN WOODROW Wilson presented the Fourteen Points summarizing his peace proposals to the American Congress in January of 1918, he ended his presentation with a general statement: "An evident principle runs through the whole program I have outlined. It is the principle of justice to all peoples and nationalities, and their right to live on equal terms of liberty and safety with one another, whether they be strong or weak."

Yet the principle of the equality of nations had not characterized United States policy in the Caribbean as it had developed since the 1890s. Nor did Woodrow Wilson's presidency see any move to change that policy; rather, Wilson became the most interventionist United States president to date. The contradiction between his pronouncements regarding Europe and his practices closer to home became as apparent to his contemporaries as they have remained to subsequent students of his administration. Contrary to mythology, Wilson acted not from a single, global foreign policy, but from multiple policies, based on differing assumptions for different regions.

One of these assumptions, inherited from his predecessors, was that the Caribbean area had a unique strategic significance for the United States. The newly completed Panama Canal spawned a kind of "life-line diplomacy" which reenforced traditional fears of European penetration of the region and led United States policy-makers to desire political stability in all of the nearby countries. In spite of this desire, the opposite condition prevailed: the Caribbean was filled with weak, chaotic states perennially in financial bondage to European creditors, and therefore perennially inviting European intervention. With the outbreak of the Great War in Europe, American security fears increased greatly, at the same time that the actual likelihood of foreign interventions was paradoxically reduced.

In addition to inheriting these strategic fears and the numerous political and financial arrangements already created to serve them, Wilson had his own convictions about the countries of the Caribbean. They were not, he felt, ready for self-government in any sense comparable to the older and more advanced societies of Europe. They were, to be blunt, backward, and their backwardness was directly related to their political instability. To Woodrow Wilson's ideologue eye, social and economic progress required United States-style representative democracy and the atmosphere of liberty and security which presumably accompanied it. If the Caribbean peoples would respect their own constitutions and turn their backs on revolution and disorder, if they would obey the rule of law rather than that of men, then social progress and economic growth would surely follow. If they would not do so, then in the name of progress the United States must make them.

It was in this spirit that the Wilson administration plunged into the increasingly troubled affairs of the region to the south. At first the president himself attempted to direct United States activity, particularly regarding the massive Mexican Revolution which overshadowed other regional developments during his first term. As events became more complex and American intervention touched more and more countries, however, Wilson had to delegate most of these tasks to his State Department and to the diplomats and commanders on the spot. While he still sought to provide them with his own perspective and frame of reference, the time came when he could do little more.

Within this Wilsonian framework, United States policy in the Caribbean worked itself out in part through conventional means: the activities of the State Department, its diplomats, and consular officials; the influence of private loans, investments, financial agreements, and purchases of local products. In addition it acted through military means, employed in the periodic use of armed interventions at crucial points. In some respects Wilsonian policy in the Caribbean can best be examined in terms of these interventions, for the moment of intervention often saw the most rapid crystallization of policy, while the method itself had no small impact on the results. Furthermore, the admirals and generals who directed these applications of force often had to form their own interpretations of their purposes, in the absence of clear directives or effective supervision from Washington. In a study of post-Spanish War Cuban policy some years ago, I found that the United States Army officers who commanded the first Cuban occupation exercised an important influence on the decisions which collectively determined the future status of Cuba, while then-Secretary of War Elihu Root held a pivotal position in shaping the resultant policy. In short, the army and the War Department constituted the vital center which produced long-range Cuban policy. Similarly, the navy (including the Marine Corps) was at times deeply involved in the formation, as well as the implementation, of United States policy in the Caribbean. Neither conventional diplomatic history nor economic analysis can fully expose this dimension of the Caribbean story, and it therefore merits more scholarly attention than it has received, for generalizations about the motives and methods of United States actions in the region can be made with confidence only after the military dimension has been integrated with the others.

The Haitian occupation which was initiated in 1915 is a particularly fruitful case through which to study the multiple facets of Wilsonian intervention, as well as accompanying problems of cross-cultural contact. As was usual in American practice, it was accomplished through improvisation on the spot rather than prior planning, and the commanding admiral acted virtually without guidance until some of the crucial decisions had been made. The civil authorities in Washington chose to leave the military almost solely responsible for making the necessary political arrangements, taking direct control only after an adequate working structure was in place. The naval commander in charge, Rear Admiral William B. Caperton, achieved a United States take-over in Haiti with relatively little bloodshed, through a skillful combination of military tactics, diplomatic negotiation, political management, intimidation, and deception. The Haitians, caught in a moment of internal crisis, were unable to unite in an effective response. Yet the initial success in fastening United States rule upon Haiti soon gave way to mounting difficulties in pursuing policies there that harmonized with constitutional democracy. Within a year, Wilsonian intervention had become indistinguishable from previous kinds, and the remnants of the Haitian political system inadequately concealed the primacy of a United States military autocracy. This, in brief, is the story contained in the following pages.

1
Introducing Haiti
and the Cruiser Squadron

THEY HAD been detained by fog in Chesapeake Bay, but now the big armored cruiser shouldered her way through the cold, rough seas of the open Atlantic. Cape Hatteras was almost abeam, somewhere off to starboard beyond the miles of tumbling water. As usual it was rough off Hatteras, but soon their course would carry them southward into the Gulf Stream, where the harsh January wind would turn soft and balmy. In the meantime the wind shrieked about the bridge, and the black latticework of the cage-type foremast swung to and fro as the ship rolled, its basket-like pattern silhouetted against the cloudy sky. Aft of it, and in unison, swung the four tall smokestacks and the military aftermast with its old-fashioned fighting tops. Last of all came the wake, churned by the twin propellors into a path of tortured foam which broadened and dispersed in sinuous eddies far astern of the ship.

U.S.S. *Washington* had been built as a flagship, specially fitted with the offices and extra quarters needed for an admiral and his staff. She was fulfilling her builders'

intention in this January of 1915, for she flew the flag of
Rear Admiral William B. Caperton, the new commander of
the Atlantic Fleet's Cruiser Squadron. It was too early in
the cruise for *Washington*'s men to know their admiral, but
most of the ship's company had already seen him about
the decks—a trim, smallish man with the weathered face of
a sailor, his hair and mustache silver-gray beneath his
gold-braided hat. As to his personal characteristics, they
would be revealed soon enough, everyone knew, for an
admiral's presence aboard ship was inevitably somewhat
overpowering. Carrying an admiral, in fact, was apt to be a
trial, for it meant too many people packed aboard, too
much ceremonial, too much "brass" coming and going; but
Washington would have to obey her orders and make the
best of it.

The ship's present orders stemmed from the circum-
stance that her admiral was taking over a new and
unfamiliar command. Dated January 5, 1915, they
directed Caperton to visit in succession Santo Domingo
City, Santo Domingo; Port-au-Prince, Haiti; Havana, Cuba;
and Tampico, Tuxpan, and Vera Cruz, Mexico. At each of
these ports he was to interview the American minister or
consul and inform himself of local political conditions, at
the same time inspecting such ships of his command as he
fell in with. The Navy Department, the orders said, would
"be pleased to receive any suggestions or recommendations
you may consider it necessary to make in connection with
the political situation in West Indian and Mexican
Waters."[1]

As these orders suggested, Admiral Caperton was to
take up duties as much political as military. The Caribbean
area had become an "American lake" since 1898, and the
administration of President Woodrow Wilson had shown
little hesitation at becoming further enmeshed in the
perennially troubled affairs of the nations which lay
in its waters. Though Wilson had come to office decrying
interventionism, his thinking had changed under the
impact of the Mexican Revolution and the Great War in

Europe. He soon echoed his predecessors in calling for stability in the regions to the south, and was even quicker than they had been to turn to intervention in order to achieve it.

In brisk succession, crises arose or tensions developed in one Caribbean country after another, and each time United States diplomats cried for warships to bring their message of American power. The seizure of Vera Cruz in 1914 by United States naval forces had brought the country to the brink of war with Mexico, and for months thereafter had diverted a division of battleships from its allotted place in the Atlantic Fleet. Other fleet units had had to go to Haiti, Santo Domingo, and Central America with a frequency which exhausted the forbearance of the navy's chiefs.

Admiral Bradley A. Fiske, then in charge of naval operations, had expostulated about the situation to the State Department only a few months before Caperton sailed. Fiske told the department's counsellor, Robert Lansing, that the constant dispersion of his ships to pursue the varied diplomatic tasks set by the State Department was wearing away the fleet's efficiency. The nation needed a powerful fleet, trained and concentrated in readiness for events. Fiske insisted that the war in Europe enhanced this need; the navy might soon be called to defend the country against formidable enemies. Yet the available forces were continually detached to special duty, sabotaging the fleet drills and maneuvers essential to combat-readiness.[2]

The alternative sought by the navy was to delegate the diplomatic work principally to the smaller and older vessels of the Atlantic Fleet, leaving the battleships and their essential consorts without distraction to constitute the fighting fleet. It was mainly from these lesser vessels that the Cruiser Squadron was made up. Though constituting a single command, the squadron was not normally expected to operate as a unit, but was meant to provide the vessels needed for diplomatic work about the Caribbean and Mexican shores. Scattered in ones and twos,

Caperton's ships were spread over a thousand miles of water, always available for the contingencies of gunboat diplomacy. Reenforcements would be needed in case of real trouble, but short of that Caperton's superiors expected him to do the best he could with what he had to safeguard United States interests and to further United States policies in the Caribbean.[3]

The sheer range of these interests and policies must have been sobering to the new commander, for they spanned the Caribbean from end to end, and they contained the potential for a rich variety of crises. There were first of all those regions for which the United States government was directly responsible, like Puerto Rico and the strategically vital Panama Canal Zone. Besides these actual possessions, there were the formal or de facto protectorates of the United States. The largest and most important of these was Cuba, but a more recent protectorate was crystallizing in Nicaragua by the end of 1914. While all of these places required close watching, the most active problem areas in January 1915 were Mexico, Santo Domingo, and Haiti, the three countries which Caperton was now ordered to visit. Mexico, wracked by a massive revolutionary struggle, had recently attracted the most official attention, while the collapse of political stability in Santo Domingo had brought the United States to interfere more and more significantly in Dominican internal affairs.

In Haiti, events had not yet run so far, but 1914 had seen a steady growth in United States involvement in the affairs of that country. Washington officials increasingly saw the poor and unstable Haitian nation as another obstacle to the United States goal of Caribbean stability, and the State Department began to consider a United States customs receivership in Haiti similar to that which had been instituted in Santo Domingo in Theodore Roosevelt's day. As in the earlier Dominican case, rumors that Germany contemplated intervention or financial participation in Haitian affairs lent urgency to State Department thinking.

As the months passed, and general succeeded general at an ever-faster pace in the presidential mansion at Port-au-Prince, Washington's suave suggestions about a new relationship gave way to blunter and more pointed prodding. The State Department sent down a draft treaty in July 1914 which spelled out the terms of the proposed customs receivership, but the incumbent government fell before negotiations could bear fruit. By October, Robert Lansing was urging the president to strengthen the naval forces in Haitian waters in preparation for more vigorous attempts to reach a settlement, while the Haitian press and public denounced the American threat to the nation's independence.[4]

The country which thus came under the scrutiny of United States policy-makers was perhaps the poorest and most isolated in the Western Hemisphere. A fabulously rich French sugar colony in the eighteenth century, the island had been populated mostly with African slaves, in bondage to a dangerously small white planter class. Weakened by the French Revolution, this precarious minority control cracked apart, ushering in a decade of savage struggles between the local whites, the free mulattos who made up a nonwhite elite, the armies and officials which came periodically from France, and, most decisively, the nine-tenths of the population composed by the black slaves. By 1804 all of the whites had been killed or expelled, and their towns and plantations lay in ruins. Haiti became a black republic, the first in the world, while the horrifying stories brought to the outside world by the white survivors made of her an international pariah.

The Haitian reality which developed in the ensuing decades, however, was far from matching the lurid tales so dear to foreigners. A simple squatter agriculture absorbed the bulk of the population in a preponderantly rural society. At the capital, black generals, usually from the rugged North, vied for the presidency, while the educated mulatto minority actually administered the affairs of government. The demise of sugar planting ended most of the country's foreign trade, while laws against foreign land-holding were designed to prevent the formation of a new white planting class. For much of the century Haiti slowly evolved from these beginnings, her shrunken foreign trade carried on by resident Europeans, her educated elite leaving the island to acquire their polish. In the later nineteenth century a succession of strong presidents and a modest boom in wild coffee led to relative national well-being and prosperity, which gave way early in the twentieth century to renewed political turbulence.[5]

In spite of its substantial isolation, Haiti was plagued with periodic foreign interference. Lacking capital and technical competence, the Haitians were obliged to undertake their few public works via the processes of bond-issuing, concession-granting, or both. Shady foreign promoters and slipshod domestic administrations produced a harvest of foreign claims and legal disputes, often attracting the diplomatic intervention of the foreigners' home governments. For a long time, France and Germany were the countries most actively involved. The United States, which refused to extend diplomatic recognition to Haiti until 1862, became interested after the Civil War in a possible naval station at the Môle-Saint-Nicolas on the northwest coast. In the 1880s one Haitian government tried unsuccessfully to sell the Môle to the United States, while in a quick reversal a succeeding regime resisted an aggressive American drive to acquire the place during the throes of a local civil conflict. United States interest in Haiti then flagged after 1891, but revived a generation later out of concern that Europeans might be acquiring excessive economic power there. French interests, and to a lesser extent German ones, held the national debt and sought to control the government's fiscal affairs. When the National Bank of Haiti was reorganized in 1910, Secretary of State Philander Knox successfully demanded that United States bankers join those of France and Germany in its ownership, and thereafter Washington kept an eye on the financial situation in Port-au-Prince. This initial interest in Haiti's internal affairs soon took on broader dimensions as her political system was undermined by an accelerating cycle of armed revolution, every year seeing the overthrow of another president.[6]

So matters stood when *Washington* and her complement sailed southward in January 1915. They would find the country which they were so soon to visit a picturesque, mountainous, poverty-haunted land, a country teeming with a rural peasantry which crowded the inland roads and villages and whose sheer numbers were slowly stripping the timber and the topsoil from the terrain. Black, illiterate, disease-ridden and sometimes hungry, the country population constituted a backward village culture, its members subsisting on crops which grew semiwild throughout the island. Few had legal title to their land, from which they gathered coffee, bananas, cotton, sugar. On it, too, they planted garden vegetables, supplementing them with chickens, a few goats, and fewer pigs. Whether in the bold northern hills of the *caco* country or on the great southern peninsula, they lived in dirt-floored huts and wore a minimum of ragged clothing. Shocked at their ignorance and poverty, an over-harsh American traveler declared these country people "little above the animal."[7] Those who knew them, however, found them courteous and kindly and hospitable beyond their scanty means. It was true, nevertheless, that there were in all of Haiti virtually no real farms or plantations, little fencing, no selective breeding of livestock or use of farm implements beyond the hoe and sharpened stick. Roads for wheeled vehicles scarcely existed outside a few cities; goods were conveyed for long distances by the women, walking on foot-paths and carrying loads on their heads.

On the coastal fringes of this poor and rugged land lay many small towns and a few cities, the two largest being Port-au-Prince and Cap-Haïtien. No one knew the exact population of any of these, but the capital was thought to contain from sixty to one hundred thousand inhabitants, and Cap-Haïtien eighteen to thirty thousand. A few more towns were judged to have populations of ten thousand or so, but most of the remainder were tiny. In the few principal cities and towns dwelt the bulk of Haiti's elite, the small minority of educated upper-class families who held virtually all public offices, monopolized the professions, and made up the genteel society of the country. Heavily concentrated in and around Port-au-Prince, this elite could be distinguished from the mass of the people by so simple an act as wearing shoes. In fact, an unbridgeable gulf existed between the peasantry and their social betters. The former did not even speak French, but a French-African *patois* called *Créole,* while the latter prided themselves on the purity with which they had preserved their borrowed mother tongue. Many of the elite had been to France; all of them were devotees of French culture, and an impressive chorus of foreign witnesses attested that they were indeed polished, intelligent, charming, and literate.

In a total population generally estimated at around two million souls, the upper class comprised, by various estimates, from 1 to 5 percent. One observer judged that about 5,000 members of this top stratum actively engaged in politics and office-holding, effectively running the country. While there was a trickle of movement across class lines, membership in the elite was so largely hereditary that a leading student of Haitian society labeled it a caste rather than a mere class.[8] There was even a corresponding color distinction: the elite tended to be brown-skinned, while the peasantry was black. Not very rich by foreign standards, the upper class manifested its culture in comfortable houses, servants, and fashionable clothes, in *musicales* and literary teas, in Sorbonne diplomas in law and medicine. Public manifestations were fewer; Port-au-Prince possessed no public library and but a single small bookstore. The one hospital was overcrowded, public sanitation almost unknown, the streets unpaved. In all of Haiti there was only one modern wharf, two lighthouses, one electric plant. This lack of development was evident in the capabilities of the elite. Educated Haitians rarely became engineers, scientists, or even businessmen. Lacking skills, capital, and entrepreneurs, the country lay open to foreign penetration, protected only by its poverty and its love of independence. The time had come when that protection would cease to become effective.[9]

The man who was destined to play a central role in the imminent impairment of Haiti's independence had reached flag rank less than two years earlier, and after forty-four years of naval service was taking up his first sea command as an admiral. William B. Caperton was not quite sixty years of age in January 1915. While known as a competent and dependable officer, he had reached his present rank through the routine discharge of his duties rather than by any show of brilliance or participation in dramatic events. When he finally achieved dramatic prominence in 1915, a feature writer from a Nashville newspaper attempted a character sketch of the native Tennessean, but confessed his inability to find much material: "A newspaper man who sets out to learn something of Admiral Caperton in Washington can dig up nothing out of the ordinary, because naval officers say there is nothing unusual about Admiral Caperton." The reporter found Caperton's prior career a "somewhat monotonous tenure of service," while the admiral himself had "the appearance more of a pedagogue than a dashing naval officer." He was, however, fit and youthful-looking and devoted to athletics. Beyond this there seemed little more to say. Even the assurance that "all . . . admire and like him and his kindly ways and quiet and unassuming manner" failed to save the portrait from a distinct dullness.[10]

There were, of course, contrasting views. The glamor of power made the admiral a far more compelling figure in Haiti than he seemed in Washington, and a Port-au-Prince politico has left a very different recollection of Caperton as the Haitians knew him at about this time: "Rear-Admiral Caperton was a slim, handsome old man, as erect as a lightning-rod; he irresistibly attracted one through I know not what fluid that spread itself from his person." Like the American reporter, the Haitian found Caperton socially active, a good mixer, and a tireless dancer, but also discerned in him a special charm which wholly eluded the American.[11]

To his new duties Caperton brought the long-acquired habit of carrying out orders, the unconscious self-confidence of the man of action, and the other ingrained attitudes and prejudices left by a lifetime in the navy. Accustomed to obeying and being obeyed, and to overcoming obstacles by direct action, there was little enough in Caperton's background or training that would seem to prepare him for political or diplomatic manipulation, for the indirection and intrigue of high-level affairs. Precipitated into the international arena, he prepared to face his new challenges with the same personal equipment that had sufficed for the earlier ones.[12]

In any case, he was to have no time for preparation; even the prospective tour of Caribbean trouble spots upon which he had embarked came to an abrupt end before *Washington* neared the first stop on the planned itinerary. On January 19th, with Cape Hatteras just passing astern, the radio shack on the flagship's upper deck received an urgent message from the Navy Department. It ordered *Washington* to proceed without delay to Cap-Haïtien, Haiti, where trouble had broken out.

2
Revolution
in Haiti

CAP-HAITIEN, the principal port of northern Haiti and the Republic's second largest city, lay along the water at the foot of rugged hills. The old town looked placid and picturesque from *Washington*'s rolling deck as she anchored in a heavy seaway on January 23, 1915, but the men on the warship's bridge feared that the situation was less peaceful than the scene suggested; eager and impatient, they chafed at the driving wind and white-tipped seas which prevented them from lowering a boat and making contact with the shore. *Washington*'s radio shack had been busy during the four days' run since she had been ordered to Cap-Haïtien. Those aboard had learned that that city was the center of a rapidly crystallizing revolution against the Haitian government. An insurgent army had approached the town in mid-January, and the local authorities had asked the foreign consuls there to intercede to ensure the peaceful entry of the revolutionary forces. The consular corps, in turn, had composed a collective request

17

to the United States for a warship to protect foreign life and property. Admiral Caperton's orders to proceed to the danger point represented his government's response.[1]

In the interval between Caperton's reception of his orders and his arrival at the city, the revolutionary army had entered Cap-Haïtien unopposed and taken possession of it. For the time being it simply stayed there, gathering recruits and support, while the government in Port-au-Prince attempted to muster its own forces and prepare to send them north. It might be only a matter of time before real fighting should develop, Caperton feared. If trouble came, however, he was not without resources. *Washington* carried a fully equipped company of marines, in addition to her own large ship's company, while other, smaller ships were near—U.S.S. *Wheeling* at Port-au-Prince, *Castine* off the far end of the island in Dominican waters. Caperton was in radio communication with both of these gunboats, as well as with the Navy Department in Washington.[2]

As the wind abated, the admiral was able to send ashore a staff officer, who sought out the local United States consul and arranged to bring him out to the ship the following day. Meanwhile Caperton mentally assessed his new problem. He was prepared to expect the worst of Haiti, which he regarded from the first, he later recorded, as a "land of seething discontent, professional revolutionaries, and ingrained political dishonesty." To him, as to most Americans, it was a place of voodoo rites, bloody barbarism, and ignorant blacks. Raised in Tennessee during the post-Civil War era, the admiral inevitably harbored doubts about the efficacy of a wholly Negro social and political system, but the image of Haiti in the entire United States was so unfavorable that the views of northerners differed little from those of southerners in regard to the "Black Republic"; to most Americans the country's name had become a synonym for backwardness and anarchy. Thus the admiral was prepared to take seriously his task of safeguarding white lives and property in this presumably black and savage land.[3]

The next day, Sunday, January 24, began with a long conference between Admiral Caperton and the consul, whom he was eager to question. Caperton found this man, Lemuel W. Livingston, intelligent and knowledgeable. A Negro, he had married into a prominent Cap-Haïtien family and knew local society and politics from the inside. The current northern uprising, he told Caperton, was virtually a continuation of the revolutionary maneuvering which had recently put President Joseph Davilmar Théodore at the head of the Haitian government. In his haste to seize the presidency, Davilmar Théodore had bought off his major rivals by giving them important posts within his administration, rather than face a test of strength. His government was therefore vulnerable from the beginning, and its weakness was multiplied by its desperate lack of funds. Even the president's own supporters had difficulty in believing that he really had no money to distribute among the hungry victors, and within a few weeks of his triumph the many defections from the Théodore faction had encouraged his rivals to take action. Now, barely two months after his inauguration, Théodore faced a growing coalition of enemies resolved to pull him down.

The leading figure in this new drive for power was Vilbrun Guillaume Sam, whose political base lay in Haiti's turbulent Department of the North. Because of his strength there, Guillaume Sam had been able to demand from Davilmar Théodore formal recognition of his status as the area's political boss. Sam soon made a new bargain, however, with the local followers of the previous president, Oreste Zamor, who had just been overthrown by the Théodore faction. Suddenly, in January, there appeared outside of Cap-Haïtien a large body of revolutionary troops. Guillaume Sam, the ostensible representative of the government in the city, called a meeting of the citizens and sorrowfully explained his inability to defend it; the government, he claimed, had failed to send him arms and ammunition. Within a few days the wily leader had openly placed himself at the head of the force he had secretly invoked, and led it into Cap-Haïtien, which he currently occupied.[4]

Caperton's first move, Livingston suggested, should be to go ashore and meet unofficially with Guillaume Sam. He should ask the revolutionist for a solemn promise not to loot or burn towns during the coming military campaign, or otherwise needlessly endanger life or property. There appeared to be grounds for concern on this score, for revolutionary troops had burned much of the coastal town of Gonaïves early in 1914. A firm warning against such practices, coming from a United States admiral whose flagship could be seen from Guillaume Sam's own headquarters, ought to give pause to everyone concerned. Livingston particularly feared the lesser insurgent generals; such leaders customarily felt free to shoot anyone who displeased them. If Caperton impressed his intentions strongly enough upon the rebels, it would do much to curb their actions. Caperton readily agreed to the plan, and Livingston promised to arrange an interview without delay.[5]

Livingston also briefed the admiral on the nature of revolutions in Haiti. The tempo of turbulence in that country had quickened noticeably in the past several years, until the success of one revolt had become the signal for the organization of another. These revolts almost invariably succeeded, and by 1915 they had developed patterns so regularly repeated as to constitute a recognized code. In the commonest of these patterns, revolt began in the north. The first step was to hire the services of the so-called *"cacos"*—rugged northern hill-dwellers who combined the roles of peasant, mercenary soldier, and clan member. It was these men who, for a price, filled the ranks of revolutionary armies. Organized in bands under local chiefs, their hierarchy ran up in theory to a supposed "Chief of the *cacos,"* or at least to a small group of top-level generals. This loosely hierarchical organization made it possible for the aspiring presidential candidate to secure the services of an entire *caco* army by striking an agree-

ment with only a few men. The revolutionary leader
normally promised a lump-sum payment in case of success,
to be distributed by the *caco* chiefs to their followers
according to rank. Everyone understood that a certain
amount of looting would also swell the profits of the campaign. When the successful revolutionist was installed in
the presidency, he paid off his army and it returned to its
northern haunts, to await the bidding of the next plotters
against the incumbent regime.

All of this, of course, cost money. To make a revolution, one must command funds estimated at from thirty to
fifty thousand American dollars. The prospective president
normally had to borrow the money, promising the lenders
a double or triple return if successful. While not without
risk, such an arrangement could bring large profits in a
short time, and there was usually someone willing to try
his hand at revolutionary finance. White foreign businessmen in Haiti were regarded as a standard source of such
funds, and some observers charged them with actually
fomenting revolution in order to multiply their profits.

Having raised funds and contracted for an army, the
revolutionist usually departed for the northeastern portion
of his country, where he would be near his new supporters,
relatively safe from governmental authority, and close
enough to the Dominican border to flee the country easily
if anything went wrong. From this vantage he issued a
revolutionary manifesto which proclaimed him "Chief of
the Executive Power"—never president, a title claimed
only after the formality of a legal election by the national
Congress. The preliminaries completed, the *caco* army
began the actual campaign by marching on Cap-Haïtien.
Occupation of this city validated the uprising as a "real"
revolution, and, since the government rarely had much
force there, it usually fell readily to the insurrectos and
became their base. It was this point to which Guillaume
Sam's insurrection had progressed, having so far conformed in general to the accepted pattern of revolutionary
procedure.

The invariable next step was for the *caco* army to move southward on St. Marc, a coastal town about half-way between Cap-Haïtien and the capital. It was here that the principal contest would come, for it was an unwritten law that the fall of St. Marc sealed the victory of the revolution. By common consent, Port-au-Prince was not defended. Once St. Marc was lost, the incumbent president fled the country, while the "Chief of the Executive Power" entered the capital in triumph to be formally elected president by Congress.[6]

Although this pattern of revolution had become relatively fixed, Livingston regarded the current situation as unusually threatening. The hatred engendered by the frequent political overturns, he had recently reported to the State Department, "may lead to desperate acts heretofore unknown in Haiti because the conditions giving rise to them have never before existed." The more substantial citizens, he thought, favored United States intervention in order to end the turmoil. "If something is not done to put an end to this intolerable situation," he warned, "the same business stagnation, suffering, pillaging, burning and assassination which have afflicted this part of the country during the whole of the present year will most probably continue indefinitely."[7]

All of this tended to confirm Caperton's initial distrust of Haitian politics and politicians. He would take a strong line with Guillaume Sam, he decided; the coming campaign would not be allowed to threaten the security of foreigners in Haiti.

By the next day Livingston had arranged the interview between Admiral Caperton and Vilbrun Guillaume Sam. Accompanied by his chief of staff, Captain Edward L. Beach of *Washington,* the admiral went ashore in his launch. The consul joined them, and the little party proceeded through the streets of Cap-Haïtien toward the headquarters of the revolutionary army. The town, the newcomers noted, looked as though it had been under siege, with buildings decrepit, streets uncared for, and business almost at a standstill. The place had perhaps 20,000 inhabitants and was the coastal terminus of a short railroad line which ran inland for twenty-five miles or so. The somewhat woebegone appearance of the town was not entirely owing to its occupation by a *caco* army; age and decay were everywhere in evidence, while the outbreak of the war in Europe had drastically disrupted the local export trade.

The revolutionary headquarters was located in a rather pretentious two-story building on Cap-Haïtien's main street, guarded by what Caperton called "a tatterdemalion soldiery." Inside the house, Caperton later recalled, the party found "a very gorgeous black gentleman arrayed like a head bellhop at the Waldorf," who directed them through a room and up a stairway, took their caps, and ushered them into a large reception room. The receptionist disappeared, and shortly afterward Guillaume Sam appeared to greet his visitors. For a moment the admiral was taken aback: "Greatly to my surprise, I recognized him as the bellhop; only this time he had discarded his coat for another but more elaborate one and an enormous sword clanked round his heels." The presidential aspirant had evidently wanted a look at his guests before revealing his own identity!

Guillaume Sam was the soul of courtesy, and seemed unruffled by Caperton's declarations as to the sanctity of foreign life and property. He promised repeatedly to preserve order in Cap-Haïtien, and announced his intention of leaving the town later in the week to continue his campaign.[8] As Consul Livingston translated, Caperton, who spoke no French, studied the rebel leader, a stern-looking man with a high forehead and a bold mustache. Vilbrun Guillaume Sam had a reputation for unusual toughness and determination and had long been prominent in national politics. At the turn of the century he had been minister of war and navy in the cabinet of his father, who was president of Haiti from 1896 to 1902. The cabinet of the elder Sam came to grief, however, under his successor, who found glaring fraud in the floating of a bond issue by which the internal debt had been consolidated in the time of the senior Sam. In a virtually unprecedented action, President Nord Alexis had those implicated tried, convicted of embezzlement, and actually sent to jail. The next president returned the situation to normal by pardoning all concerned. Among those thus released from prison were no less than three future presidents of the republic, one of them Guillaume Sam.[9]

The interview ended cordially, and in the days following his talk with the rebel leader, Admiral Caperton went vigorously to work familiarizing himself with the town and its people. Often ashore on sightseeing tours, he mentally noted everything which would bear upon a landing of his forces, rapidly assembling charts, notes, and sketches. By the end of the week he felt ready to draw up actual landing plans against the time when he might need them. Meanwhile he cultivated local society, both Haitian and foreign. On three occasions he invited groups aboard *Washington* for band concerts played by the ship's band, a device to please the Haitians while giving him a chance to study them. In this exercise he made use of his chief of staff, Captain Beach, whose knowledge of French helped to make up for the admiral's lack of it. So things went until January 26, when Caperton received news of complications at the capital from Commander Roscoe C. Moody, who commanded *Wheeling* there.[10]

The admiral had been relying on Moody for news of events in Port-au-Prince. The latter's daily reports by radio, and especially that of the 26th, ultimately convinced Caperton that he should turn his attention from Guillaume Sam's insurrectos to the incumbent government of Davilmar Théodore. The virtually bankrupt national authorities, Moody said, were contemplating the illegal seizure of funds from the foreign-owned National Bank of Haiti in order to secure the means to oppose their revolutionary foes. The two gunboats which constituted the Haitian Navy represented one of the goverment's few trump cards, but they could not move for lack of coal, making an empty gesture of the government's announced blockade of rebel-held ports. An American schooner laden with the necessary coal was tied up near the gunboats, but her captain refused to discharge his cargo until it was paid for. It was possible that the government might simply seize the schooner if its situation became desperate enough. Further, Théodore's supporters were making some serious threats. The gunboats, they said, would go north to Gonaïves, the already scarred coastal town north of St. Marc through which the *caco* forces must march on their way south, and bombard it to prevent the rebels' passage. And if St. Marc itself should fall, they threatened to burn that town before they withdrew. The main threat to foreign life and property might well come from Théodore's side rather than that of Guillaume Sam.[11]

Moody's sobering assessment was given added weight by a Navy Department despatch which Caperton received on the same day. It directed the admiral to go to the capital and accompany the United States minister to an audience with President Davilmar Théodore, the purpose of which was to warn him against any attempt to seize the assets of the National Bank of Haiti. The Wilson administration was determined to prevent such action and instructed Caperton to support the minister in his representations.[12]

Admiral Caperton accordingly moved to concentrate his little force on Port-au-Prince. *Washington* sailed to join *Wheeling* at the capital while *Castine,* the gunboat still in Dominican waters, was ordered around the island to the same destination. By the next day, January 27, *Washington* was steaming through the sparkling waters of the channel between the mainland and the large, mountainous island of Gonâve, crossing the bay of Port-au-Prince, and dropping anchor before the city and its backdrop of steep green hills. In the harbor nearby lay the angular form of *Wheeling,* with her single tall smokestack.[13] Small boats darted out from the shore carrying vendors of fruit and curios, while coasters and fishing boats passed showing curiously patched sails. At a little distance, the port's single long pier thrust out into the bay, the focus of the comings and goings of small craft.

As seen from *Washington's* quarterdeck, the city of Port-au-Prince sloped gently upward behind a low-lying waterfront, its ranks of roofs dominated by a gleaming white cathedral in the center of the town. To the north was the narrow but fertile plain of Cul-de-Sac, lying between the city and a range of rugged mountains which ran out of sight in both directions. Behind Port-au-Prince the hills drew together, with more mountain-tops just showing behind them, while on the south the city stopped abruptly at the foot of a green, thousand-foot ridge. Ordering a boat lowered, the admiral headed for the municipal pier on his way to the United States Legation. Ashore, he passed through a succession of urban zones, the sheds and warehouses along the water giving way to small one- or two-story wooden houses, many with an overhanging balcony at the front of the second floor. In the midst of these were the "open" and "closed" markets, the one a wide and dusty square and the other a large iron pavilion with arched and latticed sides. This part of the town was crowded with black humanity, for the most part lean and raggedly dressed. Both markets were jammed with stalls and hawkers offering fruit, vegetables, live but bedraggled chickens tied by the feet and hanging head-down; there were baskets and hats, sandals and cloth, racks of goat's ribs roasting above smoking braziers, stems of big green bananas. The senses were assailed by the glare of the sun, the incessant chattering of the market crowds, the pungent stench of open gutters and garbage heaps, while through the scene paced numerous women bearing burdens on their heads, erect, barefoot, and strangely dignified.

On the rising ground behind the middle of the city stood the better residential areas. Here the vegetation increased, the streets becoming lined with graceful palms and the walled yards shaded by a variety of trees. The houses grew more pretentious, most of them big victorian structures with an abundance of gables, porches, and ornate iron-work. Some more solid-looking mansions were white-walled and red-tiled; all were set off by the flowers which bloomed everywhere in tropical profusion—bright poinsettias and hibiscus, purple bougainvillea, *flamboyant* trees flaming with great red masses of blossom.

On these higher slopes lived the capital's elite. Here, too, dwelt United States minister to Haiti Arthur Bailly-Blanchard, the man to whom Caperton must apply for information and advice, and with whom he was to enter upon the diplomatic side of his mission. The admiral's carriage turned in at last through the grounds of the American Legation, a surprisingly large and handsome edifice of two stories which surrounded an arcaded courtyard containing a formal garden. The minister quickly appeared, welcoming the party warmly and leading them inside. He had been in his post only since the previous summer, but his many years as secretary of legation in Paris had given him assurance, as well as polishing the accent of his native Louisiana French. Before his promotion and appointment to Port-au-Prince, he had served as legation secretary at Tokyo, while earlier service in Russia and elsewhere made him a true cosmopolite. Now aging and in doubtful health, Bailly-Blanchard appeared lacking in vigor, but he talked readily about the local situation. Seated together in a quiet room, he and Caperton went over their instructions together, and the minister explained to the admiral the present state of Haitian-United States relations.[14]

The sheer instability of Haitian politics was a leading source of United States concern, and current events in Haiti did little to lessen the disapproval of North Americans on this score. Experienced observers in Port-au-Prince thought the Théodore government bound to fall within a few weeks. Davilmar Théodore was a feeble old man who lacked energy, money, and supporters. His military commanders were attempting to gather troops to send to the north, but the results were not encouraging.

According to common report, civilian "recruits" were rounded up by press-gangs, tied together with ropes, and marched off, still roped togather, toward the threatened area.

Mercenaries would have been more effective, but Théodore could afford none; he was unable to pay all his debts from his own successful revolution. It was said that on a recent occasion he had faced a group of dangerously restive *caco* chiefs in the presidential palace itself and confessed that he had no funds for them. Looking at the luxurious furnishings of the mansion, the simple men of the north refused to believe that the possessor of such opulence could really be penniless. In desperation the aged president told them to help themselves to what they saw. Nothing loath, the *caco* generals left the building carrying mirrors, pictures, and pieces of furniture upon their heads.[15]

What each Haitian regime in turn found particularly galling was this poverty in the midst of at least relative plenty; it was frustrating that most of the public revenues were unavailable to the government. A series of financial scandals and crises had resulted in 1910 in a new arrangement between the Haitians and their foreign creditors. The National Bank of Haiti, formerly a French corporation, was reorganized under international auspices and, by solemn contract with the government, invested with the functions of a national treasury. This new National Bank refunded and consolidated the government's previous debts, though only at a large discount, and in return received all of the customs collections, paid outstanding obligations out of them, and turned over the surplus to the government. Unfortunately, there was sometimes little or no surplus.

The new National Bank had been established under the auspices of the governments of France, Germany, and the United States, the Europeans' goal being primarily to protect those of their citizens who held Haitian bonds, and the American government's to check undue European influence. At the insistence of the State Department, United States banking interests assumed a major role in the new arrangements, led by the National City Bank of New York. The resulting instrument had the direct support of three formidable nations, while the bank's contract put it beyond the legal control of the Haitians. By 1914 relations between the bank and the Haitian government were tense. The complaint of the Haitian authorities was that the bank, while acting as a national treasury, actually served only foreign interests. It was bad enough that it received most of the state revenues, and then on occasion loaned the government back its own funds at 12 percent interest. It was worse that it insisted on paying off the bond-holders first even if it meant leaving the government penniless. The economic upheaval resulting from the outbreak of war in Europe and the rising costs of revolutionary politics had jointly caught the Haitians in a crushing grip: something would have to give.[16]

In the course of the year 1914 the Haitian government had become involved in two separate financial disputes in which the United States State Department took an interest. One grew from the terms of a railroad concession acquired in 1910 by an American promoter named James P. McDonald. Under this McDonald contract, the railroad company was to build a line from Port-au-Prince to Cap-Haïtien, while the Haitian government guaranteed the payment of 6 percent interest on the cost of construction, which could go to a maximum of $33,000 per mile for the mountainous sections. By 1914 the company claimed to have built 110 miles of road, and put the cost of all of it at the maximum $33,000 per mile, even though it built only the easiest and cheapest portions in three unconnected segments.

The Haitians, who had made the requested interest payments in two previous years, now balked on the ground that construction on the line had come to a stop with the road still incomplete. By this time McDonald had surrendered control, and leadership of the railroad company had passed to one Roger L. Farnham, an officer of the National City Bank of New York, and through it, of the National Bank of Haiti. Farnham, who had connections in the State Department, argued that under the contract the Haitian payments were due on whatever mileage of track was built and were not contingent upon completion of the entire line. Further, he blamed the halt in progress on the constant revolutionary disturbances which agitated the country. Rejecting these contentions, the Haitian government had threatened to foreclose on the completed portion of the railroad when the State Department entered the picture. Secretary of State William Jennings Bryan strongly supported the railroad interests, asking the Haitians to accept United States arbitration of the dispute and warning them against taking hasty action. Although the Haitians protested this diplomatic intervention, which the railroad's contract expressly renounced, new revolutionary overturns in Haiti had brought the whole matter to a halt.[17]

The second and more crucial dispute concerned the National Bank of Haiti, which was central to all of Haiti's financial questions. The tension between the bank and the government had been brought to the crisis level in the summer of 1914 by a deliberate act of the bank. Standing on the letter of its contract, the bank's management declared that they would no longer honor the monthly drafts of the government to meet current expenses, but would settle their mutual accounts only at the end of the current fiscal year. The immediate effect of this policy would be to cut off all payments to the government for months to come, leaving it without the means to carry on. The United States minister to Haiti reported that in his opinion the bank hoped either to force the government into complete submission or to precipitate an American intervention to establish a customs receivership on the Dominican model.

In its desperation the Davilmar Théodore regime challenged the power of the bank by printing paper money to cover its expenses. This violated the bank's contract with the government, which gave it a monopoly of note issue, and State Department protests brought the government to a halt before more than a fraction of the paper had been put into circulation. The Haitians next turned to the government gold reserve, which was deposited in the vaults of the bank; they could use their own bullion to save themselves. But the bank officials demurred; the gold, they said was legally reserved for the redemption of previous paper issues and could not be used for current governmental expenses. Facing destruction, the Théodore government seemed ready to act in defiance of both the bank and of United States protests, but once again the bank's management forestalled them. The by-now frightened bank officials feared that the Haitians meant to take their specie forcibly from the bank's vaults and asked the United States government to secure the gold before this could happen. On December 17, 1914, a party of United States Marines landed in Port-au-Prince, marched to the National Bank of Haiti, and removed gold to the value of $500,000. The bullion was subsequently put aboard the United States gunboat *Machias* and taken to New York, where it was deposited in the National City Bank.[18]

This forcible removal of the gold from Port-au-Prince was symptomatic of the Wilson administration's increasing willingness to intervene actively in Haitian affairs. The chronic instability in Haiti and the deterioration of that nation's finances had led the State Department from the beginning of 1914 to serious consideration of possible United States action there. Boaz W. Long, chief of the department's Latin American Division, was a leading proponent of forcible measures to stabilize the troubled Haitian Republic. He was strongly encouraged in these views by his personal friend Roger L. Farnham, the National City Bank official who was already so deeply involved in Haitian financial questions. Both men were sympathetically heard by an administration already active in the internal affairs of Haiti's neighbor, Santo Domingo.

After a time, indeed, each new move in the Dominican tangle sugested a parallel action to be taken in Haiti. In particular, the kind of United States customs receivership established some years earlier in Santo Domingo seemed to Washington officialdom a logical tool with which to begin rationalizing the Haitian situation.[19]

Secretary of State Bryan first suggested such an arrangement to the Haitians in February 1914, but he did not push the point until fears of European involvement added urgency to Washington's view of the situation. These fears stemmed in the first instance from the French and German official reactions to Bryan's February suggestion of a United States customs receivership. Both governments declared that the economic interests of their nationals in Haiti entitled them to demand participation in any customs control which the United States might establish. Rumors that the Germans were negotiating for a coaling station in Haiti further upset Wilson and Bryan and made them the more determined to take unilateral action.[20]

The outbreak of Joseph Davilmar Théodore's revolt against President Oreste Zamor at about this time had clinched the determination of the State Department to act. Zamor lacked the money to put down his foes; perhaps he would strike a bargain in order to save his regime. When Arthur Bailly-Blanchard came to his new post in July, he brought south with him a draft treaty which provided for American collection of Haitian customs, as well as the appointment of an American "financial adviser" with broad controls over government disbursements. Acceptance of such a treaty would gain Zamor the active support of the United States against Davilmar Théodore, and Charles Zamor, the president's brother and adviser, seemed initially to be interested in the proposal.

A temporary improvement in the Zamors' position, however, led the brothers to reject the treaty plan and attempt to go it alone, until the final collapse of their fortunes in the autumn of 1914. By then desperate, they reopened the subject with Bailly-Blanchard, and the Washington authorities raced against time to launch an intervention on Zamor's behalf before that worthy was forced from office. They lost the race; when the transport *Hancock* arrived at Port-au-Prince carrying eight hundred marines, it was to find Davilmar Théodore in possession of the capital and Zamor on his way to exile abroad.[21]

It had been a near thing, however, and the intervention so narrowly averted in October continued to be a possibility in the months thereafter. As Caperton discussed the situation with Bailly-Blanchard, it became evident that the new crisis created by Guillaume Sam's revolution might well see another attempt by the United States to introduce its authority into Haiti. The Wilson administration had already attempted to reach a settlement with Davilmar Théodore's government by means of conventional diplomacy. The first move had been to notify the Haitian regime that United States diplomatic recognition would be conditioned upon Haitian acceptance of a treaty similar to that pressed upon Zamor, but this scheme had come to grief when word of it got out in Port-au-Prince. In a volcanic session of the Haitian Senate on December 3, the minister of foreign affairs had admitted under questioning that Théodore's government was even then in negotiation with the United States, but refused to disclose any details. When a hostile senator produced "leaked" drafts of the United States and Haitian proposals, an uproar resulted which ended in a mass physical attack on the foreign minister, who barely escaped with his life. The senatorial mob was finally calmed by the dramatic declaration of the minister of interior, Dr. Rosalvo Bobo, that "the Government will shroud itself in the folds of the National Flag rather than to consent to the least attaint to the Haitian autonomy."[22]

The demonstration of Haitian nationalism set off by this incident made it politically impossible for Davilmar Théodore to pursue the subject and brought a statement from Bryan that the proposed customs receivership and financial supervision had been offered to the Haitians purely in the spirit of helpfulness, to be accepted or rejected as Haiti chose. Théodore still lacked money, however, and he proposed to Bailly-Blanchard a scheme by which his government would grant mining and commercial concessions to United States citizens in return for State Department help in securing a large foreign loan. The proposal looked to Bryan like plain bribery, and he indignantly rejected the idea. This brought negotiations to an impasse, forcing the unhappy Théodore and his ministers to consider new attempts to break the financial death-grip imposed on them by the contract with the National Bank of Haiti.[23]

The State Department, on the other hand, was determined to uphold firmly the current financial restrictions on Haiti and to introduce others as soon as possible. They were stiffened in this resolve by President Wilson himself, who had composed a vigorous letter to Bryan on January 13, 1915. "The more I think about that [Haitian] situation," Wilson wrote, "the more I am convinced that it is our duty to take immediate action there such as we took in San Domingo [sic]. I mean to send commissioners there who will . . . say to them as firmly and definitely as is consistent with courtesy and kindness that the United States cannot consent to stand by and permit revolutionary conditions constantly to exist there." The president proposed a popular election, to be held under United States supervision, the resulting government to be guaranteed in power by the United States. While the president's advisers soon showed him the need for alterations in this plan, it nevertheless reflected his conviction that something must be done about Haiti in the near future.[24]

Bailly-Blanchard led the admiral through all these matters in their long conference, and the two ended by agreeing that Caperton must be ready for action. The admiral decided to dispatch *Wheeling* to St. Marc that very day, to check on persistent reports that government troops meant to burn the town if forced to abandon it. In a dispatch to the Navy Department he expressed a desire for additional troops: "In case of landing at Port au Prince, I consider my force rather small, if the Government is to be opposed. My total available landing force with the *Castine* will be about four hundred and fifty men. There is no doubt of course such a force could defeat the force that it might encounter; but I should prefer to have at least a regiment of marines more to make the matter promptly decisive. Any calculations based on a weak resistance by the Haitians, are not to be relied upon and from my knowledge of these people I believe more than a nominal resistance will be made."[25]

The next day Caperton formally requested that two battalions of marines be sent at once on *Montana,* which he ordered to Guantanamo Bay, Cuba, to embark them. With the assurance that 650 marines were on the way, he ordered *Castine* back to Dominican waters and worked out plans for the possible landing of troops in Port-au-Prince. Bailly-Blanchard, he reported to the Navy Department, had not yet delivered the State Department's note warning the Haitians against new moves in defiance of the bank. Secretary of the Navy Josephus Daniels promptly replied that Caperton's cooperation with the minister was to extend to the landing of marines and sailors if necessary, while the next day at the State Department Lansing reiterated the desire that Caperton act with Bailly-Blanchard in the matter.[26]

As these preparations matured, the Haitians acted in a way that seemed calculated to trigger the threatened United States intervention. On January 29 President Théodore announced that henceforth the customs receipts would not be deposited in the National Bank of Haiti, but with designated private merchants instead. The government had decided to ignore the bank's contract and take charge of its own revenues. That same day the two Haitian gunboats, galvanized into action by the acquisition of funds, began loading coal from the waiting American schooner. The Théodore regime seemed about to take a new lease on life; a thousand government troops were to go north with the gunboats to St. Marc, it was said.

At the same time, the Americans moved to regain the initiative. On the last day of January *Montana* arrived with 650 marines aboard, and Caperton issued preliminary orders to the marine commander for the prospective seizure of Port-au-Prince. Also, the admiral and the minister finally delivered the State Department's virtual ultimatum to Théodore's government. Contemplating the United States forces in the harbor of his capital, the dispirited president knew that continued action against the bank could be fatal. Once again, the situation seemed stalemated. The Haitians asserted their willingness to submit the entire matter to arbitration, Caperton held his troops in readiness, and everyone awaited news from the north.[27]

As the days passed, the ragged troops of Guillaume Sam moved southwest over the mountains to occupy Gonaïves and pushed on toward the vital goal of St. Marc. Tension rose in the capital, while the country showed increasing signs of the imminent collapse of the Théodore government. There was an uprising southwest of the capital at Petit-Goâve, while rumor said that Rosalvo Bobo, until recently Davilmar Théodore's minister of the interior, was going north to start a wholly new revolution. It seemed to some of the nervous politicians in Port-au-Prince that the time had come to arrange sanctuary for themselves in the foreign legations and consulates, a customary precaution in times of danger. Others, made of sterner stuff, sought to grasp the key to the situation and play a part in deciding their own destinies. Many of these men saw that key in Admiral Caperton.[28]

Coincident with the departure of the marines, who were recalled after a week by the commander-in-chief of the Atlantic Fleet, the admiral found himself being dragged unwillingly into various Haitian plots. One intrigue centered about two prominent generals named Monplaisir and Défly, both of whom Caperton considered "undesirable characters." On February 9 he reported to Washington his belief that the two meant to seize power. "It is possible attempt may be made by this faction to force intervention by the United States by creating insufferable conditions at Port au Prince," Caperton wired. "They are counting on the backing of the United States if [they] are in power at that time. They have made attempts to approach me with proposition to intervene." A second scheme involved the proposal of ten senators that Caperton prevent the entry of Guillaume Sam into the capital and let the senatorial group arrange a "free election" to choose a new president. This man would presumably be guaranteed in office by the United States, along the lines already followed in Santo Domingo. He had rejected all such advances, Caperton said, but he was obviously feeling the pressures of his position. "I urgently request information as to the Government Haytien Policy," he concluded anxiously.[29]

The admiral did not seem averse to intervention, however, and was soon convinced that many of the Haitians themselves would support it. "Better class Haytiens keep aloof politics, desire American intervention to stabilize government but do not openly promote such ideas for fear of execution by politicians. Scheming politicians promote revolution for their own personal gain . . . ," he explained to the Navy Department.[30]

While Admiral Caperton tried to master the Byzantine complexities of affairs at the capital, his subordinates saw to it that Vilbrun Guillaume Sam kept the promises he had made at Cap-Haïtien. When *Wheeling* arrived at St. Marc on January 28, the entire consular body there came to the ship to request naval protection for foreigners. The continued presence of his gunboat, Commander Moody reported, eventually restored local confidence and brought back those citizens who had fled the town for fear of the expected fighting. Further to the north, Caperton had diverted a small cruiser, the *Des Moines,* to watch events in Cap-Haïtien; her commander found the city quiet and the rebel army departed for Gonaïves. When Guillaume Sam arrived there with a thousand men on February 5, he found *Wheeling* awaiting him. The rebel leader had hardly entered Gonaïves when Commander Moody saw him and reiterated the urgent need for preserving order and protecting life and property. Guillaume Sam once again pledged his good behavior, but at this point the Théodore government announced that Gonaïves was under blockade, while Caperton directed his commanders not to interfere with the blockade rights of the Haitian gunboats as long as they conformed to international law.[31]

The focus of the campaigning, however, soon shifted to St. Marc. So far there had been little real fighting; the government meant to make its stand at St. Marc, and *Des Moines* duly went there to help oversee events. But in a surprise move Guillaume Sam bypassed St. Marc to occupy Arcahaie, a coastal town south of St. Marc and only twenty miles from the capital. From this point his troops threatened both St. Marc and Port-au-Prince itself. The revolution was clearly nearing a climax; were the Americans to intervene or not?[32]

Uncertain of his course, Caperton once again went ashore, disembarked at the long pier, and rode through the town to the American Legation. There he and Bailly-Blanchard sought to reach a decision. The Théodore government was entering its final days; upon that everyone agreed. Guillaume Sam, on the other hand, had so far done nothing offensive to the United States authorities. Caperton's men had carefully shepherded him from town to town, a gunboat standing by at each successive coastal point which Guillaume's troops entered. Each time, the American commander had exacted a repetition of Guillaume's pledges as to the safety of life and property. The Haitians, government and insurrecto alike, were bemused at Caperton's novel approach to their revolution, but so far they had never seriously deviated from the admiral's guidelines. The campaign had been eminently orderly, furnishing no obvious occasion for a full-scale intervention by the United States. Ultimately, the admiral and the diplomat decided to let events take their natural course. Both Guillaume Sam's and Davilmar Théodore's people had promised to respect life and property; both were doing so. As long as this continued the Americans would not intervene. His decision made, Caperton returned to his ship, having promised to keep in close touch with the minister.[33]

From this point on, the revolution ran swiftly to a successful conclusion. The Théodore government had managed to get its troops to St. Marc, hoping to hold the town with them and their supporting gunboats. But on February 17 the army of Guillaume Sam, some three thousand strong, pounced decisively on the little seaport. As Guillaume's force entered the town, the government troops rushed in panic to board the Haitian gunboat *Nord Alexis* and escape by sea. Dozens were drowned while trying to swim to the ship. The scheming but resolute General Monplaisir, currently minister of the interior, was killed trying to stop the rout, it appearing afterwards that he had been stabbed by his own men.[34] Crammed with survivors, the *Nord Alexis* steamed slowly away, leaving Guillaume Sam master of the town. His victory had been witnessed, as usual, by the United States Navy, both *Des Moines* and *Wheeling* lying at anchor in the harbor of St. Marc. On the day after the town's capture, commanders Blakely and Moody went ashore together to receive the usual pledge of good order from Guillaume Sam. This guarantee was fully met, Blakely reported, finding the fact "somewhat creditable in view of the first day or two, when his [Guillaume's] troops were pitiably hungry, dirty, and tired; and thrown upon the resources of a small town incapable of handling them."[35]

The revolutionists stayed in St. Marc for several days, while their leader sought to borrow further funds with which to finish his campaign. In this he was ultimately successful, receiving an advance from a wealthy local resident. By February 21 it was all over; Port-au-Prince was virtually surrounded, its water supply cut off and provisions becoming scarce. On that day Guillaume sent word to Davilmar Théodore that he must leave the country by noon the following day. At the appointed hour, the departing president boarded a Dutch ship bound for Curacao, accompanied by his family and a lone ex-cabinet minister. The men wore frock coats and silk hats, while a government battery fired a salute; the revolution was decorous to the last.[36]

With the previous regime safely gone, the incoming president made his triumphal entry into the capital on February 25. Accompanied by about two thousand foot-soldiers and four hundred horsemen, he soon found his forces almost doubled by the assimilation of the government troops in Port-au-Prince. The national army normally joined the forces of successful revolutionaries; among other considerations, it was the only way for the officers to insure their continued pay. A proclamation, the posting of placards in the streets, and quiet was restored. The water was again turned on and business resumed, while a committee of the Senate called a special session of Congress to elect a new president. In due course Congress met, and Vilbrun Guillaume Sam became the constitutional head of the Haitian government. From first to last, Caperton judged, the change of government had involved only modest bloodshed and done very little harm. The admiral thought Haitian conditions such as to warrant the withdrawal of his flagship, and so reported. *Washington* and some of the other ships needed target practice, and there were still the projected visits to be made to the other areas of Caperton's new station.[37]

The Wilson administration had watched these Haitian political developments closely, and as Guillaume Sam's revolution moved to its close, Wilson and Bryan acted to implement the president's decision to send a commission to Port-au-Prince. Bryan notified Bailly-Blanchard on February 20 that two commissioners, ex-Governor John Franklin Fort of New Jersey and Charles Cogswell Smith of New Hampshire, would leave for Haiti on the 27th. Both men had served on the United States commission to

Santo Domingo the previous year. They were to act with Bailly-Blanchard, who would be the third member of the group, to seek means to stabilize the Haitian situation. The American minister recommended waiting until the new government had had time to establish itself, but Bryan replied that the president desired the commission to go at once. Fort and Smith arrived aboard the cruiser *Tacoma* on March 5, the day after Guillaume Sam's formal election to the presidency. They were obliged to wait a week before the new regime was ready to enter into what proved to be brief and wholly unfruitful talks. Guillaume Sam steadfastly refused to participate in negotiations until his government had been formally recognized by the United States, while the three envoys were instructed that recognition of the new Haitian government was to be conditional upon its making the necessary concessions to American demands. Since nothing could be done, Fort and Smith returned home.[38]

Much to the distress of Washington, however, the governments of Germany, France, and Italy promptly recognized Guillaume Sam. At the same time Roger Farnham, the National City Bank official so interested in the National Bank of Haiti, alarmed Secretary of State Bryan with stories of French schemes to seize financial control of the island. Farnham even spoke of Franco-German cooperation to drive out American investors there, and unlikely as the story appeared in 1915, with these two powers at war, Bryan seemed to believe it. After consulting President Wilson, he sent Paul Fuller, Jr., to Haiti in May on another special mission.

Fuller was to offer United States aid in stabilizing the Haitian political situation in return for Guillaume Sam's promise to be guided by American advice in fiscal matters. On May 22, Fuller presented to the Haitians a draft agreement which included a commitment to use United States armed forces, if necessary, to suppress foreign attacks or domestic insurrections against the Guillaume Sam government. Included in the price which the Haitians must pay

for this support were promises to deny concessions at
Môle-Saint-Nicolas to any third parties, and to submit to
arbitration all United States and foreign financial claims
against Haiti. After two weeks, the Haitians submitted a
counter-proposal which Fuller regarded as hopelessly far
from the United States position. He therefore returned to
Washington in June, recommending in his final report that
Haiti should be temporarily occupied by the marines, after
which the administration of the country might be
entrusted to Haitians acting under permanent United
States controls.[39]

During all this diplomatic maneuvering Admiral
Caperton's naval forces were absent from Haitian waters.
Caperton had been ordered to Mexico on March 9 in
response to a new crisis in United States-Mexican relations,
remaining there throughout the spring of 1915. At the end
of June, however, the admiral received an urgent summons
to return to his former station, for reasons which already
sounded familiar. French marines had landed at Cap-
Haïtien to quell disorders, the Navy Department radioed;
Caperton was to go there at once aboard *Washington* and
restore order.[40]

3

The Fall
of Guillaume Sam

WHEN *WASHINGTON* reached her new scene of
action on July 1, 1915, Cap-Haïtien looked just as it had
on her first arrival nearly six months earlier, and to those
aboard the cruiser it must have seemed that events were
repeating themselves. Once again they had come to the
little seaport to protect foreign life and property, and once
again their coming was occasioned by a confrontation between government forces and a revolutionary army in the
area. From their former anchorage off Point Picolet, three
miles north of the city, *Washington*'s crew looked over the
wind-swept waters of the bay to the town at its head. To
the southward, much nearer the town than *Washington*'s
great depth allowed her to go, lay the French cruiser
Descartes. French marines from this vessel had landed
some ten days before, and *Washington*'s despatch to the
scene reflected the unease of the State Department at any
prospect of European intervention in the Caribbean.
Admiral Caperton's orders were to thank the French com-

mander for his services, at the same time that he rendered them unnecessary by taking control of the situation himself.[1]

That evening, the captain of the *Descartes* paid an official call on *Washington.* The Frenchman, Captain Lafrogne, explained his presence to Caperton at some length. He had been ordered to Cap-Haïtien by his own minister at Port-au-Prince and had arrived on June 19 to find the town occupied by a revolutionary force led by Dr. Rosalvo Bobo, President Davilmar Théodore's one-time minister of the interior. That very day, however, Bobo had evacuated the place in the face of a strong government force under General Probus Blot. Fearing disorder as Blot's soldiers replaced those of Bobo, Lafrogne landed fifty men to protect the French consulate, the local office of the National Bank of Haiti, and a monastery operated by a French order, as well as foreign interests in general.

His government had no desire to interfere in Haitian politics, Lafrogne earnestly assured Caperton, nor in any way to subvert the influence of the United States there. The Frenchman evidently found his situation embarrassing, even though he had recalled his landing parties to their ship on June 24. Both the Haitian government and the German minister to Haiti had protested his presence in Cap-Haïtien as a violation of Haiti's wartime neutrality, and now Caperton hinted that his departure would be agreeable to the United States. Politely putting himself at the admiral's disposal, Lafrogne asked Caperton directly if the latter's instructions interfered with his remaining at Cap-Haïtien. Equally politely, Caperton replied that they did not, and thanked the Frenchman for his exertions in protecting American interests in the area during the past days.[2]

Captain Lafrogne's departure was followed almost immediately by the arrival of Lemuel Livingston, the United States consul with whom Caperton had worked during his previous stay in Cap-Haïtien. Again the knowledgeable consul explained the current political situation to the admiral, and discussed future possibilities with him.[3]

The story he told was in many ways a familiar one, but it contained new elements as well.

Rosalvo Bobo had entered Cap-Haïtien late in April at the head of five hundred *cacos*. In the inevitable manifesto he declared that the purpose of his revolution was to prevent the Guillaume Sam government from betraying Haitian independence to the Americans, and he called on all true patriots to reject the bondage that threatened them. "There is no people whose genius and industrial activity I admire more than theirs," Bobo proclaimed. "To introduce into our country its industries, its capital, its methods of work—is one of my most ardent and constant dreams. But to turn over to them our custom houses and our finances, to put ourselves under their tutelage, never, never, NEVER." Pointing to the "iron collar" which the United States had already fastened upon the neck of Santo Domingo, the manifesto concluded with a ringing call to arms. It was signed: "Rosalvo Bobo, Graduate of the Faculties of Law and Medicine of Paris, former Envoy Extraordinary to Santo Domingo."[4]

By previous standards, Bobo's movement should have been well on the road to success. The conventional first step, the seizure of Cap-Haïtien, had been achieved, while the anti-American issue which Bobo raised was well calculated to elicit popular support for the insurgent leader. Bobo himself had been prominent in the outcry of December 1914 against the treaty proposed by the State Department to the Théodore government. Furthermore, President Vilbrun Guillaume Sam was now under strong American pressure to accept a new treaty arrangement with the United States. A special envoy, Paul Fuller, Jr., had gone to Haiti in May in an attempt to repair the failure of the earlier Fort Commission to achieve any progress. Fuller was authorized to water down the American demands considerably, leaving the Haitians in at least formal control of their own customs and finances. In return for limited American direction of Haitian finances, Guillaume Sam would be guaranteed the support of the United States against his domestic enemies.

The offer put Guillaume Sam in a dilemma. The record of his predecessors showed how precarious was the presidency of Haiti, while the burgeoning Bobo revolt lent urgency to the situation. To be maintained in office by the power of the United States was a tempting prospect. Yet acceptance of any treaty arrangement with the Americans, even such a mild one as Fuller offered, would validate Bobo's charges of a sellout and discredit Guillaume with his countrymen. When the hard-pressed president had attempted to bargain, Fuller had broken off the talks in disgust and returned to Washington, leaving Guillaume no alternative but to fight it out alone.[5]

Vilbrun Guillaume Sam, however, was a ruthless and determined man, and he prepared to make an all-out fight against his enemies. Using a large issue of paper money that had originally been authorized by the Théodore government in defiance of the National Bank contract, Guillaume raised troops for a surprise offensive in the north, and his energy was rewarded in June with the expulsion of Bobo's army by the government forces. After that, events remained deadlocked: General Blot held the city for the government, but Bobo's men were still camped a few miles inland, biding their time as their leader attempted to widen the base of his support.[6]

As Admiral Caperton saw it, his duty was to protect foreign interests in Cap-Haïtien and to maintain the primacy of the United States. His long evening of conferences with Lafrogne and Livingston had given him the data he needed, and he mentally outlined a plan of action to be put into effect the following day. His first step was to visit the *Descartes* and return Lafrogne's call of the previous night. The admiral had decided that the French cruiser had best leave; its continued presence would be "undesirable on account of [the] primary interests of the United States and the neutrality of Haiti . . . ." He informed Lafrogne that the United States had now assumed charge of protecting foreign interests, French included. Lafrogne, therefore, was relieved of further responsibility in the matter, and should he decide to go he could do so with an easy mind. While expressing appreciation for Caperton's assurances, the Frenchman raised objections to this unmistakable invitation to depart. He would prefer to leave soon, he said; his open violation of Haitian neutrality, and the possibility of consequent friction with the United States, were all too obvious to him. Unfortunately, his requests for sailing orders had so far been ignored by his superiors, and now he was running short of coal as well. To add to his perplexities, he had given refuge aboard his ship to Bobo's chief-of-staff and five other Bobo adherents who had been too slow in leaving the city when the government forces entered. The French minister at Port-au-Prince had ordered them surrendered to General Blot, but Lafrogne. could not bring himself simply to hand them over to be shot. How could he dispose of his embarrassing guests?

Curious, Caperton asked to speak with the Bobo general. This worthy spoke confidently of his leader's strength, which he estimated at between three and four thousand men, well supplied with ammunition. Since such a force could easily have held Cap-Haïtien, the admiral gave little credence to the Haitian's information, nor did he suggest a determination of his fate. For the moment, he was through with Lafrogne, and, returning to *Washington*, he moved to the next step of his plan.[7]

This was a bold one, though by no means unprecedented. Caperton had decided that the only certain way to insure the safety of life and property in Cap-Haïtien was to forbid the Haitians to fight there. On his own authority, he would make the town a sanctuary, its status enforced if necessary by *Washington*'s guns. Captain Beach, *Washington*'s French-speaking commanding officer, went ashore that very afternoon to inform the government commander of this decision. Since fighting in Cap-Haïtien must inevitably endanger foreign life and property, he told General Blot, no such fighting would be permitted within the city limits. While the United States was completely neutral as between the two parties, and had no wish to intervene, the admiral would not hesitate to do so to enforce his decision. Word of this decision would also be transmitted as soon as possible to the rebel commanders, Beach told Blot. The latter assured Beach that he too was full of concern for foreign safety, but added that the revolutionary forces were in any case too weak to be taken seriously. Blot apparently made no objection to Caperton's arbitrary ruling, perhaps because it greatly simplified his own mission of barring the rebels from Cap-Haïtien.[8]

Upon Beach's return, Caperton composed a letter, identical copies of which he addressed to Blot and Bobo. After explaining his ban on fighting in Cap-Haïtien, Caperton wrote that he was prepared to land troops to enforce it. "I trust that, by confining your military operations to the country well clear of the town and by continuing to respect the lives and property of foreigners in your vicinity, you will make it unnecessary for me to take action," the admiral concluded.[9]

It was a simple matter to deliver this letter to General Blot, who was already aware of its contents; the more urgent problem was to get it to Rosalvo Bobo before he should attempt a new attack on the city. As usual, this task was entrusted to Beach, who promptly enlisted the aid of Consul Livingston. An excursion into the interior was necessary; the rebels were supposedly near Petite Anse, a village three or four miles across the bay from Cap-Haïtien, and there was nothing to do but go there and find them.

Beach and Livingston started out on foot from Cap-Haïtien on the morning of July 4, accompanied by a marine officer and six armed marines. They reached Petite Anse in an hour or so, only to find the place deserted. Following the road to the far side of the village, they discovered an armed sentry. Like most ordinary Haitians, this man did not speak French, but the native *patois* called *Créole*, a mixture of French and African linguistic elements. On hearing the name "Bobo," however, he pointed down the road, and the little party went on. Soon they

passed more sentries, and as the road narrowed into a jungle
trail a number of men fell in behind them, following
silently. For another hour they walked through the steaming countryside, accompanied ahead and behind by an
ever-growing escort of Haitians.

By the time they reached Bobo's main camp, the
Americans considered their situation dangerous, and they
were not reassured by the appearance of the men who
swarmed about them. "A more villainous appearing set of
men were never gathered together," Beach later recalled.
"All were but slightly clad, and each was armed with a
musket, a pistol, a sword, and a long, vicious-looking
knife." It was the Americans' first sight of the famed
cacos, the feared hill-fighters of northern Haiti who constituted the mercenary soldiers of each new revolution.
Beach told the marines to keep their weapons ready, an
order that was hardly necessary, since all were already
tense and on the alert.[10]

They were met in the *caco* camp by a well-dressed
general who addressed Beach in French. Bobo was gone
but would soon return, the general said; they must sit
down and wait for him. Stools were brought, everyone sat,
and the general launched into fulsome praise of Bobo,
while his auditors refreshed themselves with oranges and
hot coffee. The Haitian cooled abruptly, however, when he
learned of Beach's errand. Bobo too was anxious to avoid
injuring foreigners, he said, but if the government troops
refused to come out and fight, it would be necessary for
his forces to go into the city and attack them. Fearing that
tempers might rise, Beach gave the general Caperton's
letter, charged him with its delivery to Bobo, and
announced that the Americans must leave.

For a moment it seemed that Beach's words would
precipitate a crisis. The general declared peremptorily that
he would not permit them to go, while the marines
nervously fingered their rifles. But when Beach remained
firm, the Haitian changed his tone, pleading with them to
wait just a little longer for the absent Bobo. Finally, seeing

their determination to depart, he presented the group with
a fat turkey as a parting gift! As they left the last of the
cacos behind, the Americans breathed a sigh of under-
standable relief; only later, when Beach knew the Haitians
well, would he declare that they had been safe all the time.
The escort of armed *cacos* had been designed to show
them that Bobo actually possessed real forces, while the
officer's reluctance to let them go stemmed from his
certainty that Bobo would be upset at missing them, Beach
believed.[11]

While Beach provided liaison ashore, the admiral
looked to his outside communications. Upon arriving in
Haitian waters, Caperton had requested the use of the
U.S.S. *Eagle*, a small auxiliary vessel that happened to be
in the area. A converted yacht, little *Eagle* was negligible in
terms of naval power, but she could be useful for running
errands. Caperton ordered her to Port-au-Prince to gather
information about political conditions there, after which
she was to join him at Cap-Haïtien. She appeared at the
latter place on the 4th, at the same time that Beach was
off on his march to the *caco* camp. Port-au-Prince was
quiet, *Eagle*'s commander told Caperton, and the
Guillaume government seemed in control of all of the
country except the small area in the north where Bobo was
operating. Were any important negotiations under way
between Haiti and the United States?, Caperton asked,
remembering his previous visit to Haiti. This time it
seemed there were none; the United States had not even
recognized the Guillaume government, though Germany,
France, Italy, and some smaller nations had done so. As a
result, there had been little official intercourse since the
Fuller mission.[12]

Reassured that no major events were pending elsewhere, Caperton landed an officer and eleven marines to
establish a radio station at the local railroad depot. The
depot dominated the landward approach to Cap-Haïtien,
and the admiral desired instant contact with the shore. The
railroad was American-owned anyway, he reasoned, so that

he was merely protecting national property, while its strategic location was a clear bonus. Informed of the American action, General Blot made no objection.[13]

July 6 brought the first real shooting since Caperton's arrival. Government and rebel units clashed some three miles southeast of Cap-Haïtien, and during the afternoon General Blot left town for the scene of the fighting with 250 soldiers. Three dead and twenty-five wounded men from the government force were brought back to the city during the day, while about 250 more toops went to reenforce Blot on the following morning. It appeared that the fighting would continue to a decision. Even though the struggle took place well away from the city, as Caperton had demanded, the admiral now became apprehensive that it might end with both sides rushing into the city in an uncontrolled melee. This had happened before, he had been told, and he decided to prevent it by landing a force to block the road into town.[14]

The main road and the railroad from the interior both approached Cap-Haïtien by way of a peninsula which was separated from the town by the Haut du Cap River. The railroad came to an end at the station which occupied the tip of the peninsula, while the road crossed via a bridge to the town side of the river. The railroad station already occupied by Caperton's radio party thus commanded the main approaches to Cap-Haïtien, and Caperton ordered additional men to the spot. This outpost, to be manned by thirty marines, was supported by the guns of little *Eagle,* whose shallow draft enabled her to anchor close inshore on the bay side of the peninsula. The American admiral could thus virtually seal off the city to the Haitians by the deployment of minor units of his forces.

This was not to be done without informing General Blot, and at Caperton's request, Consul Livingston sought him out and asked his assent. Blot obviously could not give it, especially as his opponents had already charged the government with failure to defend Haitian independence from American encroachments. The general insisted that his

own forces could adequately protect foreign life and property, and that there was no occasion for United States
troops to land. Finding the admiral firm, Blot asked for
time to consult President Guillaume, but Caperton refused
to wait; the additional marines landed on the morning of
July 9.[15]

The next few days passed more quietly. On the 12th
the *Descartes* at last weighed anchor and steamed out of
Haitian waters. Her departure, however, was followed by a
period of sudden excitement. Heavy firing could be heard
outside the city, and by the next evening everyone was
talking of a great government victory over the rebels. By
July 15 the defeat of Bobo's army was confirmed; the
cacos were retreating into the hills and moving toward the
Dominican frontier. General Blot shrewdly proclaimed
amnesty to all who surrendered except the chief revolutionists, and Bobo seemed reduced to carrying on guerrilla
warfare in the hills. Two of Caperton's officers sent via
Eagle to the border region to gather information learned
that Bobo was believed to be short of money and ammunition, while the government had sent a second force to
cooperate with Blot's men in rooting out the rebels.[16]

By late July it appeared that Vilbrun Guillaume Sam
and his generals had achieved the unprecedented by
putting down a revolution already in full swing. This break
in the almost automatic rebel successes of recent years
might well check the spiral toward chaos which had characterized Haitian politics, and the Americans were corre-
spondingly pleased. "It is certainly very gratifying to hear
of the satisfactory termination of the trouble in Haiti,"
Admiral William S. Benson, the chief of naval operations,
wrote Caperton from Washington, "and we hope we will
soon be able to permit you to return to your old cruising
ground off the Mexican coast."[17]

These optimistic assumptions collapsed abruptly on
the morning of July 27, when *Washington* got word from
the cable station at Cap-Haïtien of an uprising in the
capital itself. Radioing the United States Legation in

Port-au-Prince for particulars, Caperton learned during the
next few hours that the president and his officials were
refugees in the French Legation, that the city was in the
hands of revolutionists, and that a last-minute mass execution of political prisoners by the collapsing Guillaume
regime had raised passions to a dangerous pitch. A warship
was needed at once, the Legation said, and the admiral
hastily prepared to sail for the new storm center. Leaving
Eagle to watch events in Cap-Haïtien, *Washington* left that
evening on her nearly 300-mile journey around the end of
the island.[18]

Even steaming at forced draft she could not reach the
capital until late the next morning, and the sun was high
by the time *Washington*'s bow cut the waters of the bay
before Port-au-Prince. As the cruiser anchored, the admiral
and his staff gathered on her quarterdeck to sweep the
shore with their binoculars. "I was about a mile off,"
Caperton recalled, "and I saw much confusion, people in
the streets, and apparently there was a procession, as if
they were dragging something through the city . . . ."[19]

What the admiral saw was the culmination of a bloody
and dramatic overturn in Haitian affairs, which ended the
remarkable efforts of Vilbrun Guillaume Sam to retain his
grip on the presidency. His policies had at first born fruit
in a sharply improved financial and military situation. In
addition to issuing eight million *gourdes* (the Haitian
monetary unit) in paper money, the government had
denounced its contract with the National Bank of Haiti
and retained the entire customs revenue for its own current expenses. Although these measures meant future
trouble with the bank, the creditors, and the United States
government, in the short run they had enabled Guillaume
to mount an unprecedented military effort against Rosalvo
Bobo's revolt. At the same time, the embattled president
fastened an iron grip on his capital, ruling through martial
law and jailing leading opponents. Suspicious that Bobo
received financial support from Port-au-Prince, Guillaume
ordered a systematic roundup of everyone even rumored

to be out of sympathy with his government. Soon some two hundred men were imprisoned, while hundreds more found customary sanctuary at foreign consulates and legations. By late July scores of the nation's principal leaders were in jail or in hiding, while ordinary citizens hardly dared venture on the streets for fear of being impressed on the spot into military service.[20]

To the growing number of dissatisfied politicians in the capital, the situation appeared grim. Their lot would be intolerable while Guillaume held power, yet Bobo's revolution was hopelessly stalled at the first hurdle; even if his troops were capable of taking Cap-Haïtien from the government forces, Admiral Caperton's decree still barred them from the city. Since revolution could no longer be made by the accepted rules, the rules must be broken, and the government overthrown in Port-au-Prince itself. This would not be easy. As tensions mounted in the city, Guillaume had brought in several hundred *caco* mercenaries to guard the presidential palace. Since these men were encamped in the palace grounds, the president was literally surrounded by his army. With the opposition scattered and in hiding, it would take a daring man to attempt an attack.

That man turned out to be Charles Delva, who had formerly been Port-au-Prince's chief of police, and, more notably, was remembered as an honest one. With others, Delva had taken refuge in the Portuguese Consulate. Somehow he managed from there to smuggle enough messages about the city to organize an uprising. His plan was necessarily short and simple, but it proved effective.[21] In the early morning of July 27, Delva and thirty-seven other armed men stole from their various refuges and made their way in the dark to the presidential palace. At 4:00 A.M. they attacked the *cacos* there, shouting and firing. Awakened in panic, the nearest *cacos* fled, while a few confederates of Delva among them helped the attackers to secure possession of some machine guns set up in the yard ready to fire. Their seizure was decisive. As the *cacos* began to rally, they were cut down in a hail of bullets that in minutes had killed fifty men and wounded scores of others. Guillaume's remaining mercenaries escaped or surrendered, while recruits swarmed to Delva's standard as fast as word of his action swept through the city. In no time resistance collapsed at the palace, and as the morning passed the government troops surrendered their last positions. By eleven o'clock the Guillaume regime had no organized defenders left in the capital.[22]

Caught by surprise, the president barricaded himself inside the palace with a handful of followers, while his attackers began preparations to fire the building in order to burn him out. In a final act of savagery, Guillaume sent orders to the commandant of the prison to kill every political prisoner if the president were driven from the palace. Having thus provided for vengeance, Guillaume made a last effort to save his own life. The grounds of the presidential palace and of the adjoining French Legation were separated by a high wall containing a single door. According to a widely circulated story, each Haitian president carried the key to this door on his person so that he could take refuge in the legation in case of need. Guillaume, too, presumably carried such a key, and when his position became hopeless at the palace he rushed to the door in the wall, hoping to get through it before anyone noticed him. Finding the lock rusted fast, he was forced to scale the wall, but the delay brought his enemies upon him and he was wounded in the leg before he escaped to the sanctuary of the French compound.[23]

In the meantime General Charles Oscar Ettienne, the commandant of the prison, carried out his orders with dreadful fidelity. Accompanied by his jailors, he went through the corridors personally supervising the slaughter. In cell after cell the occupants were shot and hacked to death, only a few surviving to tell what had happened. One survivor, struck by a machete, fell to the floor to be instantly covered by the body of a fellow victim who fell across him. He lay still and feigned death, even when the jailors pretended to be a rescue party and called for the living to come out at once and escape. He listened as most of the hidden survivors exposed themselves and were killed. For hours he lay on the floor, soaked in his own blood and that of the corpse atop him, hearing horrors that made him forget the pain of his wound. The worst of these was the slow demise of a young man in an adjoining cell, who had somehow incurred the enmity of a jailor. Aided by his fellows, the jailor pulled out his victim's teeth one by one, and then gouged his eyes out, as the sufferer screamed prayers for death. In all, almost 170 men died in the prison, including members of many of the most prominent families in the republic. Among the victims were two ex-presidents of Haiti, one of them Oreste Zamor, who had left office barely six months before.[24]

The slaughter at the prison was completed during the morning of the 27th and discovered by the townspeople soon afterward. An enormous crowd quickly gathered about the prison door, watching the appalling stream of mangled corpses carried out upon planks, one by one. As more and more of the watchers discovered the bodies of their own relatives, curses against the president and General Oscar Ettienne rose above the moans and cries of grief, and emotions rose to an unbearable pitch. Someone reported that Oscar had taken refuge in the Dominican Legation. Under normal circumstances this would have ensured his safety, but the events of the morning had swept away all traditional restraints. Edmond Polynice, a leading citizen who had just seen three of his sons carried dead from the prison, led the way to the legation, forced his way into it, and shot Oscar Ettienne dead before the door. For the next twenty-four hours the body lay on the sidewalk, cursed, spat upon, and riddled with the bullets of passersby. Finally it was soaked in oil and burned in the street.[25]

Rather than sating the mob, the killing of the prison commander only excited it further, and strengthened its eagerness to settle with Guillaume Sam himself. By early afternoon a crowd had collected about the French

Legation, where the fugitive president had gone. Justifiably alarmed, the French minister notified his British counterpart and the young American chargé, Robert Beale Davis, Jr., both of whom went immediately to join their colleague. Davis found a tense group gathered in the legation. The minister was particularly concerned for the safety of his wife and two daughters, but so far he had been equal to the situation. When the crowd outside had attempted to force an entrance, the Frenchman reminded its leaders of the many occasions when they themselves had found refuge in diplomatic sanctuaries. He appealed with special effect to Charles Zamor, influential brother of the ex-president who had been slain that morning at the prison. Zamor, who ten months earlier had owed his own life to the shelter of the French Legation, finally agreed to withdraw and to take his followers with him, but warned that he could not promise to control the enraged populace.[26]

Guillaume Sam, wounded and terrified, fully realized the desperation of his situation. With action no longer possible to him, his iron resolution broke, and he crept about the house like a hunted animal, crawling on hands and knees past spots exposed to outside view. As night came on his companions in hiding deserted him, choosing to attempt to escape in the darkness rather than await the vengeance of the people. Yet, so strong was the tradition of asylum and the inviolability of legations that the night passed without any further move to enter by the crowds that alternately gathered and dispersed until a late hour. By morning the town was quiet, and the crisis seemed past. Davis, the American chargé, returned to his own legation to find out when the warship he requested would arrive, and the British minister also departed on his own business. Beginning to relax at last, the French minister and his family sat in their drawing room with the doors open to the morning breeze. Suddenly, without warning, the house was full of men.[27]

Ironically, the *Washington* was unwittingly reponsible

for this incursion, the participants of which were mostly younger men of the upper class who had just attended the funeral of General Polynice's three murdered sons. The sight of the big cruiser on the horizon, black smoke pouring from her stacks and a huge white wave at her bow, had crystallized their intentions. The Americans would land to protect the legations, someone shouted, and then it would be too late; they must dispatch Guillaume Sam before the cruiser anchored![28]

The group, some seventy-five or eighty strong, rushed to the legation and took it by surprise. A quick search of the house turned up a man who closely resembled the president, but someone recognized him as the wrong man just as he was being dragged off to death. A more thorough search had almost failed as well, when the fugitive was betrayed by the smell of iodoform from a dressing on his wounded leg. Following this odor, the mob discovered a door hidden by the head of the minister's big bed, which had been moved to cover it. In the bathroom thus disclosed cowered Guillaume, whose end had come. He was dragged out of the house, beaten, stabbed, and pleading for his life, as his wife and children watched. Outside, he clung to a buggy in the driveway until his arm was broken by the blow of a club. The gates of the high iron fence being locked, the president was then thrown over the fence to a much larger crowd waiting outside the grounds. Once in their hands, he was literally torn to pieces. Davis, who had heard from afar the terrible howling of the mob, returned at this moment to see a man burst from the crowd flaunting a severed hand, the thumb of which he had stuck in his mouth. Others carried feet, the other hand, the head, and other portions of the body, while the remainder was dragged through the streets on a rope by crazed, screaming men and women.[29]

With the exception of Guillaume Sam, no one at the legation had been harmed, but the streets of the capital were swarming with frenzied crowds, and responsible observers, Haitian and foreign alike, were apprehensive that the almost unprecedented savagery of the past two days might find new outlets. To foreigners, the violation of the Dominican and French legations was particularly alarming, as it suggested that no haven of safety remained for them. Furthermore, other members of the fallen regime still hid in several of the legations. Would there be a general hunt for them? Would the mob eventually turn on the foreigners themselves? By the time *Washington* came to anchor, the diplomatic corps of Port-au-Prince was united in wanting immediate protection.

The chief diplomats were boarding his flagship soon after Admiral Caperton opened communication with the shore. The representatives of the United States, France, and Great Britain found the cruiser's decks crowded with a large landing party already mustered under arms, and they joined in insisting that these men be landed as soon as possible. The French minister was particularly exigent; deeply shaken by the lynching he had just witnessed, he reiterated that his legation had already been violated and his wife and daughters were unprotected; he had recalled the *Descartes* but she could not arrive for some time. More soberly, the others supported the Frenchman's position. There was no effective authority in the city, they said, while blood-crazed mobs ran everywhere. The Americans must take control of the situation, for at the moment there was no one else to protect life and property.[30]

All this only verified Caperton's own impressions, and he decided at once to land the troops, a decision which was reenforced within a few hours by a direct order from Washington. Detailed plans for a landing were ready at hand, for he had drawn them up during his previous visit to the capital in February. It would be wise, however, to insure that the landing was unopposed, at least by any organized force. The government having fallen, Caperton knew that the customary Committee of Safety would be in temporary charge in the capital. The admiral promptly composed a letter to this committee which explained his purpose, and entrusted it to Captain Beach for delivery and explanation ashore.[31]

Once more Beach found himself acting as Caperton's

emissary in an unknown situation. Accompanied by Lieutentant John N. Ferguson, the admiral's flag lieutenant, he took a boat to the waterfront and landed in the city. The two officers crossed the town through scenes of wild excitement and safely reached the presidential palace, where, as they had hoped, they found a Committee of Safety ensconced. Some of its members were uncomfortably close to the day's events: Charles Delva, who had started the revolt; Charles Zamor, whose brother had been murdered; Edmond Polynice, who had lost three sons at the prison and killed General Oscar Ettienne to avenge them—these and several others made up the committee. To them, Beach gave Caperton's letter, accompanied by a quick verbal summary of what the Americans expected of them.

"The Committee was told that the town was under the *Washington*'s guns and that a hostile reception of the Admiral's troops would endanger the city's existence," Beach wrote later. The Americans came in friendship, but any attack on them would be severely punished. The committee should endeavor to get the people off the streets and the soldiers back into their barracks. In his letter, Caperton expressed the hope that the committee would cooperate with him in bringing order out of chaos in Port-au-Prince. Beach's verbal supplement indicated that it would be the worse for them if they did not. Finally, Beach asked that a high-ranking Haitian official, preferably one of the committee members, should meet the Americans upon landing and guide them into town, using his influence to prevent any clashes on the way.[32]

After some discussion the committee assented in principle, although they insisted that they could not guarantee the safe entry of the Americans. They designated one of their number, General Erman Robin, as the requested guide. In the meantime *Washington* had been brought closer in to shore and moored broadside to the city, with her decks cleared for action and her guns trained out. At five in the afternoon, *Washington*'s boats began to ferry the landing party to a stretch of beach at Bizoton on the south side of the bay, about three miles west of the center of town. This meant marching into a strange city as night fell, but the admiral felt that the situation gave him no choice; in his opinion, "reasons of policy greatly out-weighed those of tactics" in this case. Some 330 men were landed, 165 sailors and 165 marines, all under the command of Captain George Van Orden of the Marine Corps. Met by General Robin, the little column entered the city about 7:00 P.M., then dispersed into smaller units posted at the legations, the market place, and other key points. There was no resistance, though random firing kept every-one on edge.[33]

As darkness settled over the city, the Americans bivouacked for the night, while those aboard *Washington* watched anxiously for signs of trouble. Uncertain as the situation was, one thing was rapidly becoming clear: after almost a year of teetering on the brink, the United States had inaugurated a military intervention in Haiti.

4

First Days
of the
Haitian Intervention

FOR THE Americans the night of July 28 seemed interminable. Both to the men ashore and to their shipmates aboard *Washington,* the little landing force seemed desperately vulnerable, camped as it was in the middle of a foreign city gone mad. While the afternoon's landing had been unopposed, the tone of the townspeople was distinctly unfriendly, and as the troops moved into the city, they had found a large crowd awaiting them which threatened to block their advance. According to an American reporter, the officers in charge led the column straight into the crowd, which gave way sullenly before them. Some men on nearby rooftops had fired a few shots over the heads of the Americans, but no harm was done; presumably the shots were intended only as a warning.[1]

After dark, however, scattered firing began, which seemed to come from every part of the city and continued through most of the night. Keeping vigil on *Washington*'s quarterdeck, Admiral Caperton grew increasingly concerned about the shooting, the sound of which carried

62

clearly across the water. Finally two lieutenants of his staff volunteered to go ashore to reconnoiter. They reported on their return that the landing force seemed to be all right, but beyond that they had learned little. No one doubted that the Haitians were firing at the Americans, and the lack of execution was attributed chiefly to the darkness. The men of the landing force, their minds full of the horrors of the previous day, believed themselves in real danger from the savage horde which they thought surrounded them. Captain Beach remembered it as "a dreadful night, filled with apprehension of impending evil."

In the morning everyone was astounded to find that not a man in the force had been hurt. Beach later learned the reason for this seemingly miraculous escape. After he had cultivated intimate relations with the Haitians, they all insisted that no one had fired at the Americans that night. On the night after a government fell, it was customary to celebrate by firing into the air; the more unpopular the fallen government, the more firing occurred. Thus the Americans had probably been in no danger, but their very different impression at the time undoubtedly influenced their actions in the period just after the landing.[2]

On the evening of the 28th Caperton had received via the Navy Department the first terse instructions from the secretary of state. American forces should land to protect life and property (they had already done so); the British and French ministers should be informed of this American protection and requested not to call for landing parties of their own; beyond this, Caperton was authorized to act at his own discretion. The admiral in turn asked for the early dispatch of whatever marines were available at Guantanamo Bay and was promised a small but immediate reenforcement from that nearby source.[3]

On July 29, the day after the initial landing, Caperton took several measures to improve his situation. The first of these was to appeal to Washington for larger reenforcements. "Men have little rest and much exposed to extreme heat," he cabled, and at any rate they were too few for

effective control of an entire city: "Earnestly request
marine regiment be sent Port au Prince." At the same time
he sent orders to Captain Van Orden, in charge of the landing force, to begin disarming the Haitians in the streets,
cooperating with their leaders when possible. Van Orden
was also to place outposts at all approaches to the city,
seizing any arms or ammunition going in or out. Fearing
attack, the admiral wished to round up the weapons in the
city as rapidly as possible and to prevent more from coming in. To do this most effectively, however, it was desirable to work through some local authority. At the
moment, the only semblance of such authority was the
Committee of Safety, or "Revolutionary Committee," as it
now called itself, and Caperton decided to attempt to use
this body for his purpose. As his agent in the attempt he
chose Captain Beach, whom he formally designated his representative ashore.[4]

Beach began his delicate mission that day, setting up
headquarters at the United States Legation. In the absence
of Arthur Bailly-Blanchard, who had been called home on
leave after the failure of negotiations with Guillaume Sam,
the legation was in the temporary charge of Robert Beale
Davis, Jr., a young lawyer from Virginia who was normally
the legation secretary. The relatively inexperienced Davis
had already received instructions from the State Department to "confer and cooperate with Admiral Caperton in
all possible ways," a hint that he was quick to take. At the
first opportunity, Davis told Caperton that he considered
the situation one where military direction took precedence
over diplomacy. Confessing himself a novice at diplomacy
besides, he put himself virtually under Caperton's orders.
The resulting relationship was a smooth one, Beach in particular coming to respect Davis's judgment and to find his
assistance valuable. Most important, Caperton was from
the beginning in complete local charge of the Haitian intervention; under the circumstances, even the State Department wished it so.[5]

From the legation Beach sent messages asking the members of the Revolutionary Committee to come there to meet him. All seven members promptly responded, and the American naval officer was soon in conference with the Haitian group, several of whom he found personable and interesting. The dashing Charles Delva, who had almost personally overthrown Guillaume Sam, showed a blunt but engaging nature, a readiness to laugh, and a total lack of pretension. Charles Zamor and the elderly Edmond Polynice, who had also played prominent roles in the events of the previous days, were polished, knowledgeable, and politically shrewd. These three men, Beach felt, constituted the leadership of the committee. Of the others, Beach thought two of minor importance, a third a "crook," and the fourth "just a horrible *caco.*"[6]

The conferees soon struck a bargain. Each member of the Revolutionary Committee agreed to recognize Caperton's authority, while the Americans would back the committee's administration of affairs in Port-au-Prince. Beach and the committee would meet daily to coordinate their actions, which were to begin at once. Flanked by Davis and Captain Van Orden of the marines, Beach outlined an initial program for the city: the committee and its agents would undertake to disarm everyone found in the streets, soldiers and civilians alike, and confiscate arms and ammunition wherever found. At the committee's insistence, all of the weapons confiscated were to be taken to the presidential palace and stored under the guard of city policemen armed with clubs. After a long discussion, the committee acquiesced in this much, but rejected Beach's further proposal that the Americans should occupy the city's barracks, displacing the government troops.[7]

While Beach oversaw the initial arrangements on shore, the admiral attempted to evaluate the flood of rumors that swept the uneasy city. Both houses of the Haitian Congress were in session and attempting to elect a president. No one candidate could command a majority, though Rosalvo

Bobo was said to be among the strongest, and the day
ended without a decision. In Haiti the president was
elected directly by the Congress, while in the absence of a
president the Congress could perform no other function
than to choose one. In the past, this had usually been a
foregone conclusion: they chose the man who had made
good his claim to be chief of the executive power by
winning a revolution. But in the present situation no one
had a clear claim, nor had anyone an army in the capital to
back his aspirations—no one, that is, except Caperton.
Congress's failure to elect a president at once, while the
intervention was in its infancy, was to prove decisive.
Caperton soon felt able to delay the election until he
could control its outcome, while so long as the national
government was thus immobilized, there was no local
authority beyond the Revolutionary Committee.[8]

Political issues were augmented by military ones. During the afternoon reports circulated that there would be an
attack on the American landing force that night, launched
from outside of the city. Coincident with these alarms
came the welcome arrival of the naval collier *Jason* from
Guantanamo Bay, carrying a company of marines. These
were sent ashore immediately, raising the total strength of
the landing force to something over four hundred men.
Captain Van Orden redeployed his scanty units to cover
the approaches to the city, while *Washington*'s crew
readied her three- and six-inch guns for any hostile targets
which might be spotted by the ship's searchlights during
the night.

The rumors of a night attack on the 29th seemed
validated when firing again broke out after dark. It was not
severe, appearing to consist merely of sniping from bushes
at the south edge of town and American counter-fire.
Nevertheless, the landing force took its first casualties in
this engagement. Two seamen were killed, one of them the
nephew of Samuel Gompers, president of the American
Federation of Labor. On the Haitian side, Caperton
reported six of the attackers killed and two wounded. The

affair constituted no threat to the American military position; indeed, subsequent investigation suggested that the
two Americans had been killed by the fire of their own
nervous comrades, and it was by no means certain that
there had even been a Haitian attack. At the moment,
however, the landing force believed itself threatened, as
did the admiral and his superiors in the United States.[9]

"It is believed here that the Haytians probably will
continue their sniping, as the Mexicans did at Vera Cruz,"
wrote a newspaper correspondent back in Washington,
"But it is expected that Rear Admiral Caperton will be
able to discourage them in this practice in a few days by
dropping an occasional shell at odd intervals from the big
guns on the Washington into the woods about the city,
where the snipers appear to be hiding."[10]

Closer to the scene, the admiral was both less bloodthirsty and less cheerful than the anonymous reporter.
"No cause for alarm," he radioed Washington the next
morning, "but absolutely necessary I have sufficient force
to handle situation." Later in the day he spelled out his
concerns more fully. "At least one regiment of marines
absolutely necessary at Port au Prince at once. City covers
large area and has population sixty thousand. Four
hundred men not sufficient to guard town . . . . Men
becoming exhausted by excessive work period." The admiral was also worried about the Haitian government
forces near Cap-Haïtien. "What action Army in North will
take when news reaches them of American occupancy not
known. They can reach Port au Prince in one week."[11]

To these messages the admiral received a quick but
unwelcome reply from the secretary of the navy. The gunboats Castine and Nashville, which he had requested for
Haitian duty, would sail to join him as soon as they could
be made ready, but no extra marines were available. Nevertheless, Caperton should "retain possession of town until
further orders." These tidings brought consternation to the
little group of officers on the Washington, but they were
superseded by a new dispatch a few hours later which

promised that five hundred additional marines would sail the next day from Philadelphia aboard the battleship *Connecticut,* along with twenty machine guns, ample supplies of small-arms ammunition, and field pieces supplied with shrapnel shells. At the end of the day a third message from the Navy Department further lightened the mood on *Washington's* quarterdeck: "Department appreciates excellent manner in which disturbance at Port au Prince has been handled," it began, and was signed "Daniels."[12]

Throughout the 30th the work of disarming the people of Port-au-Prince continued uninterrupted. In the course of the day five wagon loads of arms and cartridges were collected and deposited under guard at the palace. Though the work was done largely by the landing force, the Revolutionary Committee gave it public sanction, posting proclamations periodically through the day. The committee's first proclamation announced its own personnel and proclaimed a state of siege, a condition amounting to modified martial law. This was followed by a broadside prohibiting the carrying of arms and the holding of political meetings, and establishing a nightly curfew in the city. A third proclamation gave further detailed rules for the maintenance of order, but here Admiral Caperton stepped in: "This I hastened to supplement by advising the Committee that our men would carry out the provisions of that particular order."[13]

In the meantime, Captain Beach was visiting the editorial offices of the city's principal newspapers in an attempt to calm their fears about the American intervention. One daily, *Le Nouvelliste,* had editorially protested the presence of the troops on the 29th, asking rhetorically if certain excesses during a time of great excitement justified the flagrant violation of Haitian territory. Fearing that the previous night's shooting affray would add to the prevailing apprehensions, Beach called personally on the editors of *Le Nouvelliste.* In the ensuing interview, the captain deplored the recent night firing and asked the editors to display calm and patience. He made a distinctly favorable impression on the Haitian journalists, who found Beach courteous and dignified; they reported to their readers that they told him they would try to be patient, but would not promise to change their attitude toward the American landing.[14]

From *Le Nouvelliste* Beach proceeded to the office of *Le Matin,* another Port-au-Prince daily, where he gave assurances that the Americans came in friendship, seeking only to restore order and to forestall European intervention; they had absolutely no designs on Haitian independence. The next day he enlarged on this theme during a second visit to the editors of *Le Nouvelliste.* The recent disorders, he said, had imposed certain international obligations on the United States, and the troops had been landed to fulfill them. They had no other purpose in Haiti. If the Haitians wished the troops to leave as soon as possible, so did the Americans, and the best way to speed this universal goal was to cooperate in the restoration of tranquillity. For so long as there was disorder, the Americans would stay; if hotheads provoked violence, therefore, they would only prolong the situation which they professed to oppose. With the cooperation of all good Haitians, however, amity could be preserved, and Beach ended by inviting the public to visit him in person at the United States Legation, promising to receive them cordially.[15]

Admiral Caperton took exactly the same line with the American press. "The occupation of Port au Prince by the forces of the United States will be of short duration," the admiral told a reporter for a New York newspaper, "if the people will calm themselves and abide by the orders which have been issued looking to disarmament and the restoring of peace." He declared that the American landing had "nothing to do with any diplomatic negotiations of the past or the future." If he had not sent troops ashore to restore order, French and British warships would have come, and their landing parties might now patrol the streets of the capital. Thus Beach and Caperton, in these and other public statements, pictured the intervention as no more than a necessary response to the events of July 27-28 and played down the long-term implications which it might have for the Haitians.[16]

While the two commanders labored to put the best face on their actions, new complications continued to arise during the last two days of July. On the 30th the *Descartes* arrived in port, posing again the question of the landing of French marines. The French minister was firm in his demand for a legation guard of his own government's troops. He fully trusted the Americans to provide security, he said, but French honor had been touched by the violation of his legation and must be vindicated. If no French troops landed, the Haitians would think that he had been abandoned by his government and the prestige of France would suffer. Caperton suggested to the State Department that they handle the matter in Washington, but the French ambassador there echoed his colleague: the landing of a French legation guard in Port-au-Prince had become a point of national honor. The French marines would be confined to the legation grounds and would carefully avoid any interference with the Americans, but they must land. Ultimately the *Descartes* sent ashore an officer and thirty men, with the reluctant approval of the State Department.[17]

A lesser incident with the German minister was easier to handle. The German lodged with Davis a protest against Admiral Caperton's order forbidding the carrying of concealed weapons in Port-au-Prince, asking by what right and authority an American naval officer could give such orders. With the impetuosity of youth, Davis returned a stinging reply: "By that same right and authority which you acknowledged when you asked for, received, and still retain a guard of American Marines at your Legation."[18]

Local politics were more perplexing. To begin with, the exact status of the Revolutionary Committee was a puzzle. The cooperation of the committee was unquestionably useful, and Davis reported on the 31st that it was "seemingly acting in good faith and practically under

[the] Admiral's direction." On the 30th, however, the entire committee had come out openly in support of Rosalvo Bobo for president. Thus it was no longer merely an administrative body, but had become a partisan political bloc as well; it would be difficult to support it in one function without seeming to endorse it in the other. The difficulty was the more apparent in that Bobo was a leading opponent of United States influence in Haiti![19] As a further complication, both the committee and the Haitian Congress were eager to elect a president, but Caperton was by no means ready to face this vital issue. On the 31st the Chamber of Deputies sent a delegation to inquire if the admiral had any objection to their proceeding with an election, and received in return his request that they delay the election until order had been more fully restored. Recognizing Caperton's practical control of affairs, the chamber acceded to his desires for the time being.[20]

The presence in the capital of a large number of *cacos* and unpaid soldiers added another factor of instability. Food supplies were running low in the city and prices were soaring, bringing extra hardship to the poor. Occasional incidents between citizens and United States troops created added stress. The mood of the populace was volatile, and in the absence of recognized leadership the inevitable jockying of political factions was already under way among the elite. The situation was extremely fluid, and to the admiral it seemed that his superiors in Washington failed to understand how tenuous was his position. He was particularly irked by a State Department instruction that under no circumstances should he hand over control of the capital to Haitian authorities, and on the 31st he read them a little lecture: "The State Department . . . evidently thinks that a *de facto* government exists here. All government functions are at present carried on by a committee of citizens practically under my direction."[21]

Assured that a battleship and another five hundred marines were on the way, Caperton could begin to feel more confident about his future control of the city.

Nevertheless, he meant to stay alert during the few days remaining until *Connecticut* arrived. The constant search for weapons turned up new stores daily, while there remained the possibility that arms were hidden in quantity somewhere outside the city, available on short notice. Believing that his men had been under fire on the night of July 28 as well as that of the 29th, the admiral saw no reason to take their security for granted. As soon as his reenforcements came, he meant to secure the city, in ways currently beyond the capability of his limited military resources.[22]

Looking further afield, there was the problem of the two armies in the north that had been contesting for political control. The fall of Guillaume's government had cut much of the ground from under General Blot, while Bobo's *cacos* were once more concentrating near Cap-Haïtien. Bobo had clearly not given up his attempt on the presidency, and he now enjoyed the open support in the capital which he had lacked before. Seeking a way out of his tight corner, Blot announced his adherence to the cause of General Darius Bourand, former minister of the interior under Guillaume Sam, who commanded government troops nearer the Dominican border. Blot's announcement nominally united all the former Guillaume forces in the area under Bourand, who now also claimed the executive power, and raised the possibility of new fighting between the rival northern chieftains. This situation had direct consequences in the south as well; the question of the presidency could never be genuinely settled so long as the main political armies survived intact in the hinterlands. Even worse, Caperton feared that one or both of these factions might decide at any moment to march their forces southward to challenge the American possession of their capital. The controlling factors of the situation, he concluded, lay ultimately not in Port-au-Prince but in the Cap-Haïtien area. Years afterward, the admiral still recalled the complexities of that time with something close to despair: "It was a very maze, a crazy quilt of a state of affairs."[23]

A plan of action emerged on July 31, in the course of a long conference between Caperton, Beach, Davis, and others. The conferees decided to despatch to Cap-Haïtien a commission of influential Haitians who would attempt to secure three pledges from the leaders there: that the government forces would embark on the Haitian gunboat *Nord Alexis* and sail to Port-au-Prince, that Bobo's *cacos* would disband and return to their homes, and that Bobo and his chiefs in particular would report personally to Caperton at the capital.[24]

Having adopted this plan, Caperton ordered it implemented at once, and it fell to Beach to recruit the commission. The selection of the group's members could determine its success or failure, and Beach promptly sought advice. Both he and the admiral had already received plenty of this commodity—Beach later recalled that in these first days Caperton interviewed scores of Haitians while Beach himself interviewed hundreds—but he now solicited the views of former Foreign Minister Jacques Nicolas Léger, who for many years had been the Haitian minister at Washington. Not only was Léger at home with Americans, but Beach respected his integrity. While willing to give advice, the ex-diplomat consistently rejected any official tie with the United States authorities on the ground that he wished to retain his freedom to oppose them if need be, a position which Beach thought both honest and proper.

Léger approved of the plan to send a commission to Cap-Haïtien, and at Beach's request he actually named the members. He chose three men from the Revolutionary Committee, including Polynice and the subtle Charles Zamor, whose influence was great in the north. Besides these, Léger selected the local archbishop and ex-President François Denis Légitime, an aged man who had briefly been head of state a quarter of a century earlier. The enterprise might well succeed, Léger thought; the government troops were certain to be eager to come home, while Zamor and the other Boboites would try to convince their candidate that he could best serve his interests by a personal appearance in Port-au-Prince.[25]

All of the nominees agreed to make the trip, and Caperton completed the commission by adding his own aide, Lieutenant R. B. Coffey, who was sent along to see that the admiral's instructions were obeyed. The party sailed on August 1 aboard *Jason,* the Haitians formally attired in black silk hats and frock coats in spite of the heat. The gunboat *Nashville* had by this time arrived at Cap-Haïtien to join *Eagle,* and Coffey had orders to secure the support of Commander Percy N. Olmstead, *Nashville*'s commanding officer, for his campaign of persuasion.[26]

The departure of the commission for Cap-Haïtien was common knowledge in the capital, and its mission was generally regarded as having great political significance. No result could be expected for several days, however, and in the interim Caperton continued to wrestle with the situation in Port-au-Prince. He was particularly concerned about the conjunction of large numbers of idle men in the city and the severe food shortage which had driven up the cost of living. He soon conceived two alternative approaches to the problem, one aimed at making food available and the other jobs. The food project was the simpler; Caperton suggested that the navy donate provisions to the local clergy, who could distribute them to those in need. This would ameliorate suffering, improve the mood of the townspeople, and enhance the American image among them. A second alternative was to provide local employment on a large scale through public works projects. The American-owned Haitian Construction Company had contracted with the Haitian government the previous year to pave the streets of the capital and lay a sewer system. The work had actually begun, but the government's chronic lack of funds had brought it to a halt. Up to 1200 men could be employed on the project if funds could be found to resume it, and Caperton believed that the money would be well spent. These proposals were received coldly at the Navy Department, however, and

Secretary Daniels quickly ruled out spending the navy's money for Haitian relief. If necessary, Caperton could *sell* naval provisions in the city at cost, but there would be no donations of government supplies. The admiral should rather encourage influential Haitians to organize relief societies of their own. "Great danger of encouraging idleness should be kept in mind," Daniels warned.[27]

Even more serious than the rejection of the admiral's relief plans was the rift which opened at this time between the American authorities and the Revolutionary Committee. This group attempted independent action on the night of August 1, when they arrested and jailed one Joseph Dessources, an ex-senator with presidential aspirations who had been publicly critical of the committee. Beach learned of the action the next morning and quickly investigated. In spite of his low opinion of Dessources—whom he described as a "vulgar chief of Cacos," a villainous and semiliterate man who affected a Prince Albert coat and silk hat—the captain urged Caperton to intervene in the case. The committee must not be allowed to exercise the power of political arrest, he argued; Caperton agreed, and ordered the prisoner released. When Captain Van Orden went to enforce this order, General Robin of the Revolutionary Committee attempted to dissuade him. Dessources was an anti-American agitator, Robin said, and was certain to make trouble if left free. Unmoved, Van Orden proceeded to remove Dessources from the prison, and Robin lost his temper: perhaps they would not meet again in friendship, he declared threateningly.[28]

Caperton regarded that statement as mere bravado, but the next morning brought the committee's response. Squads of unarmed soldiers appeared at posts throughout the city, challenging passersby and demanding countersigns in the name of the Revolutionary Committee. Again the committee was attempting to assert an independent authority, and the city was tense with the prospect of a clash. Perplexed, the admiral considered his alternatives. "Revolutionary Committee at first acted practically under

my direction, but now frequently give orders without my
knowledge and act more independently," he complained
to Washington on August 3. Yet dismissal of the group
would bring further difficulties: "I must have some agents
for the direction of affairs or else must assume entire civil
and military control which is undesirable at present."[29]

Captain Beach, the admiral's principal adviser, was by
this time convinced that the Revolutionary Committee
meant to become the real power in any new Haitian government. It began with two solid assets: a recognized
authority and a close working relationship with the Americans. It still had a number of soldiers under its nominal
control, and was even able to expend government funds,
though Beach freely admitted that it spent little, all of it
for proper purposes. The committee's aim, he thought, was
to determine the presidential succession by persuading the
Americans to support their candidate, for with Caperton
behind them they could hardly fail to secure the election
of whomever they chose.

The group had originally hoped to rush their man into
office before the Americans could exert any influence on
the matter, thus presenting the admiral with a fait
accompli. However, a widespread nervousness in the wake
of the recent bloodletting was manifest among leading
politicians, and the result was an unprecedented scarcity
of first-class presidential candidates. Rumor had it that the
committee had hurriedly canvassed a dozen local prospects, all of whom declined interest, before settling almost
by default on the candidacy of Rosalvo Bobo. If Bobo was
not their first choice, he was an active and well-known
candidate with important backing of his own, and once the
committee publicly joined forces with him its die was
cast. But it proved impossible to elect him quickly, while
the growing United States intervention changed the
situation fundamentally. Committee members lost no
opportunity to praise Bobo to the Americans, but they
were handicapped by Bobo's previous anti-American platform and disquieted by Caperton's noncommittal stance.

At the least, the Haitians needed the admiral's acquiescence; as Beach said, "All assumed he would practically determine who was to be elected President."[30]

A growing fear that Caperton would not accept Bobo's election, coinciding with the departure of the shrewdest members of the committee for Cap-Haïtien, led the remaining members to contemplate changing their tactics from persuasion to pressure. While they had no wish to fight, they were astute enough to see that Caperton was almost as eager as they to avoid a clash. The admiral's zeal in safeguarding life and property was by now well known to the Haitians and appeared to impose further limits upon his options. The Haitians doubted, for example, that Caperton would ever order *Washington*'s big guns turned on the city; the resulting death and destruction would represent precisely what he was there to prevent. They thought it might be time to hint at their own fighting potential, to suggest that blocking their plans might bring serious trouble. Perhaps they could present the election of Bobo to the Americans as the price of peace. The arrival of the new marine regiment on August 4, therefore, came at a sensitive moment. In Beach's view, the committee "was acting for the Admiral where it had to, and for itself where it could," while the people of the capital were uncertain of the limits of its authority.[31]

The five hundred men of the Second Marine Regiment were a welcome sight to the weary sailors and marines of *Washington*'s little landing force, who had been on duty day and night for a week. Worn down by heat and anxiety, their tensions dropped away magically with the knowledge that United States forces in the area had more than doubled in strength. Nor was this fact lost on the Haitians. The commander of the palace guard sought an interview with Caperton while the new force was still landing. He professed to be wholly pro-American and completely at the admiral's disposal, avowedly speaking for both himself and his soldiers. Offering Capteron the keys to the presidential palace, he asked only guarantees for the safety of himself and his men. The Americans were there to guarantee the safety of everyone, Caperton responded, so long as they committed no hostile acts; he had no intention of occupying the palace, however, and no need for its keys. Dismissing the Haitian, Caperton told him to return to his post.[32]

By the time the *Connecticut* dropped anchor with his new reinforcements, Caperton had planned a series of decisive moves. Under the command of Colonel Eli K. Cole, the Second Marines began to disembark on the afternoon of the 4th, landing stores and men steadily through the night. Without waiting for their fellows, the first units to land entered the city and marched straight to the Casernes Dessalines, a central military post marked by Caperton for early seizure. Startled by the sudden appearance of the armed and business-like marines, the Haitian soldiery decamped, leaving behind most of their arms and ammunition. The next day Cole and his men continued their rapid deployment. On the afternoon of the 5th Cole himself led three companies, one of seamen and two of marines, out to Fort National, which crowned a hill just outside of the city. The fort held both a garrison and an important arms depot and was another of the points whose seizure had a high priority on Caperton's agenda. Once arrived at the fort, the marine colonel halted his men and went into parley with the Haitian general in charge. After prolonged persuasion and vacillation, the Haitian agreed to surrender ʱ fort peacefully, and he finally reentered it accom- ̣ ied by the navy lieutenant from the bluejacket ̣pany. Upon hearing their general's tidings some of the ̣ison surrendered, but most simply jumped over the ̣pet and ran away, a course which Cole made no effort ̣ iscourage. Inside the fort the Americans found four- ̣ cannons of varying vintage, 450 rifles, and over a ̣on rounds of ammunition.[33]

̣hat night Charles Delva, as president of the Revolu- ̣ry Committee, sent Admiral Caperton a formal ̣n protest. He had originally told Captain Beach, he

said, that the American landings should be limited to plac-
ing two to five men each in the various legations and
consulates. Instead there had been a mass incursion of
United States troops, which had seized official places
"after having forced the door and tramped under foot the
national flag." Today it was Fort National; next the
National Palace might be menaced. Such actions constituted an illegitimate occupation "which outrages the
sovereignty and rights of the nation." In addition to his
protest to Caperton, Delva said, he was sending a similar
letter to Davis at the United States Legation, in the hope
that the State Department would intervene to rectify the
situation.[34]

There was much truth in what Delva said; it was
becoming difficult to speak of the growing American
presence as mere protection of life and property. Yet in
the absence of guidance from Washington, it was impossible for Caperton to call it anything else. He had been told
only that he must not hand back the city to Haitian control, and he firmly believed that in order to stay on safely
he must have full control of it himself. That control
achieved, there remained the twin political questions of
the presidential election and the progress of affairs at Cap-
Haïtien.

The Congress had submitted gracefully to Caperton's
request on July 31 that they postpone the choice of a
president. As the days passed, however, the pressure for an
election grew on all sides. The Revolutionary Committee
wished to hold it quickly while Bobo still lacked major
rivals. The Congress was eager to fill the presidency so that
it could function again; there was a jealous hostility
between the congressmen and the Revolutionary Committee, each refusing the recognize the other's authority. The
election of a president would end the life of the rival Revolutionary Committee and restore congressional powers,
though the committee members in turn hoped to survive in
power as the principal ministers of the new chief execut-
tive. Beyond these purely tactical considerations, most

Haitians in and out of politics felt that the nation was helpless and vulnerable so long as it lacked a functioning government. As Beach put it, "There was an uneasy feeling that perhaps the United States might make demands that Haiti could not, with self respect, agree to, and that there should be a Haitian government in existence, prepared to negotiate with the United States."[35]

In order to ease the pressure, Admiral Caperton let it be known on August 4 that presidential aspirants could now come forward and publically announce their candidacies. A number of figures at once tested the political winds, and on the following day the Haitian Congress formally announced that the election would occur on the following Sunday. Again the admiral interceded, and again the election day was indefinitely postponed, but this time the Congress was notably reluctant to comply. The truth was that Caperton himself was becoming desirous of securing a president as soon as possible and had postponed the election only because he thought it necessary. On the day he took the action he reported to Washington the desirability of setting the Haitian government to running again: "Progress toward good government could soon be commenced with protection and influence by the United States. At present time, except as directed by me, there is no central government and the Haytian people are anxious to have a president elected. Haytians also fear at present that the continuance of their independence may not be permitted by the United States."[36]

In addition to awaiting the return of the mission to the north, a major reason for holding off the election was the Americans' fear that Congress would be intimidated by the *cacos* who remained in the city. Guillaume Sam had brought in some 1500 of these mercenaries, and disarming them had been one of Caperton's first concerns. Most of them now supported Bobo's candidacy, having made common cause with the Revolutionary Committee. Beach was certain that the committee's eagerness for an early election now stemmed from their intention to use these *cacos* to control the outcome. In his eyes, the Americans were working against time to disarm and neutralize the *cacos* before an election was held. Caperton fully shared Beach's fears, reporting that "the election of Bobo as president has been demanded by them [the *cacos*], and Congress, terrorized by the mere demands is on the point of complying but my request [for postponement] restrained. No other man could be elected under present conditions on account fear of cacos." To counter this influence, the admiral maintained his pressure on the *cacos* until many left town in disgust. As he drily commented, "No obstructions were put in their way."[37]

Each day the political pressures mounted in the capital, but Caperton was determined to prevent a decision until his "peace mission" returned from Cap-Haïtien. If the mission were successful, all the threads of the political tangle would cross in Port-au-Prince, where the admiral could grasp them and weave them to his purpose.

5

Tightening the Grip

AS EVERYONE awaited the return of the mission to the north, the question of the presidency became daily more pressing. While various Haitians tested the political waters, the Americans labored to keep up with events and to judge the alternatives open to them. It became Beach's duty to gather information about the men most prominently mentioned and sound out their attitudes regarding the United States. At first the presumptive candidates seemed to disappear as fast as they fell under the scrutiny of the Americans; man after man quickly removed himself from consideration. Among these early dropouts was Charles Delva, the president of the Revolutionary Committee. Delva had declared for Bobo with the rest of the committee, but some of the politicos at the capital pointed out in private that Bobo had so far accomplished little, while Delva had overthrown the previous president almost alone. Thus Delva had first claim on the succession, the argument ran, and should be persuaded to drop Bobo's cause and espouse his own. Intrigued, Beach called on Delva and

82

brought the matter up, but the dashing Haitian refused to discuss his own candidacy. Instead, he strongly reaffirmed his loyalty to Bobo, a position to which he adhered until the presidency was filled.[1]

As the Haitians clamored for an election and Caperton feared the imposition of Bobo by the *cacos,* Beach searched for a safe alternative among the nation's elder statesmen. He first tried J. N. Léger, the former minister to the United States, but Léger had no interest in the presidency. "I am for Haiti; not for the United States," he told Beach; "Haiti's president will have to accept directions and orders from the United States and I propose to keep myself in a position where I will be able to defend Haiti's interests." Francois Légitime, the aged former president, was also approached before he left on the mission to Cap-Haïtien, and also rejected Beach's advance. A third possibility was the incumbent Haitian minister at Washington, Doctor Solon Menos, but his chances were gravely lessened by his absence from the country, and at any rate he declared himself unwilling to enter the race.[2]

Of those who desired to run, few were attractive to Caperton and Beach. One man, however, seemed suitable. Philippe Sudre Dartiguenave, the president of the Senate, was first mentioned publicly as a candidate on August 2, and in the ensuing days Beach looked him over. Accompanied by Lieutenant E. G. Oberlin, one of the admiral's aides, the captain met privately with Dartiguenave and one of his leading supporters at a house outside the city. The prospective candidate declared with becoming modesty that there were men better qualified than he for the presidency; he did not seek the post, he said, but was willing to serve if elected. More important, he was ready to accept long-term controls over Haiti by the United States. According to Beach's version of the discussion, Dartiguenave declared that "all thinking Haitians" foresaw the presentation of a treaty by the United States which would provide for the control of customs by the Americans, as well as sufficient military control to insure order and stability.

They were prepared to accept such a treaty, he said, so long as it involved no cession of territory or independence.[3]

Though never a faction leader, Dartiguenave was a man of substance in congressional politics, and Beach and Caperton soon concluded that he was the candidate they wanted. By August 5 Caperton was singing his praises to Washington as a man of honor and ability who was anxious for the regeneration of Haiti. Unlike most of the candidates, he had never been involved in any revolutionary activity, nor was he hostile to the Americans. "He realizes that Haiti must agree to any terms demanded by the United States," Caperton explained pointedly, "and he professes to believe that any terms laid down by us will be for Haytian benefit." Dartiguenave had also given his assurance that he would use his influence in the Haitian Congress to secure the agreement of that body to American demands. This would be no slight advantage, for in Haiti the president of the Senate customarily disbursed patronage and money to its members, and possessed a corresponding influence. Caperton believed Dartiguenave to be personally honest, but he too had acted as the dispenser of government spoils and perquisites. "Should he be elected," the admiral said, "he must be sustained by the protection of the United States."

This condition, however, also applied to anyone else who might be elected, since Admiral Caperton had not yet ruled out Rosalvo Bobo, the other principal candidate. Nevertheless he did not favor him; Bobo's election, he thought, would lead only to more revolutions unless the United States stepped in. And while the admiral did not say so in his report, Bobo promised to be less manageable than his senatorial rival.[4]

So matters stood when the *Jason* returned to Port-au-Prince on August 6, bringing several dozen politicians and generals from Cap-Haïtien. The mission to the north had been a complete success: both Rosalvo Bobo and Darius Bourand had answered the admiral's summons to the capital. The commission which had achieved this happy result called upon Admiral Caperton on the *Washington* before going ashore, to receive his enthusiastic congratulations upon their work. It had not been easy, as Caperton realized when he heard the full report of Lieutenant Coffey, the aide whom he had sent along with the group.[5]

There had been problems from the very start. During the trip to Cap-Haïtien, Coffey became convinced that the three delegates from the Revolutionary Committee intended to use the mission for Bobo, rather than for neutralization of the north. Their real aim, he concluded, was to bring pressure on General Blot to evacuate the Cape and turn it over to Bobo's troops, thereby enhancing Bobo's status as a presidential aspirant. Furthermore, Coffey had feared actual violence once the commission landed. Charles Zamor and Edmond Polynice were still inflamed by the deaths of their brother and sons, respectively, in Guillaume Sam's massacre, and they hated Probus Blot as an agent and colleague of the murderous late president. Blot, on the other hand, could be expected to harbor an almost equally intense ill will toward those who had overthrown and killed his leader and destroyed his own position. When *Jason* dropped anchor at midday on August 2, therefore, Coffey had told Zamor, Polynice, and the third member from the Revolutionary Committee, Colonel P. Chevalier, that they were not to be allowed ashore for the moment. Zamor in particular had protested angrily and at length; aside from anything else, he wanted to see his wife and children, from whom he had been separated for months. Coffey met this problem by arranging to have Zamor's family brought out from the town to visit him, and months later Zamor admitted to Coffey that his action may well have saved the Haitian's life.[6]

From this point on, Lieutenant Coffey had dominated the activities of the commission, deriving his authority from his status as the personal representative of Admiral Caperton. With the remaining members, ex-President Légitime and Archbishop Conan, Coffey went ashore to begin his work. Consul Livingston joined them, and that evening the group had a conference with Probus Blot and a number of his advisers. Coffey told them that the United States had assumed military control of the capital and that Admiral Caperton was determined to restore order in the north as well. He went on to explain the mission's goal of securing the disarmament of all factions and the return of their leaders to Port-au-Prince, where a political settlement could be peacefully achieved. The Blot party listened calmly enough to the lieutenant's proposals, except for an outburst of excited remonstrance at the mention of Zamor's name which confirmed Coffey's earlier fears. They agreed to consider Caperton's program while Coffey conveyed the admiral's guarantee of personal protection for all who came to Port-au-Prince at his behest.

On the next morning Lieutenant Coffey renewed his discussions with the Blot party, accompanied this time only by Consul Livingston as interpreter. Blot feared that his departure from Cap-Haïtien would insure a take-over by Bobo's forces, and he refused any parley with Zamor or Polynice on the grounds that they represented the hated enemy faction. Coffey promised in reply that the Americans would keep out Bobo's troops while he was away, causing some of Blot's followers to waver. At this point the meeting very nearly broke up when one Blot general, angry at the waverers, attempted to leave in what Coffey described as "a hasty and aggravating manner." His fellows restrained the irate general and the meeting went on, but Blot still failed to reach a decision.[7]

After this meeting Coffey went off to the *Eagle*, which lay closer inshore than either *Jason* or the recently arrived gunboat *Nashville* could get. A message soon arrived from Blot announcing that Bobo's troops were approaching the city and asking that United States forces land at once to keep them out. The same missive, however, conveyed Blot's decision not to go to Port-au-Prince under any circumstances, leading Coffey to return a sharp answer. His refusal to accept the admiral's invitation, Blot was told, "could not be considered other than an unfriendly act," and he must expect the Americans to act accordingly. There would be no more American troops landed.[8]

During the afternoon General Darius Bourand arrived from the region of the Dominican border, where he commanded some nine hundred additional troops of the former government. Torn by doubt and indecision, Blot gained no visible confidence from the arrival of his nominal chief, and finally asked to be deposited on Dominican territory by a Haitian gunboat which lay in the harbor. The presence of so many Boboites among the admiral's commission undoubtedly alarmed him, and he feared treachery at the capital; it was rumored as well that his rivals had paid him to leave the country. That night General Blot passed off the scene, while Bourand attempted to reorganize the forces in Cap-Haïtien and to repair the damage done by Blot's desertion. Seeing the Americans as his best remaining hope, Bourand readily agreed to go back with Coffey to Port-au-Prince. He pledged as well that all of the forces under his command would remain in their present positions and refrain from offensive action, fighting only if attacked.[9]

As the Blot-Bourand faction neared collapse, Rosalvo Bobo emerged more clearly than ever as the central figure in the politics of the north. Arrangements had already been made for the commission to meet Bobo at Caracol, a coastal village some fifteen miles east of Cap-Haïtien, and on the morning of August 4 the entire group proceeded to the point aboard *Jason*. Here the Boboite half of the commission participated in negotiations for the first time, helping to smooth the course of the discussion. As previously with Blot, Coffey opened the meeting by explaining the nature of the mission and the proposals of his admiral. Fearing that Bobo might be misled by the strength of his adherents among the commission, Coffey took pains to stress that the entire arrangement was neutral in intent and that Caperton promised nothing to any of the factional leaders beyond their own personal safety. Bobo and his generals seemed unconcerned by this warning, and they agreed in principle to all that Coffey asked. Bobo declared that his troops would go to the capital and lay down their arms, one division marching by the coast road via St. Marc and the other directly through the interior, while he himself would go on ahead in a United States vessel.

This presumably met Coffey's objectives, and yet the lieutenant was not entirely happy about the results of the conference. He felt certain that Zamor and Polynice had secretly assured Bobo that the presidency was his if Bobo would come to Port-au-Prince and that this explained the latter's ready acceptance of the plan. Furthermore, there were manifest disadvantages in having Bobo's army follow him south in a body, to arrive armed and intact at the capital. But Bobo held to this specific arrangement and Coffey could see no alternative to accepting it; to challenge Bobo's good faith and bring on an open break would be more dangerous, he thought, than taking a chance on the promises freely offered by the Haitians.[10]

While the commission and Bobo were in parley at Caracol, affairs at Cap-Haïtien changed with dramatic suddenness. Learning from informers of Blot's flight and the disarray of his abandoned troops, the Bobo commanders on the spot attempted to take the city by a sudden advance. As the Bobo forces came into sight the town's defenders panicked, hundreds of them taking refuge in the grounds of the bishop's palace and others jumping into the sea to swim to the Haitian gunboat *Nord Alexis.* At this point, however, Admiral Caperton's dispositions of many weeks earlier came into play. Caperton had left standing orders that no armed forces would be permitted to enter the town, but the Boboites apparently believed that the few Americans in sight could do nothing to stop them. The main force of *cacos* marched toward the town on the main road, entering the narrow neck of land commanded by the marine outpost and the guns of little *Eagle.* Their advancing column received its first warning of danger when a six-pounder shell from *Eagle* carried away the fore-legs of the horse of the general leading the charge. A few more shells routed the advance, and the *cacos* streamed back to the woods in full flight.

As the senior American officer present, Commander Percy Olmstead of the *Nashville* immediately ordered ashore a landing party of 250 men taken from the complements of his own ship and *Eagle,* and by the end of the day they had occupied the city and disarmed the Haitian troops within it. When envoys from the Bobo forces returned to explore the situation, they were told by the marine outposts that *cacos* could enter the city only if they deposited their weapons with the Americans for safekeeping. Asserting that they merely wished to attend church services, many left their arms and passed on into town, where they were enthusiastically received. The citizens at the Cape had long since grown restive under General Blot's six-weeks' occupation, and many hailed the Boboites as their deliverers, while the disarmed Blot troops were huddled under American protection. The United States occupation was a new element in the situation, and everyone wondered how long it would last, meanwhile anxiously awaiting Rosalvo Bobo's arrival on the morrow.[11]

The morning of August 5 saw Bobo arrive at the Cape as he had promised. An escort of United States troops brought him safely into town, where he was met by Olmstead, Coffey, and the Haitian commission. The large crowd that had gathered gave Bobo a noisy ovation, so that he and his generals made a triumphal entry to the sounds of their shouting. Once indoors, the group held another long conference, during which Bobo showed no ill will for the shelling of his men by *Eagle* the previous day.

Like Lieutenant Coffey, Admiral Caperton had been upset at the prospect of having Bobo's *caco* army appear intact at Port-au-Prince, and he had radioed Coffey during the night that this provision must be renegotiated. After some discussion, Bobo agreed that his troops would remain in their present positions for the time being, leaving the details of their disarmament to be settled at Port-au-Prince. Bobo himself would sail on *Jason* to meet the admiral, accompanied by a group of his principal generals. But at this point new difficulties arose. Bobo desired to board *Jason* after leading a grand parade of his army through the streets of Cap-Haïtien, and he planned to take with him on the journey no less than forty of his generals. It was only after long argument that Lieutenant Coffey scaled these demands down to a level he deemed acceptable; twenty-six generals would go with their leader to Port-au-Prince, and the military parade would be reduced to a procession of Bobo and the chosen twenty-six.

At last the arrangements were complete, and Coffey began hasty preparations to load everyone into *Jason.* After the recent clash between Americans and *cacos,* Coffey was eager to take Bobo off before another shock should alienate him entirely. The lieutenant's nervousness was further increased by the progress of the Boboites' scheming; by now they assumed that their leader would be hailed in the capital as he had been at the Cape and were so certain of Bobo's elevation to the presidency that cabinet posts had been distributed, with portfolios tentatively allotted to Zamor, Polynice, Léger, and Delva.[12]

Commander Olmstead, who remained in charge at Cap-Haïtien, found pro-Bobo sentiment there so universal that he radioed Caperton for instructions. The local Committee of Safety claimed jurisdiction and wished to put itself at the disposal of Bobo or Zamor, but Caperton ordered Olmstead to retain military control and to recognize no faction. The admiral had already decided to ask Washington for an additional regiment of marines with which to occupy Cap-Haïtien. At Olmstead's request, he agreed to send *Connecticut* to the Cape in the interim. The big battleship had finished landing the Second Marines and their equipment, and her seaman battalion would provide enough men to ensure a safe hold on the city until more marines could arrive from the United States. As the *Jason* steamed southward, *Connecticut* would come north to take her place.

The return voyage of the *Jason* to Port-au-Prince made a fitting conclusion to her odyssey. It being necessary to separate the factions, General Bourand was quartered forward with his small party, while Bobo and the twenty-six generals were put as far away as possible in the after end of the ship. Between the rival leaders *Jason* carried seventeen Catholic nuns, who wished to quit Cap-Haïtien for Port-au-Prince but could find no civilian transport. The Haitian commission was also theoretically separated from the factions, but its three Boboite members spent much of their time planning the future with their chosen leader. Bobo himself talked a great deal of his plans for the regeneration of Haiti, the vague and grandiose character of his pronouncements leading Coffey to doubt his mental balance. According to Coffey, Zamor and Chevalier expressed their own doubts on this score but nevertheless stuck to their intention of making Bobo president. And so, buzzing with plans and apprehensions, the *Jason* steamed toward Port-au-Prince, where the weary Coffey could turn over his difficult charges to the care of Admiral Caperton.[13]

The admiral, for his part, was already planning for their coming. Once assured of *Jason*'s imminent arrival with Bobo on board, he and Captain Beach worked feverishly on the night of the 5th to prepare for the morrow. The American naval occupation of Cap-Haïtien and the departure of the northern leaders, they thought, would bring at least a temporary halt to disturbing events in that part of the country. As Caperton had hoped, everything was coming into focus at the capital; the danger now was that Bobo would be received there as a patriotic hero and set off a popular movement too strong to be contained. Warned by Coffey's reports of Bobo's formidable popularity at the Cape, the two planners hastily arranged to complete their take-over of Port-au-Prince the very next morning, before *Jason* could arrive. The recent operations of the Second Marines would continue on the 6th with the boldest moves so far in Admiral Caperton's dangerous game.

When Colonel Cole had started his whirlwind movement through the city on the 4th, there were numerous military barracks containing several thousand troops and considerable arms, still formally under the control of the local authorities. One of the Revolutionary Committee's sources of power was the presumption that it could command these troops, and even after the seizure of the Casernes Dessalines and Fort National, eight such barracks remained. On the morning of the 5th, Cole's newly landed marines found eight big wagons commandeered from the street-paving project waiting on the dock. Early the next day a wagon, accompanied by a detachment of marines, proceeded to each of the eight remaining barracks, where the marines quickly collected all the arms and ammunition in sight. The Haitian soldiers present were informed that their army service was at an end. Those who lived in town were ordered to go home and take off their uniforms, while those from the countryside were marched out of town, told to return only as civilians, and dismissed. The Haitian troops, for the most part miserable conscripts, made little objection to their sudden release, especially since the Americans accompanied it by giving them the first proper issue of rations they had had in days.

Beach held one of his regular meetings with the Revolutionary Committee at the very time the barracks were disarmed, and when routine business was finished he announced that action to the Haitians. "This was greeted with a howl of frenzied rage," he recalled. "Each committeeman jumped to his feet; wild, indignant protestations were shouted. The ground under them was being torn away. Their power had vanished in a moment." They were even angrier when Beach informed them that the troops were to be disbanded as well; anyone returning in uniform would be arrested and punished. Nor was the navy spared; the Haitian gunboat *Pacifique* arrived during the morning to be boarded and seized by a party of bluejackets.[14]

There was further bad news for the Revolutionary Committee. On that same morning, Caperton ordered the occupation of the city's police station and government offices, with the intention of assuming direct supervision of the officials involved rather than working through the Revolutionary Committee. In addition, he foreshadowed a move for control of the national finances by notifying foreign legations that Beach was to become the general administrator of the customs. "Because it did not keep the faith, I have curtailed the power of the Revolutionary Committee," he notified Washington, reporting that "my orders are gladly accepted and executed by the civil officials of the late Government."[15]

As a third move on that eventful morning, the admiral publicly ordered all *cacos* to leave at once for their home in the north; any *caco* found in the city after 11:00 A.M. would be arrested, he warned. By the appointed hour the entire city had heard of the momentous events of the day, and the crowds which had gathered in the streets were wild with excitement. At eleven sharp, nevertheless, marine detachments began rounding up *cacos* and marching them to a central detention camp. It was this act which triggered mob action; within minutes, a riot had begun. Armed men, who had infiltrated a crowd near the customs house, fired at a marine patrol. The marines fired back into the crowd, and in the confusion the *caco* prisoners made a run for it. In moments two *cacos* were dead, numerous rioters wounded, and the crowd was in flight, while elsewhere in the city the issue of submission or bloodshed balanced on a knife edge.

In the event, Caperton's bold moves won the day. By hitting all centers of resistance almost simultaneously, by rapid movement and effective show of force, the Americans overawed the city and made good their domination. "Haytians now realize that the occupation of Port-au-Prince by the American forces is complete," wrote a correspondent for the New York *Herald*. "Port-au-Prince to-night has the appearance of a conquered city. American marines and bluejackets are everywhere." Caperton, he

reported, had ordered an 8:00 P.M. curfew, with all doors
and windows to be closed at night. Many houses had been
searched for arms and ammunition; the city lay under
complete military control.[16]

It was in this context that Beach and the admiral prepared to receive Rosalvo Bobo at midday on that crowded
6th of August. Bobo now represented the principal threat
to their control of the situation. Although he had never
gained possession of Cap-Haïtien, he had no effective rivals
in the north. There was no question as to his popularity
with the people, as had been demonstrated at Cap-Haïtien.
For months he had claimed to be chief of the executive
power, he had powerful allies in Port-au-Prince, and he was
widely viewed as a bulwark against the pretensions of the
United States. Even Beach, who was to play a central role
in blocking his ambitions, recorded that Bobo was "greatly
beloved" in Haiti, and judged him intelligent, honest, and
well-meaning—an infinitely better man than Guillaume
Sam, Beach thought. Bobo had practiced medicine for
years, willingly treating the poor without pay, and thus
embodied humanitarian as well as patriotic ideals. But the
Captain denied that Bobo was fit to be president, charging
that his ambitions had turned his head: "He was an idealist
and a dreamer and believed he was destined to be Haiti's
saviour." In Beach's opinion he was fatally lacking in
judgment, and so unable to perceive reality as to be
mentally incompetent.[17]

However true this was, Caperton and Beach had
apparently decided that the election of Doctor Bobo to
the presidency would be inimical to United States interests
in Haiti, for they now moved quickly and decisively to
prevent it. Caperton had earlier scheduled a conference
ashore for that very afternoon, during which he would
interview both Bobo and Dartiguenave, his own favorite
candidate. Fearing, however, "lest a public demonstration
turn Bobo's head," the admiral arranged to have Bobo
brought directly from *Jason* to the *Washington,* so that he

could settle with the Haitian even before he set foot on land. Beach and Caperton between them rehearsed the coming confrontation, planning it in detail, and it was with suppressed excitement that they watched *Jason's* sailing launch bear Bobo toward them over wavelets sparkling in the midday sun.[18]

Then in his forties, Doctor Rosalvo Bobo was a mulatto, like almost all of Haiti's educated elite, and notable for his head of red hair. His accomplishments were substantial: many years in Europe had made him fluent in several languages, while he held degrees in both law and medicine and was reputed a highly competent physician. He had already gained some success in politics, having served as Haitian minister to the Dominican Republic and as minister of the interior before turning to revolution. That he now regarded himself as separated from the presidency only by the necessary formalities was evident as the boat from *Jason* approached *Washington's* side. Rising to his feet in a commanding attitude, Bobo removed his high silk hat and faced the flagship with a hand thrust in his coat *a la* Napoleon. Then he mounted the gangway with slow steps and stopped on the quarterdeck, awaiting the honors due to a head of state. He knew nothing as yet of events ashore and undoubtedly expected to negotiate with Caperton as one dignitary to another. Behind him stood the four generals whom Coffey had allowed to come along, dressed like their chief in frock coats and silk hats. Each of the five carried in his hand a suitcase with a legend painted on its side; Bobo's read "Dr. Rosalvo Bobo, Chief of the Executive Power," while the others bore the titles of various cabinet posts. Beach and Coffey, who headed a group of officers waiting to greet the Haitians, studiously ignored these pretensions. One of the officers, stepping forward, said merely, "Howdy do, Doctor, glad to see you, come below." Visibly nettled, Bobo stalked into the cabin to which he was conducted, where Beach commenced the remarkable interview of which he has left this account:[19]

"Are you a candidate for the presidency?," Beach asked abruptly.

"Sir, I am more than a candidate," Bobo replied, "I am Chief of the Executive Power; I command an Army in the North of Haiti which is now unopposed. My friends here, in Port au Prince, overthrew the vicious Vilbrun Guillaume. The Haitian presidency is already mine; the election is a mere formality."

"Are you a patriot?," Beach next asked Bobo. Pained by the question, the latter framed a lengthy answer alleging himself to be the greatest patriot in Haiti, whereupon Beach launched into his attack: "Dr. Bobo, I deeply regret my words may seem harsh. For you personally I have nothing but kindly feeling, and admiration for your own accomplishments. But Admiral Caperton directs me to inform you that you are not a candidate for the Haitian presidency. And further, that instead of being a patriot, you are a menace and a curse to your country."

"What do you mean by these harsh words, sir? by these intolerable insults?," cried Bobo, leaping to his feet. "Why am I not a candidate? Why do you say I am a menace to my country?"

Reseating the presidential aspirant, the captain at last explained himself. Bobo was not a candidate for president, Beach said, because the United States forbade it. He was a menace to his country because he maintained a revolutionary army which threatened the nation's peace. All Haiti cried for an end to disorder, for a free election; Bobo would blast these hopes, although he had not even made good his claim to power in the customary way. Thus, charged Beach, "You propose again to force Haiti into the throes of agony. That is why you are a curse to Haiti, Dr. Bobo." The United States would tolerate no more revolution in Haiti, the captain announced sternly, and so long as he was a revolutionist Bobo was also a public enemy of the United States.[20]

This blast left Bobo cowering in his chair, Beach claimed, "like a small schoolboy in the relentless grasp of a

hard-hearted master." When Beach next threatened that
Bobo would not even be allowed to land, the doctor broke
into expressions of despair: "What must I do, oh, what
must I do; I am a patriot, I love my country, I came here
to save her." At once Beach laid terms before the brow-
beaten Haitian: Bobo must renounce his claim to be chief
of the executive power, by going before his followers and
telling them that he was now merely a private citizen and
ordinary candidate, subject to the free choice of Congress.
He must also disband his army; Beach dictated two telegrams on the spot to be sent over Bobo's signature, which
the latter copied out in a trembling hand. The first,
directed to the Committee of Public Safety at Cap-Haïtien,
said: "I hereby order all generals of the Caco army to enter
town and surrender their arms to the American captain.
Carry out my orders that we may save our menaced father-
land." The second telegram repeated the same order
directly to Bobo's generals: "Lead your men into town
and surrender your arms to the American Captain. Carry
out my orders without hesitation or restrictions in the
name of our threatened country, which we should save at
any cost and sacrifice."[21]

When these messages were duly signed, Bobo was taken
into the admiral's inner cabin to meet Caperton, who had
been eavesdropping behind the door all the while. Captain
Beach solemnly informed the admiral that Bobo had con-
sented to go ashore as a mere citizen, and Caperton
appealed to Bobo to confirm the statement. The latter did
so with obvious reluctance, but Caperton shook his hand
warmly and expressed his deep satisfaction. He might well
be satisfied, for his final stroke had been a success, and the
momentum of Bobo's progress toward the presidential
palace had been fatally slowed.

Even so, it was an anxious moment when Doctor Bobo
stepped ashore to mingle at last with the people of Port-au-
Prince. By his own admission, Caperton watched Bobo
through a telescope as he landed in the city. It was now
past noon, and the rioting of the late morning had ended,

though tension still gripped the city. Thousands of Haitians waited at the pier to give an ovation to the new-comer; an exhortation from Bobo could have set off new outbreaks. But the admiral's reception had served its pur-pose in shaking the doctor's confidence, and at any rate Bobo as yet knew nothing of what had been happening in the capital, having spent the day aboard *Jason* and the flag-ship. As a final precaution, Caperton permitted only the four generals who had come with Bobo to *Washington* to accompany him ashore, the others being detained on *Jason.* All twenty-six generals of the Bobo party had been armed, and the Americans wanted no such nucleus of trouble introduced into the seething crowds of the capital that day. Thus the appearance of the leader aroused great popular excitement, but no new acts against the Americans occurred.[22]

After Bobo's departure to his residence, Beach and Caperton turned their attention to the rival Bourand party, which still waited aboard *Jason.* During the afternoon this group was brought to the flagship and given much the same terms as Bobo, to which they readily assented. Bourand sent telegrams to his generals at Ouanaminthe and Fort Liberté, worded as follows: "In the interests of peace and to hasten the free election of a new president, I wish you to surrender to the American Admiral [*sic*] at the Cape your forces and arms. Best wishes. Bourand." In addition, plans were initiated to bring back General Blot's troops from Cap-Haïtien as soon as possible. After the conference Bourand and his party returned to *Jason* to spend the night, but the next day it was judged safe to put them ashore, where they stayed under guard in Bourand's own house.[23]

The night passed quietly, while the only violence the next day occurred some miles outside the city when a marine party captured a group of brigands who had been pillaging the countryside. Feeling still ran high, however, and the air was full of protests at the actions of the previous day. "The American eagle extends his wings more and more over our territory," proclaimed a headline in *Le Nouvelliste*. The accompanying editorial was bitter in tone. How could the Haitians believe any longer that United States intervention was intended only to restore order, it asked, when by now actual colonization was threatened, and Admiral Caperton held Port-au-Prince under absolute military control? The Americans had expressed great concern over the violations of the sovereignty of Belgium and Serbia in the European war; when would they apply similar principles to events in "this hemisphere and this country?"[24]

From Congress the chairman of the Haitian Senate's Committee on Foreign Relations, Senator L. C. Lhérisson, appealed for justice from the American people and their president via a correspondent of the New York *Herald*. An explanation of United States intentions was due Haiti, he declared, and President Wilson ought to make it at once. Protests were heard in Washington, too, where the Haitian minister called upon Secretary of State Robert Lansing that same day. The presence of American troops in Haitian towns was a direct incitement to disorder, he told Lansing, and until they were withdrawn the disturbances would continue. According to press reports, Lansing took the position that nothing could be done until a Haitian government had been established, but Minister Menos warned that the mounting threat to their sovereignty might drive the Haitians to antiforeign outbreaks.[25]

Such statements, it was true, were somewhat undercut by the ostentatiously pacific sentiments of the two presidential candidates. Senator Dartiguenave still thought the negotiation of a new treaty between Haiti and the United States essential; "Unless we do so we cannot save Haiti," he said. And Rosalvo Bobo, in a sudden about-face, now vied with his rival in courting the Americans. If elected, he promised, he would "establish the strongest kind of relations with the Washington government." The Americans, after all, were the elder brothers of the Haitian people. "We are the younger brothers," Bobo explained, "and we should accept their advice and counsel."[26]

These new views must have been surprising to Bobo's fellow citizens, most of whom continued to complain of the steady United States take-over of their country. In an attempt to calm the atmosphere, Beach made another visit to *Le Matin*'s offices. The captain pictured the recent actions of the Americans as aimed still at the preservation of life and property. That aim, he explained ingenuously, embraced the lives and property of the occupying forces themselves, which were threatened by the continued presence of armed groups in the capital. A military occupation was necessarily a harsh experience, he continued, but the Americans were trying to be as considerate as possible; for example, they had rejected the idea of a general house-to-house search for arms because it would give offense to the Haitians. As to the duration of the occupation, no one could predict it with precision, but it would not end before order was reestablished and a government installed which respected individual liberty and could guarantee profitable enterprise. The Americans, however, had no chosen candidate to head the new government; the choice of a president was an affair for the Haitians, Beach assured the editors.[27]

While Beach labored at soothing Haitian opinion, Caperton pondered the recent rush of events and wondered about the state of mind in Washington. To a remarkable degree he had acted on his own initiative, for his instructions to date added up to little more than commands to hold the capital and keep order. It was by decision of the admiral that everything else had been done, both military and political. His government had supplied and reenforced him, and indicated approval after the fact, but to his requests for policy guidance it had turned a deaf ear. Now, however, Admiral Caperton felt such guidance to be essential, and he appealed to his superiors for it once again:

Relative to: Customs control, Mole St. Nicholas, Landing forces to suppress revolution, and any other matter the U.S. Government would care to take up at this time, I request to be informed in detail at the earliest practicable moment what are the full and exact terms that would be acceptable to the United States.

The most favorable time for concluding with Haiti convention relative to all these matters is the present. It seems that the people and the leaders are inclined to meet any demands of the United States. It is advisable that I know this before the Presidential Election is held.[28]

A Haitian president must be chosen within the next few days. The admiral intended not only to supervise the choice, but to do so as part of a broader settlement with the Haitians as to their future relations with the United States.

6

Election
of a President

EVENTS CAME rapidly into focus in the days following the return of the mission to the north, but at first little progress was visible. Admiral Caperton's appeal to Washington for instructions brought a quick response on August 8, but not an entirely satisfactory one. On the favorable side Admiral Benson, the chief of naval operations, announced approval of the admiral's request for another marine regiment and disclosed that 850 more marines would soon be on their way. Would this give Caperton enough force to hold the city and the surrounding country from which it drew its food supply?, Admiral Benson asked rather anxiously. Less welcome was the news that the election of a president must be further postponed. The Haitians had hoped to hold the election on the 8th, prompting Caperton to ask for early guidance, but now Benson put him off without answering his questions: "Before granting permission to hold election await . . . instructions from Washington. In a very few days definite instructions concerning the entire question will be sent to you."[1]

In lieu of information, the Navy Department sent a proclamation, which Caperton duly issued over his own signature. This document, obviously meant to soothe the Haitians, read as follows:

I am directed by the United States Government to assure the Haitien people that the United States has no object in view except to insure, establish, and help to maintain Haitien independence, and the establishment of a stable and firm government by the Haitien people.
Every assistance will be given to the Haitien people in their attempt to secure these ends. It is the intention to retain United States force in Haiti only so long as will be necessary for this purpose.[2]

With this Caperton had to be content. Working fast, he was able to put off the election once again, but it was no longer easy to do so. Everyone, he reported, was clamoring for it, and he feared that any further delays would require the use of force. It was also possible that Congress might meet suddenly and without notice to choose the new president before the Americans knew what was happening. Congressional leaders now insisted that the election must be held no later than August 12. It must be held soon in any case, for according to law the current session of Congress ended on August 17, and the next did not begin until nine months later. Before adjournment it was necessary not only to install a president but to conduct much additional legislative business. Even if the election were held at once, the time left for necessary congressional actions would be very short, the admiral warned. At the very least, he asked that the administration set an early election date and notify him of it at once. Only thus could he allay the apprehensions of the Haitians and head off further outbreaks.[3]

In the meantime the investigation of the candidates went on. A second meeting between Beach and Bobo was varied by the presence of Dartiguenave as well; the two front-runners met by prearrangement on the 8th at the

United States Legation, each accompanied by a friend. There they listened as Beach gave a little speech about the condition of Haiti. The United States was determined to end revolution and disorder in the country, Beach said; the new president must recognize this fact and attempt to demonstrate a new and higher patriotism in working for his nation's future. One of his two listeners would probably be elected president, he continued; were there any others equally qualified for the post? There were many others, answered Dartiguenave, who denied that he had actively sought election. Bobo, however, declared that no other Haitian possessed as he did the love and confidence of his people, and therefore concluded that no other candidate was as well qualified as himself.

Beach next asked Dartiguenave whether, if Bobo were elected, he would "promise to help him loyally and earnestly in his efforts to secure the welfare of Haiti." Dartiguenave promised readily, and Beach put the same question to Bobo. Knowing that the Americans supported his opponent, Bobo not unnaturally saw this request as a device to secure in advance his acceptance of his own defeat. His reply as recorded by Beach was uncompromising: "No! If I am not elected it will be because the presidency is stolen from me. I am by rights now President of Haiti. . . . If I am defrauded of my rights I will leave the country, I will go away, I will abandon Haiti to her fate. She can never survive without me." Unmoved by this melodramatic announcement, Beach reported to Caperton that the Haitian was "looney," and both Americans became colder than ever to Bobo's candidacy.[4]

The day of this interview was also notable for the arrival of the *Nord Alexis,* carrying from Cap-Haïtien the men of General Blot's former garrison. The small Haitian gunboat was crammed with 766 soldiers, who proved to be in a state of extreme misery. Engine trouble had prolonged the normally short voyage to four days, during which none of the wretched soldiers had had anything to eat, although the Americans had supplied the ship's commander with funds to buy food for the troops before he sailed. When news of their plight reached the *Washington*, the American bluejackets donated their entire breakfast, which was already prepared but not yet served. Since *Washington* carried about 1100 men, it was a substantial meal which her ship's boats took over to *Nord Alexis,* including among other items several thousand loaves of bread. The famished Haitians fell fiercely upon this unexpected bounty, wolfing down all of it before they finished.

Once fed, the soldiers were landed at the Haitian naval base at Bizoton, on the south shore of the bay near Port-au-Prince. Here they found the ubiquitous Beach waiting to speak to them. The United States was a good friend to Haiti, the captain declared, and therefore meant to put an end to revolutions and fighting in the country. This being the case, there was no further necessity for keeping the soldiers in service; all of them were discharged on the spot and told to go home. If anyone attempted to force them back into the army, they need only tell the Americans, who would protect them. They must tear off their insignia and leave it off. As they left the naval base, they would each be given ten *gourdes* (about two dollars) in back pay. They need not give any of it to their officers; all of it was theirs alone.[5]

Already cheered by their feast, the miserable conscripts were even happier when they found that they were to be free, but the almost unprecedented distribution of ten *gourdes* apiece in cash brought on a mass delirium; such a sum was equal to a *caco*'s salary for a successful revolution. Cheering, the soldiers tore off the rad tapes which decorated their uniforms and threw them on the ground. "They shouted and howled and yelled, danced, and ran about, kissed each other, and were as crazy a lot of men as ever got together," Beach recounted. In all, 730 men left the compound as civilians, while 36 sick and wounded went temporarily to a hospital ashore. A few days later the New York *Sun* expressed wonder at the event. "Imagine 736 musket-carrying Haytians coming in

on board the famous gunboat Nord Alexis and demobiliz-
ing at the request of an American naval officer whom they
had never seen before!," the *Sun* marvelled. But its writer
had underestimated the navy; the soldiers had been disarmed at Cap-Haïtien before they ever boarded, while the
"famous gunboat Nord Alexis" was stripped of her arma-
ment and sent back to the Cape to report for orders to
Connecticut's Captain E. H. Durell.[6]

With everyone now assuming that the new president
would be chosen on the 12th, the political pot came to a
full boil. Caperton held daily conferences with congressional leaders and other prominent Haitians, while Beach
spent almost all of his busy schedule on political affairs.
Both candidates made it increasingly clear that they would
meet nearly any American demand in return for the admiral's support. Dartiguenave virtually said as much in the
presence of a number of other congressional leaders,
arguing that no Haitian government could stand except
through the protection of the United States. This being
the case, the Haitians must be prepared to grant customs
control, allow the United States to intervene at need, even
cede Môle-Saint-Nicolas to the Americans for a naval base,
the Senate president believed. Caperton reported that
other congressmen thought the same thing.[7]

Though less forthright about it, the Bobo camp was
equally ready to accede to American demands. While still
at Cap-Haïtien, Charles Zamor had told Consul Livingston
in confidence that an arrangement with the United States
would be necessary and that Bobo must be brought to
accept the fact. As Caperton's preference for Dartiguenave
became clear, the Boboites made a desperate effort to out-
bid their opponents. At a private meeting with Beach, the
doctor's managers proposed a deal through which
Caperton would cooperate in having Bobo named provisional president, without at present holding any election.
In return Bobo would undertake to govern as the admiral
directed, ready to make any or all of the concessions
already offered openly by Dartiguenave.[8]

The idea of choosing a temporary provisional government to settle matters with the United States and supervise the election of a permanent successor had been mooted about the capital for some time. The pro-Bobo Revolutionary Committee now cabled Washington to call for the adoption of the plan on the ground that it had the support of the people and the leaders of Haiti, but Caperton countered with strong opposition. While the plan had once been popular, he hold the Navy Department, it was now merely a device of the Boboites to stave off defeat in a legitimate election. American protection would free the members of Congress from their fear of coercion, Caperton thought, resulting in victory for Dartiguenave. To cancel the election would be "in effect another revolution in favor of General Bobo," and the admiral saw no reason to reverse his original choice of candidates. He would not discuss the Bobo proposal.[9]

With this American rejection of their latest scheme, the Bobo faction faced defeat. Although a coup seemed impossible in the face of the United States troops at hand, it appeared to be the only device left them, and it was widely believed in Port-au-Prince that Bobo would attempt to regroup his scattered *cacos* in the capital and make the effort. Men in the streets exchanged rumors of an impending *caco* raid which would bring down arson, pillage, and murder on the city, while assassination threats were so rife that Caperton placed a marine guard at Dartiguenave's residence.[10]

The Americans had already done much to forestall such attempts, particularly in strengthening their military control of the capital. In addition, Admiral Caperton took an important administrative step to further weaken Bobo's chief remaining prop, the Revolutionary Committee. Early in the year the then-President Davilmar Théodore had denounced the contract with the National Bank of Haiti and begun depositing the government's revenues in selected private banks, a move amounting to a declaration of financial independence from foreign control. The

United States had protested at once on behalf of the bank, but the continuous upheaval since January had prevented meaningful negotiation. Thus private banking houses, primarily that of Simond Frères, held Haitian government funds and on demand turned them over to whoever seemed at the moment to represent the government. Caperton believed that the Revolutionary Committee was financing its activities through the use of these funds, the holders of which would feel no great obligation to defy the threats of force by which the committee strengthened its claim to the money. Particularly in the provincial towns, pro-Bobo agitation was reportedly linked to the use of local customs receipts. On the 9th, therefore, Caperton ordered the restoration of the Treasury service to the National Bank of Haiti "on account of military necessity," as he told his superiors. Though taken as a tactical move in the contest over the presidential election, this change also reflected a movement back toward foreign control of Haiti's government finances.[11]

On August 10 the admiral at last received the long-awaited instructions from Washington, while permission to hold the election came from the secretary of the navy: "Allow election of President to take place whenever Haitians wish. The United States prefers election of Dartiguenave." The entire question of the relations between the United States and Haiti would be taken up after the election, the secretary explained.[12] Relieved that he would not have to postpone the election again, as well as by this first written approval of his support of Dartiguenave, Admiral Caperton saw his situation further clarified later in the day by a dispatch from Secretary of State Lansing to Davis at the American Legation. In the crisp tones of authority, Lansing outlined what he expected of the Haitians. Since an election was now imminent, he said, Davis should confer with Caperton "to the end that, in some way to be determined between you, the following things be made perfectly clear" to the Haitians:

First. Let Congress understand that the Government of the United States intends to uphold it, but that it cannot recognize action which does not establish in charge of Haitian affairs those whose abilities and dispositions give assurances of putting an end to factional disorders.

Second. In order that no misunderstanding can possibly occur after election, it should be made perfectly clear to candidates as soon as possible and in advance of their election that the United States expects to be entrusted with the practical control of the customs, and such financial control over the affairs of the Republic of Haiti as the United States may deem necessary for an efficient administration.[13]

The first section of Lansing's terms seemed designed to rule out Bobo, and the second to insure that whatever candidate might be elected would take office with full knowledge of what was expected of him. To oppose these expectations in advance would invite the enmity of the Americans and jeopardize an aspirant's chance for the presidency, while to do so only after the election would raise charges of bad faith and lay open the new president to reprisals from Washington. As Lansing confided to President Wilson, "I do not see why it would not be as easy to control a government with a president as it is to control the Haitien Congress and administrative officers."[14]

Meanwhile the Bobo camp had not yet given up. On August 10th a noisy demonstration on the doctor's behalf occurred in the capital. "Down with Congress, long live Bobo," shouted a crowd of his supporters as they surged through the narrow streets. Their slogan reflected the Boboites' new tactics; despairing of their leader's election by Congress, they now proposed to defy the legislative branch and assert the power of the rival Revolutionary Committee. Anticipating trouble, Caperton ordered *Eagle* and the gunboat *Castine* to Port-au-Prince and landed blue-jackets to reenforce the marine patrols in the city.[15]

On the following morning the Bobo demonstrations continued, threatening to become disorderly, and in an effort to control them the Americans dispersed the crowds in the streets, arresting seventeen men identified as *cacos*. At this point the Revolutionary Committee made its long-awaited bid for power. The walls of the city blossomed with its proclamations, which decreed the dissolution of Congress and the convocation of a provisional government, presumably to be composed of the members of the Revolutionary Committee. The provisional government, the notices declared, would convoke a constituent assembly to revise the constitution and elect a president. In an attempt to enforce the dissolution of Congress, the committee posted armed men outside the Palace of the Chamber of Deputies and attempted to seal its doors, a move which brought a force of marines on the run. After a tense confrontation the Haitians withdrew without firing, leaving the marines in control.[16]

The Revolutionary Committee next seized the telegraph office, closed it to the public, and launched a flood of telegrams to every part of the country calling for action on behalf of Bobo. Again a marine patrol hurried to the scene and cleared the building, after which Caperton installed a marine as sole telegraph operator and threatened the director of the telegraph company with jail if he did anything more at the bidding of the Revolutionary Committee.[17] But no sooner was this accomplished than a fresh alarm sounded; Haitian informers brought word that the Bobo party planned to prevent the next day's election by starting a riot in the capital, complete with gunfire and the burning of selected buildings. If successful, this course would not only stave off the morrow's expected defeat but might frighten congressmen into compliance when the election was finally held. After a quick conference with Captain Beach, Caperton summoned Bobo and the members of the Revolutionary Committee to a meeting that afternoon at the American Legation, where Beach would represent the admiral. Contacting the marine commander, Beach made hasty preparations for the confrontation.

When the Haitians arrived at the legation they were
conducted to a rear veranda on the second floor, where
they found Beach and Lieutenant Oberlin awaiting them.
Also in evidence were two marines who had been chosen
for their expertise with a pistol, while the visitors were
seated in chairs carefully arranged to give the two marks-
men the best fields of fire in case of trouble. Since the
Haitians themselves normally carried pistols, Beach meant
to take no chances. After these precautions had been
observed, Captain Beach informed the group forcefully
that the actions of the Revolutionary Committee had
proven it to be "unworthy of the confidence and authority that Admiral Caperton has hitherto given you." The
committee was therefore dissolved, while any attempt to
continue its functions would bring "severe penalties,"
Beach warned. Furthermore, Beach announced, the
Americans knew of the plot to foment rioting on election
day, and if his auditors valued their lives, they ought to
know that the first shot fired on the morrow would be the
signal for the immediate execution of every one of them.
To insure their own safety, they "had better endeavor to
make sure that tomorrow is the most peaceful day in
Haitian history." As Beach had expected, this announcement caused a sensation among the Haitians, although
according to the captain none of them denied the plotting
of which he had accused them. Everyone spoke at once,
babbling excitedly. Only Charles Delva remained coolly
realistic; he merely laughed and said "you win."[18]

From this unlikely scene, the seemingly iron-nerved
Beach hurried off to still another confrontation. On the
previous day the admiral had requested that every member
of Congress assemble during the late afternoon of the 11th
at the Théâtre Parisiana in downtown Port-au-Prince. The
purpose of this deliberately informal meeting was to convey to the legislature the terms just received from the
secretary of state. Again Captain Beach was to be the
American spokesman, accompanied this time by Davis, the

secretary of the legation. Upon arriving, the Americans found most of the 39 senators and 102 deputies waiting in the theater, still abuzz with consternation at the morning's attempt to unseat them. The Revolutionary Committee's abortive coup had frightened and alienated the legislators, who now looked to the Americans as their protectors. As a result, Beach found the atmosphere particularly cordial as the meeting began.[19]

Davis opened the proceedings with a paraphrase of Lansing's message of the previous day. The congressmen seemed unsurprised at the contents of the message and listened quietly until Davis was finished, whereupon Beach addressed them at some length. He repeated and emphasized the two main points of the message: there must be an end to factional strife in Haiti and the United States must be granted "practical control" of the customs and of government finances. This, he said, was "the first exact, direct, authoritative message you have received officially" from the United States, and one of the most important messages in Haiti's entire history. If the congressmen accepted its terms, Admiral Caperton would authorize them to elect a president on the next day; in that case, the admiral would "take your action as formal agreement on your part that you do accept and will abide by the requirements of the message just given you." On the other hand, Beach warned, "The Admiral refuses to permit the election unless you agree to abide by the demands of the message." This ultimatum set off what Beach described as a "lively conversation," marked by a number of questions from the audience. But no one voiced serious objections, the captain reported, while there was audible relief at the lack of territorial demands on the part of the United States. Ultimately the congressmen agreed to accept the terms, so that the election was definitely to be held as scheduled on the following day.[20]

The admiral took elaborate precautions to see that the election went off peacefully. The morning of August 12 saw marines take station at key points all over the city, while guards stood at every street corner within two blocks of the Palace of Deputies, where the election would be held. In some places the marines were entrenched behind sandbags; in others they had emplaced field guns to command the streets. Even so, fresh rumors held that the *cacos* had hidden arms, including machine guns, near the election site, with which they planned to massacre the assembled congressmen. The latter took their danger seriously, asking and receiving permission to carry pistols on their persons. As Caperton noted dryly, "It must have been a pleasant sensation to cast a ballot under such circumstances."

The situation made the traditional presence of a public audience in the visitors' gallery a rather delicate consideration, dealt with by limiting admission to those with passes signed by Colonel Cole of the marines. Even these persons, however, were searched and disarmed by the guards at the doors, a process which aroused vigorous protests from the Haitians, while filling a small wagon with their firearms. As a final precaution, a squad of armed marines remained inside the chamber during the entire session.[21]

The election was by joint session of both houses of Congress. Balloting began at 10 o'clock, and proceeded to a finish without incident or surprise. Of 116 votes cast, Philippe Sudre Dartiguenave received 94. The remaining votes were scattered among three other candidates, of whom Rosalvo Bobo ranked lowest with only three votes. Some two dozen members stayed away entirely, while one of those present cast a blank ballot. When the result was announced, Dartiguenave, tears streaming from his eyes, was led to the platform to take the oath of office. This done, he told the congressmen in a short address that he had never been a factional leader nor pursued personal ambition, that his sole concern was for the national welfare, and that in the present crisis everyone must bury the past and work together to save the country.

Coming down from the platform, the new president went to Beach, took his hand, and made a second speech expressing gratitude for the American protection which, he said, had made possible an election free from intimidation. The Americans had come to Haiti at a time of terrible misfortunes, he continued, but already Admiral Caperton had restored peace and was rebuilding confidence in the country. "Instead of lowering an already lowered Haitian pride, he has made us feel that he knows that there are good men in Haiti, he has endeavored to learn from these men what Haiti needs, and he is helping to build up Haitian pride," Dartiguenave proclaimed, stressing once more his conviction that no government could long survive in Haiti without United States support. To Beach it appeared that the new president was putting his cards on the table at the start, perhaps to let the Haitian elite know that he planned to work with the Americans and could count upon their support.[22]

At noon everyone left the Palace of Deputies for the customary inaugural procession through the streets, ending at a private home where a close friend of the president-elect acted as host at a reception. Preceded by a company of United States Marines, the president rode in an automobile surrounded by a gaily uniformed Haitian guard of one hundred men, Captain Beach sitting beside him on the seat. After them came hundreds of horse-drawn carriages bearing members of Congress, the diplomatic corps, and distinguished private citizens. The procession having arrived safely at its destination, the reception began, but soon a sense of suspense became noticeable among the guests. The unvarying finale to the inauguration of a new chief executive was the firing of a salute from the guns of Fort National, but at the appointed time no salute boomed out. Everyone knew that it had been ordered, and in the strained atmosphere of the day apprehensions instantly revived. The president himself became so nervous that Beach finally sent off Lieutenant Oberlin of Caperton's staff to see what was wrong.

Upon arriving at the fort, Oberlin found that there was no powder or firing apparatus on hand, the Americans having seized it all a week previously. Eventually locating some empty shells and powder, he set the gunners to work, and at length was able to load the guns, using mud for wadding and arranging to touch off the charges with lighted cigarettes. After two hours of frantic improvisation, Oberlin got off a halting twenty-one gun salute and the joyless inaugural celebration broke up. In a fitting day's climax, the elegantly attired guests were forced to fight their way home through the onset of a hurricane which howled through the night, bringing floods of rain and doing heavy damage in the area; by morning it had driven ashore half of the Haitian Navy, the gunboat *Pacifique.*[23]

In the United States the holding of the election seemed further evidence of the success of the American pacification program. One magazine writer found President Dartiguenave a particularly appropriate choice because he was thought to be on good terms with all of the Haitian factions and because he could "be depended upon to do what he is told by the United States authorities."[24] *World's Work,* the magazine which carried this analysis, fronted the issue with a handsome full-page photograph of Admiral Caperton, who was widely praised for his management of Haitian affairs. An editorialist in *The Outlook* found that the intervention illustrated "how much this country must at times depend upon the judgment, discretion, and administrative ability of its naval officers," while the New York *Sun* declared that Caperton had "restored order, conciliated the revolutionists, and won the confidence of the politicians as if by magic." The admiral had won over the Haitians by "a shrewd mingling of firmness, tact and benevolence," said the *Sun:* "When Caperton persuaded them that he had not come to seize the government and murder them in their beds; that, in fact, it was his mission to abolish war, settle politicians' feuds and provide work by cleaning house in fetid Port au Prince, their hostility vanished and the American occupation became popular."[25]

American gratification at Caperton's success stemmed in part from the belief expressed by the *Sun* that he had gained Haitian assent to his actions through tactful persuasion, seasoned perhaps by firmness, but essentially diplomatic. This belief seemed borne out by the relatively small loss of life that had so far resulted from the intervention, and at which President Wilson was particularly gratified. The country at large regarded Dartiguenave's election as a unique exercise in free balloting in contrast to the normal imposition of a candidates through the intimidation of the Congress. This view was strengthened by the categorical assurances of both Caperton and Beach that they had made no attempt to dictate to the Haitian Congress or to force the selection of any one candidate. Their only concern, both agreed, had been to prevent the intimidation of Congress by the *cacos* and thus enable it to make a genuine choice. "There had been no bargaining of any sort and no pressure had been brought to bear upon any elector in Dartiguenave's behalf," Admiral Caperton wrote.[26]

Even if this assertion were technically true, it is impossible to accept it at face value. The Haitian Congress had been accustomed to choosing presidents on the basis of which faction could currently bring the most force to bear on it. Without the American presence they would probably have elected Rosalvo Bobo, whose control of the Revolutionary Committee and the *cacos* would normally have been decisive. Bobo failed of election because Admiral Caperton blocked his drive for office and demonstrated that his own power was superior to Bobo's. It could have been no secret to the congressmen that the Americans wished the election of Dartiguenave, while most of the politicians in Port-au-Prince had assumed all along that the admiral would be a major factor in deciding the presidential race. It was openly and visibly American force which controlled the capital, and Congress duly elected the man whom the Americans supported. It may have been true, as Beach insisted, that the United States would have abided by the result had another candidate won—Lansing, after all, had attempted to commit all the candidates in advance to American terms, thus lessening the risks involved—but this hardly justifies the claim that no pressure was exerted to influence the election.[27]

The members of Woodrow Wilson's cabinet neither misunderstood these realities nor were they bothered by them. When Caperton's civilian superior, Secretary of the Navy Josephus Daniels, went to cabinet meetings that summer he found himself the object of jocular references to his new-found power. "Make way for Josephus the First, King of Haiti," cried Secretary of the Interior Franklin Lane one day, rising and salaaming, while others asked about the forthcoming presidential election. "Will the candidate you and Lansing picked out manage to squeeze in?," one man asked, bringing a general laugh. Such remarks hardly constituted policy statements, but they did tell something of the atmosphere in which the policy was made.[28]

7

Public Opinion
and Government Policy

WITH THE inauguration of President Dartiguenave, Haiti regained a fully functioning national government. The way was now open for the United States to secure a treaty from this government, giving it the special powers in Haiti sought by Washington since early in the previous year. It was well understood by the Haitians that the United States would demand control of the customs and general supervision of government finances; the Haitian Congress had been told as much by Beach and Davis at their meeting of August 11. It was further understood that the Americans would tolerate no more revolutions and that they would protect the new regime of Sudre Dartiguenave from forceful overthrow. Within this broad framework, however, lay room for considerable debate as to how these ends were to be accomplished, to what extent the Haitians were now to resume charge of their own affairs, and what was to be the future duration and influence of the American military occupation.

Admiral Caperton had so far taken the lead in giving form to American activities in Haiti, cutting through the political tangle there to restore order and install a president at Port-au-Prince. Within a few days of the original troop landings, the admiral also began urging the negotiation of a firm treaty relationship which would guarantee American purposes, though he did not presume to suggest the specific terms of such a compact. He did, however, propose that Captain Beach be made the sole negotiator for the United States; it was largely Beach who had dealt with the Haitians so far, Caperton said, and he had already won their confidence. Beyond that, he thought that the American military presence alone prevented a relapse into anarchy and therefore believed that it must continue indefinitely: "The United States must, in my opinion, expect to remain in Haiti until the native government is self-sustaining and until the people are educated to respect and abide by the laws."[1]

As Caperton saw it, the principal obstacle to the peaceful development of Haiti was the power of the *cacos,* which had made revolution possible for any ambitious politician with enough money to hire them. "The Cacos," he reported, "are organized in bands under irresponsible and lawless chiefs who side with the party offering greatest inducement and only nominally recognize the government." Claiming that "they practically control politics," Caperton insisted that "a stable government in Haiti is not possible until Cacos bands are broken up and their power broken." The armed forces disposed by the Haitian government were clearly inadequate for that purpose; if Caperton's forces were withdrawn, the *cacos* would simply resume their old ways. The Haitians knew this perfectly well, Caperton declared, and they therefore welcomed the American presence as a barrier against renewed anarchy.[2]

The admiral was strengthened in these views by Captain Beach, his political manager ashore. Beach, who by now was acquainted with most of Haiti's political leaders, concluded that they were "heartsick of continual disorder" and knew that they must accept some kind of foreign dominance in order to end it. They reached this conclusion with heavy hearts, however, hoping fervently to retain their essential independence whatever transpired. They were, in fact, ambivalent: all of them disliked foreign occupation, but at least some of them believed it essential and hoped that it would prove beneficial.[3]

There was certainly no dearth of suspicion of American intentions. Even when United States forces first landed, a New York newspaper correspondent found the ordinary people of the capital strongly disapproving, while the daily newspaper *Le Nouvelliste* regularly challenged the newcomers' usurpation of power. In August a group of the local elite founded the *Union Patriotique,* dedicated to defending the national sovereignty and territorial integrity of the country against Yankee encroachment. Educated Haitians were particularly disturbed by the prevalence of racism in the United States, and demagogues even pictured the Americans as plotting the reestablishment of chattel slavery. In addition, the election of Dartiguenave as president left some important political factions disgruntled at finding themselves cut off from power. Many Haitians opposed the American occupation from the start and practically all of them regretted its necessity.[4]

Yet it remained true that in many hearts, this regret was mixed with hope for the future. The daily press of Port-au-Prince reflected an impressively full and thoughtful discussion of the national crisis during the month of August 1915. Though *Le Nouvelliste* editorially opposed American intervention, *Le Matin* printed letters from its readers on both sides of the question, along with numerous excerpts from newspapers in the United States. One letter, reprinted from another local journal, insisted that opponents of the occupation had no monopoly on patriotism, since those who accepted it and worked with the Americans were also acting for what they believed to be the country's best interests. This view was implied in many of the almost daily expressions on the subject which *Le Matin* carried.[5]

The most pro-American of the capital's journalists was Charles Moravia, managing editor of *La Plume,* who less than two weeks after Dartiguenave's inauguration wrote a fiery defense of the occupation against its enemies: "The day after July 27, Port-au-Prince, in distress, trembled; the arrival of the *Washington* on the 28th restored calm in peoples' spirits: seeing that the Americans had landed, one could sleep in peace, normal life was restored, order was assured. But this benefit once realized, the press having become free, thanks to them, each one able to speak freely, thanks to them, people wrote and people spoke. But, what did one read and hear? These benefactors are invaders, they are the enemy." Who could say, the editor demanded, "that without the arrival of the Americans . . . Port-au-Prince, a prey of factions, would not have been the scene of fire, of massacre and of pillage; who will say that without them, the troops of Dr. Bobo would not be at that moment at arms with those of Probus Blot, of Jean-Gilles, of Bourand, while the South marched on the capital, where terror would reign no matter which party was in command . . . ?"

Brusquely dismissing appeals to Haitian liberty and independence, Moravia denied that they had every really existed except in the rhetoric of self-serving politicians. Where were the country's schools, hospitals for the poor, modern prisons, he asked. They were not to be found in empty slogans, but in the adoption of a calm and rational point of view, the rejection of ridiculous agitation and violence, the formation of an honest government made up of patriotic men of all factions. It was thus that the people could save their honor and dignity, without slighting their duties as citizens and patriots.[6]

A few days later Moravia actually defended the American record of race relations, claiming that "of all the peoples of the white race, the Yankee people is that which has done the most for the rehabilitation of the black race."

Citing John Brown, the settlement of Liberia, and *Uncle Tom's Cabin* as examples, he predicted that in Haiti black and white would learn to know each other, to forget mutual prejudices, and to work together for progress.[7]

Several years later, an American observer who was in Haiti to investigate the occupation concluded that "a large percentage of leading Haitians" had been "thoroughly despondent over the situation and were ready to welcome any force that promised to give them peace and order. They fully expected that the Americans would take complete control and work order out of chaos."[8] However, the Haitian elite had never wished to see "complete control" in the hands of foreigners. Rather they had hoped that the United States presence would act as a stabilizing influence and promote social and economic development while leaving day-to-day control in Haitian hands. If Haiti could enjoy the benefits which the United States could offer, while escaping total subjection, many upper class Haitians were prepared to accept the result with equanimity.

Admittedly, a great deal depended upon the intention of the Americans, and an early probe into the Yankee state of mind proved less than encouraging. *Le Nouvelliste*'s Ernest Chauvet went to New York to sound out journalistic opinion and found it cool toward his own country. He was courteously received everywhere in the New York newspaper world, he reported upon his return, but everyone there thought Haiti a backward land of graft and revolution and believed the intervention both necessary and helpful to Haiti. Since every class of American supported United States policy in Haiti, Chauvet concluded, "irrational opposition" by the Haitians would be futile.[9]

While Chauvet's report of American opinion was substantially correct, it barely scratched the surface of anti-Haitian prejudice in the United States. There, the blood-letting which attended the fall of Guillaume Sam, and which had so upset the Haitians as to reconcile many of them to intervention, was pictured as simply characteristic of the society in which it occurred. "Haiti has broken out again," declared an editorial in *The Outlook*. "In the insurrection, riots, wholesale executions, assassinations, and anarchy there the United States is deeply concerned." The *Literary Digest* announced that "murder, in accordance with century-old customs, is the outstanding feature of the accession of a new President in the Republic of Haiti." The New York *Herald* stated: "Once again the Haytian 'lid' has blown off," and opined that "Port au Prince is undergoing one of its periodic reigns of terror. . . . What Hayti most needs is a strong contingent of American marines to preserve peace within its borders . . . ." Later the *Herald* inquired whether "the authorities at Washington realize the ignorant and barbarous character of the population of Hayti?" Expressing its horror in italics, the *Herald* reported that *"the ignorant negroes are being told that American marines in Hayti mean the first step toward reintroducing slavery,"* as a final proof of Haitian ignorance. But the Chicago *Tribune* put it all most succinctly: "Haiti, as most Americans know, is a rebellion called a republic."[10]

The *Tribune* also advanced an argument for continuing the occupation that soon came to be heard from other sources. United States policy in the Caribbean had long been aimed at keeping out the influence of rival great powers. By 1915 all of these were involved in the European war, which while it lasted ruled out any serious Caribbean threat from any of them. Foreseeing that the war would destroy the world's power balance, the *Tribune* editorialist predicted that a new era of colonial rivalry would follow closely upon its end and warned that the United States had best be prepared for it: "If we are wise we shall get a better control over events in Central America and the Caribbean than we have now, and get it while we are comparatively free from interference."[11]

Public support for American control of Haiti stemmed from a combination of racial prejudice, concern over hemispheric security, and disapproval of the turbulence and instability of Haitian politics. A Minneapolis *Journal* editorial which called the Haitians "half civilized blacks" and found in them "a White Man's burden of no inconsiderable weight" was a fair sample of the ordinary tone of the press. Other writers stressed the prevalence of voodooism in Haiti, conjuring up the delicious horrors and cannibalistic rites which Americans erroneously but invariably ascribed to that religion. The Haitians were widely assumed to be a bloodthirsty lot, sunk in corruption and incapable of self-advancement. If they also jeopardized Caribbean security by their anarchy and weakness, then they must be reduced to order and tutelage by the United States. As an editorial said in *World's Work:* "It has taken the United States a very long time to intervene in Haiti. To find an example in recent history of greater forbearance, greater patience, would be difficult."[12]

Such statements were not isolated expressions, but rather represented the position of the great majority of American newspapers in 1915.[13] Furthermore, a similar assessment of the situation and capabilities of the Haitians had led Washington to decide long since that Haiti must be reduced to order by United States influence and to consider intervention for a year before it actually occurred. Thus there was substantial agreement between government and public as to the nature of the Haitian problem.

Unfortunately, there was also substantial ignorance. Even the State Department lacked expertise on such small Caribbean countries, partly as a result of the sweeping turnover of personnel which accompanied the advent of the Wilson administration in 1913. After sixteen years out of power the Democrats meant to regain the federal offices, while the experienced men in the diplomatic service were overwhelmingly Republican. William Jennings Bryan, the incoming secretary of state, replaced incumbents in his department on pure patronage principles. The new chief of the Latin American division, Boaz W. Long, for example, was a businessman whose only formal qualification for the post was that his company had a branch office in Mexico City. The more experienced Robert

Lansing had recently succeeded Bryan as secretary of state when Admiral Caperton landed his troops in Haiti, but neither Lansing nor his subordinates in Washington and Port-au-Prince had any great mastery of Haitian affairs. As a result, their thinking was strongly influenced by the general assumptions about that country which they shared with ordinary Americans, while the specific data upon which they acted came primarily from the reports of Admiral Caperton. Thus handicapped, the president and his foreign policy advisers struggled to define the nature of the intervention now under way.[14]

This effort actually began before the intervention. Paul Fuller, Jr., who in May had unsuccessfully attempted to negotiate an agreement with Guillaume Sam, returned to recommend a course similar to that followed earlier in Cuba. The United States, he thought, should land marines long enough to stabilize Haiti's political turmoil and then secure a treaty similar to the Platt Amendment. That pact, imposed on the Cubans some fourteen years earlier, had authorized continuing American controls over Cuba together with a formal right of renewed military intervention at the discretion of the United States. Fuller's memorandum went to Woodrow Wilson with the endorsement of Boaz Long. "It gives me a good deal of concern," the president wrote of the matter to Bryan on July 2. "Action is evidently necessary and no doubt it would be a mistake to postpone it long."[15]

July's sensational events in Port-au-Prince crystallized official thinking at the end of the very month in which Wilson had expressed a determination to act. Boaz Long immediately asked minister to Haiti Arthur Bailly-Blanchard, then in Washington, for a written expression of his views. Bailly-Blanchard replied on July 31 with a call for "a complete armed intervention" which would install a provisional government headed by Charles Zamor.[16] Aided by the advice of Fuller, Bailly-Blanchard, his friend Roger Farnham of the National City Bank, and others, Long formulated the stance of the State Department's

Division of Latin-American Affairs. Like Bailly-Blanchard, he urged American military control in Haiti, rejecting Fuller's scheme of a temporary intervention followed by a special treaty relationship. Calling Fuller's plan a "half-measure," Long declared that it had failed in Santo Domingo and would fail equally in Haiti. The history of Haiti evidenced a continuing lack of political competence and public responsibility, he said, while recent years had witnessed a growing demoralization there. "These facts," wrote Long, "all point to the failure of an inferior people to maintain the degree of civilization left them by the French, or to develop any capacity of self-government entitling them to international respect or confidence."

What was needed, Long thought, was a full-scale military government, headed by a United States Army general who would report to the War Department's Bureau of Insular Affairs. Ignoring Bailly-Blanchard's device of a Haitian provisional government to make United States control more palatable, he planned to dispense entirely with Haitian participation. Nor was this regime to be any slap-dash temporary affair; Long recommended that "the intervention be for a period of 33 years at the end of which period, and each succeeding 33 years, it shall be decided by the President and Congress as to whether the United States shall withdraw . . . ." He listed the reasons for this virtually permanent take-over of another country as: the United States' predominant interest in the Caribbean, its duty to an inferior people, its duty to European powers (especially France, which had refrained from intervening at the request of the United States), and "the general belief of those familiar with conditions in Haiti in favor thereof."[17]

Long's superior, the secretary of state, was slower to arrive at definite conclusions, although he too sought advice from all quarters. Lansing was willing at least to consider Fuller's plan as well as Long's. He also conferred with Roger Farnham, though confessing to Wilson that he was "a little suspicious as to the City Bank's attitude toward the Republic of Haiti." Farnham had been to Haiti several times, and seemed knowledgeable, but Lansing had heard that the banker had "shown more or less arrogance in treating with [the Haitians]." At any rate he was an interested party representing the bank's interests, and "statements in their behalf must be received with caution."[18]

While Lansing was very much interested in the financial aspects of Haitian affairs, his interest stemmed largely from a traditional fear of European influence. In the summer of 1914, as counsellor of the State Department, he had written a long memorandum on the dangers of foreign economic influence in the hemisphere. "Has the time arrived," he then asked, "when the Montroe Doctrine, if it is to continue effective, should be restated so as to include European acquisition of political control through the agency of financial supremacy over an American republic?"[19] Commercial and financial domination might prove as permanent and effective as more traditional forms of power, and Lansing was concerned lest these more subtle influences should foreshadow a European resurgence in parts of Latin America. The French and German economic roles in Haiti particularly worried him, and in the autumn of 1915 he sent Wilson a copy of his 1914 memorandum accompanied by a more specific exposition of its applications:

Recently the financing of revolutions and corruption of governments of the smaller republics by European capitalists have frequently thrown the control of these governments into the hands of a European power.

To avoid this danger . . . which may be as great a menace to the national safety of this country as occupation or cession, the only method seems to be to establish a stable and honest government and to prevent the revenues of the republic from becoming the prize of revolution and of the foreigners who finance it. . . . The possession of the Panama Canal and its defense have given to the territories in and about the Caribbean Sea a new importance from the standpoint of our national safety. It is vital to the interests of this country that

European political domination should in no way be extended over these regions. As it happens within this area lie the small republics of America which have been and to an extent still are the prey of revolutionists, of corrupt governments, and of predatory foreigners.

To all of which the president indicated full agreement in his reply of a few days later.[20]

Wilson, too, was bombarded with advice. At the end of July he received a missive from John Franklin Fort, who had headed the president's commission to Haiti in March. "I see marines have been landed and I am delighted that this has happened," Fort began. The government's aim should be to secure the election of an acceptable president of Haiti, while keeping the marines there to maintain order. Now that the occasion had presented itself, Fort thought it a simple matter to resolve the Haitian situation. None of the "rebel leaders" had any force worth noticing, Fort said: "They are simply a conglomerate lot of poor ignorant half clothed men and boys, who are forced into the army . . . ." For one or two dollars apiece, the United States could buy up every rifle in Haiti, while dominating the country with "five hundred to one thousand marines and two machine guns." Calling the letter "interesting," Wilson sent it on to Lansing.[21]

On August 3 Lansing wrote Wilson that he found the situation in Haiti "distressing and very perplexing," and that he was not yet certain what to do about it. The secretary seemed particularly concerned with the problem of justifying an American take-over. He did not see, he said, how anything could be accomplished without control of the customs receipts, both to keep them from "irresponsible persons" and to do something about economic breakdown in the country. People were starving to death in Port-au-Prince, and if the United States were to take control it must relieve suffering through direct use of the public revenue. There was "no excuse of reprisal as we had at Vera Cruz," the secretary reasoned, leaving but one justification for the United States taking administrative control in Haiti, "the humane duty of furnishing means to relieve the famine situation." He then rehearsed the difficulties of the case, among which he numbered the ignorance and illiteracy of the mass of Haitians and the threat of Rosalvo Bobo, whom he thought "mentally unbalanced and brutally savage." A lesser problem was the obstructionism of the German merchants in Haiti, whom he accused of blocking the previous attempts to secure a treaty by the use of slander and false report. Lansing ended by appealing to the president for suggestions.[22]

Replying promptly, Woodrow Wilson confessed that "my own judgment is as much perplexed as yours." "I fear we have not the legal authority to do what we apparently ought to do," the president agreed, and to act without it would constitute a case similar to Theodore Roosevelt's actions in Santo Domingo. Yet action was imperative: "I suppose there is nothing for it but to take the bull by the horns and restore order." A long-term program, however, would require congressional action and the cooperation of the Senate in treaty-making. In the meantime, Wilson thought, three things must be done at once. First, the navy must dispatch to Port-au-Prince "a force sufficient to absolutely control the city not only but also the country immediately about it from which it draws its food," and Lansing was instructed to inquire of the secretary of the navy whether this had been done, or how soon it could be. Second, "we must let the present Congress know that we will protect it but that we will not recognize any action on its part which does not put men in charge of affairs whom we can trust to handle and put an end to revolution." Third, the Haitians must be made to understand "that we consider it our duty to insist on constitutional government there;" there must be no payment of debts contracted to finance revolution, and if necessary ("that is, if they force us to it as the only way") the United States must "take charge of elections and see that real government is erected which we can support."[23]

Not only was none of this wisdom as yet transmitted to Admiral Caperton, who remained in the dark for almost

a week longer, but so far it fell a good deal short of constituting a genuine blueprint for Haitian policy. While waiting
for high-level clarification, the press speculated busily as to
what would be done next. As early as July 31 the New
York *Herald* reported that Washington officialdom was
openly discussing the imposition of a treaty upon the
Haitians which would secure American control of finances
there and apply terms similar to those of the Platt Amendment. A few days later, however, the *Herald* opined that
the president had not yet reached a decision as to Haitian
policy, a conclusion echoed by the New York *Sun.* "So far
as the President is concerned no order has been given that
the American forces shall undertake any permanent solution of the Haytian problem," the *Sun* stated. Yet the New
York *Tribune* declared on August 8 that "it is an open
secret that this government plans to exercise a protectorate
over Hayti similar to that now binding Santo Domingo,
administering the finances and custom houses of the
republic and reserving the right to intervene in the event of
disorder." Contradictory as it was, this reporting accurately reflected the discussions and indecisions of the
administration.[24]

While Lansing's message of August 10 enabled
Caperton to authorize the presidential election and provided minimal guidelines as to American intentions to the
Haitian Congress, discussion continued in Washington on
other issues. One subject considered at this time was the
future status of the Môle-Saint-Nicolas, the small but well-
protected and strategically located harbor which flanked
the Windward Passage between Haiti and Cuba. The United
States Navy had long been intrigued by its potential as a
naval station, and at times the government had made active
efforts to secure it, especially in the 1880s. These efforts
were revived briefly in 1913, while both then and in the
following year the United States had asked for assurances
from Haiti that the Môle would never be alienated to a
third power. The outbreak of the war in Europe renewed
concern on this score, and Admiral Caperton had been

ordered during his previous Haitian visit to check on rumors that a German raider was using it for a base. The rumors were never substantiated, however, while the navy's own interest in the Môle had remained slight after the acquisition of Guantanamo Bay on the Cuban side of the Windward Passage.

Lansing had wished to include a disavowal of any American designs on Môle-Saint-Nicolas in his August 10th message, having ascertained from the navy's General Board that the navy still saw no need for an additional station there. Unaccountably, Wilson rejected Lansing's suggestion and ordered that the issue of Môle-Saint-Nicolas be held over to be taken up with the new Haitian administration, a position which may have reflected the president's fear of German use of the Môle if it were left unoccupied.[25]

With the election of President Dartiguenave, Lansing launched the logical next step, the conclusion of a treaty between Haiti and the United States. On August 13 he submitted a draft convention for Wilson's approval. It was, he explained in his covering letter, cast along the lines of the treaty proposed to the Haitians the previous year, but "covering the ground far more thoroughly and granting to this Government a much more extensive control than the original treaty proposed." Lansing intended that the Haitians should approve this draft without modification or delay, and he meant to allow no bargaining or give and take between the two parties. "I confess that this method of negotiation, with our marines policing the Haytian Capital, is high handed," he told the president with notable candor. "It does not meet my sense of a nation's sovereign rights and is more or less an exercise of force and an invasion of Haytian independence." The secretary also recognized the danger that a treaty so secured might meet a hostile reception in the United States Senate when submitted for ratification. Yet he saw no alternative: "From a practical standpoint, however, I cannot but feel that it is the only thing to do if we intend to cure the anarchy and disorder which prevails in that Republic."

The terms of Lansing's proposed treaty would give the United States sweeping powers over Haiti's government finances, law enforcement, and other functions central to sovereignty; as Lansing observed, it marked a position "considerably in advance of our Dominican policy." "This is, I think, necessary, and has my approval," the president responded. Even so, there was a qualm in his assent: "Do you think it will affect Latin American opinion unfavorably?" A treaty there would be, however; the decision was firmly made that Haiti must become a protectorate of the United States.[26]

8
The Signing
of the Treaty

ON AUGUST 14, just seventeen days after the Americans landed at Port-au-Prince, *Washington*'s radio room received the instructions of the secretary of state regarding the proposed agreement with Haiti. Addressing himself to legation secretary Robert Beale Davis, Jr., Lansing ordered the immediate preparation of a draft treaty in accordance with a detailed outline which accompanied the message. The Haitians had dropped their objections to the terms proposed to them the previous year, Lansing said, and now seemed willing to go a good deal farther, even as far as ceding the Môle-Saint-Nicolas. In view of this attitude, Davis should submit his draft to President Dartiguenave as soon as possible, at the same time advising the president of the department's belief that, "as a guarantee of sincerity and interest of the Haitiens in orderly and peaceful development of their country, . . . the Haitien Congress will be pleased to pass forthwith a resolution authorizing the president elect to conclude, without modification, the treaty submitted by you." Only when the Congress had passed the required resolution should Davis extend United States recognition; he would then get the treaty signed and submit it for ratification.

The accompanying provisions went far beyond the comparatively mild terms of July 1914. The president of the United States was to name a general receiver of customs, who would collect and disburse the customs revenues of the country. These were to be applied successively to the expenses of the customs administration itself, which were not to exceed 5 percent of receipts, to the service of the public debt of Haiti, to the costs of a national constabulary, and finally to the current expenses of the government. In addition to a customs administrator, the United States would name a financial adviser, who was to supervise Haiti's government fiscal operations. Further clauses provided that the Haitians could neither increase their public debt nor change their customs duties without the approval of Washington. In sum, the government of the United States was to exercise sweeping controls over nearly every major aspect of Haitian public finance. These economic powers were augmented by additional controls, the most important of which was the creation of a national constabulary designed to replace both the army and the civil police, and whose commander and other officers were to be named by the American president. Thus both law enforcement and military functions would be placed firmly under United States direction. The treaty was to be in force for ten years, after which it could be renewed for another ten years if *either* party desired it. The dose was a strong one, and Lansing judged it best that the Haitians swallow it quickly at a single gulp.[1]

President Dartiguenave's initial reaction to the treaty terms was mild, the president indicating a belief that congressional approval of the treaty could be secured. The treaty negotiations, however, promptly bogged down. H. Pauléus Sannon, the foreign minister, led a strong cabinet opposition to the American demands, while the sessions of the Congress began to echo with denunciations of the proposed United States powers. Days passed in fruitless discussion, and the authorities in Washington quickly grew impatient. Upon the orders of the State Department, Caperton accompanied Davis in a call at the national palace on August 21, during which the two men delivered a virtual ultimatum to the president, cabinet, and congressional leaders: the Haitian Congress, they announced, must approve the treaty without modification by August 25. It was Sannon who gave the formal reply. If the United States insisted upon acceptance without modification, the foreign minister declared, then the government must resign. The Haitian offered to submit to Congress a resolution approving the conclusion of a treaty with the United States "for the best reciprocal interests of the two countries," the details to be negotiated, but that was as far as he would go.[2]

The Haitian regime's new stubbornness reflected the sentiments of its citizens. There had been a rising tide of anti-American feeling in the capital, and as the nature of the American treaty demands became public knowledge, foreign observers noted a good deal of excitement among the people. Resolutions of protest circulated freely, while the local press expressed opposition to the treaty terms. One editor, Elie Guérin of *Haiti Intégrale,* became so unrestrained in his attacks that a detachment of Waller's marines arrested him, setting off a public demonstration. A Haitian protest ultimately secured Guérin's release, but the Haitians were left more certain than ever that they faced a serious threat to their independence.[3]

This unforeseen defiance called into question the entire situation in Haiti. An angry message from the State Department declared that continued resistance by the Dartiguenave regime would necessitate either its replacement by some other Haitian faction or the temporary imposition of an American military government. To Admiral Caperton it seemed unlikely that a satisfactory new Haitian government could be found. The Dartiguenave group had been selected specifically because it was divorced from faction, but this made it by its very nature weak and lacking in solid support. An alternative regime must be drawn from one of the recognized partisan groupings, which meant that it would probably refuse to make a treaty on American terms. A government weak enough to be coerced would almost by definition lack popular support, while one which represented public opinion would not be amenable to current American purposes.[4]

In addition, the admiral charged bitterly, Haiti's best political leaders lacked the courage to defy their own public for what he regarded as the nation's good. "It is to be remembered that there are practically no patriotic people in Haiti, in the sense of people being willing to unselfishly sacrifice their own personal interests for the good of the country," he reported. "There are many well meaning and morally upright men who think they are patriotic, but who will not . . . dissociate themselves from the faction leaders, their Cacos, and the revolutionary methods." Men like Léger and Zamor, Caperton said, expressed sympathy with United States aims but refused to support Dartiguenave because "it would be detrimental to their own personal political fortunes."[5]

By August 24 it became clear that, although no immediate action could be expected from the Haitians, neither was the government eager to resign. On that day two separate emissaries from Dartiguenave privately visited Davis to convey the same message: the president could accept the substance of the treaty, but he could not appear before the public as bowing to dictated terms. The tactless American insistence on acceptance "without modification" had made it all the more necessary that the treaty should seem to be the product of genuine negotiation if the government was to retain any standing at all with its citizens. At the suggestion of one of the emissaries, Davis again saw Dartiguenave at the palace, where the president assured him that the concession of a few changes of wording would serve to clear the path to ratification. Davis at last agreed to forward desired changes to Washington, although he was not authorized to do so, so long as they involved mere matters of wording and detail rather than basic principles. The Haitians would work out the proposed changes as quickly as possible and it was hoped that the treaty issue would soon be resolved.[6]

In the meantime the Washington authorities had given thought at last to the state of the Haitian economy. As soon as possible after ratification of the treaty, they informed Davis on the 18th, the State Department would use its good offices to secure the renewal of the stalled railway construction, thereby providing jobs for the needy. For the moment, however, Davis was to confer with Admiral Caperton as to public works projects which could be instituted for the same purpose. These instructions came in response to the admiral's repeated appeals for action to relieve destitution in the capital, a subject which he had already raised in Washington without much success. Like the rest of Haiti, Port-au-Prince suffered from the dislocation of trade and shipping caused by the European war, from the effects of disorder and revolution, and from a shortage of rain which had hurt the food supply. On the morning of August 13 a woman was found dead of starvation in the marketplace with a nursing child in her arms, while reports of other deaths from starvation in the city came in almost daily. Malnutrition was accompanied by an increase in disease, as the widespread poverty which normally characterized the city began to assume truly grim proportions.[7]

Caperton hoped that the erection of a new government would in itself help to restore normal economic activity, including renewed public works programs, but in the days following the inauguration of Dartiguenave he took energetic stopgap measures to help the really destitute until conditions should improve. Since Secretary of the Navy Daniels had previously ruled out the use of navy money for relief, the admiral asked the secretary to solicit funds from the American Red Cross. This Daniels did, and

Caperton received $1,000 at once, followed by $500 per month for the next several months. The bulk of this money was expended in Port-au-Prince and the balance in Cap-Haïtien. To use the funds with maximum effect, the admiral recruited a committee of prominent local citizens and churchmen to disburse them. Headed by Archbishop Conan, the group worked closely with church charitable institutions, which were already in contact with the local poor. To eke out these slender means, the admiral also used what navy resources he could. Working through a Wesleyan missionary named Turnbull, he organized a system for providing free hot meals from a central kitchen in the city. Much of the ingredients for these came from the messrooms of the *Washington,* where all unused food was collected and sent ashore after each meal, to be supplemented with rice purchased with a portion of the Red Cross funds. According to Beach, some eight hundred women and children came twice a day to share the stew thus produced.

The navy medical establishment was also pressed into service, opening a free public clinic in the city. Forbidden to give away navy supplies, Caperton did the next best thing by ordering medicines sold at cost. In addition, the navy organized a day nursery for the infants of working women and ventured into other territories previously unfamiliar to it. In all of these efforts, however, the scarcity of means imposed stringent limits upon what could be done. Dollars would go far in Haiti, but there were never enough of them, and the admiral often dipped into his own pocket to aid the work. Worst of all, the business recovery and renewal of construction projects for which everyone waited proved desperately slow to appear.[8]

The State Department's new interest in the condition of the Haitian economy soon bore fruit in a decision to have Caperton take over Haitian customshouses in order to secure immediate funds for public works. If possible, the department instructed, this should be done "upon the

invitation of the *de facto* authorities.'' The objects of this
move were to develop the economy and pacify the people,
thereby easing the task of the occupation and strengthening the position of the Dartiguenave regime. Admiral
Caperton promptly received an order to take over the customs administration in ten coastal cities, using the
proceeds to maintain order and carry on public works.
Davis was to try to persuade Dartiguenave to request the
take-over, but the admiral was to act whether the president
did so or not. United States personnel should take charge
of each customshouse, and each must be supplied with a
marine guard force. In each city, the collections were to be
deposited in the local branch of the National Bank of Haiti
in a separate account in Caperton's name.[9]

Although this measure was meant to be helpful,
Caperton viewed it as a distinctly unpleasant surprise. As
the admiral realized immediately, such a program constituted a drastic step which altered his entire situation. The
Haitians had assumed that the inauguration of a president
had made possible the return of governmental functions to
their own authorities and that the treaty terms which they
received from the United States would provide for certain
American controls over an essentially Haitian administration. Not only had the draft treaty injected an unexpectedly large foreign element into the civil administration of
the country, but now it appeared that the military occupation, far from being phased out, was to expand its physical
grip on Haiti while continuing to usurp the powers of the
government. Furthermore, the Haitians had watched in
apprehensive disapproval the operation of the United
States customs receivership in the neighboring Dominican
Republic, with the result that customs administration had
come to symbolize to many the very essence of national
independence. Although reconciled to the supervision of
their customs service by American agents, the public
would object to its simple seizure by foreign troops. This
new shock to Haitian pride might jeopardize the acceptance of the treaty or even renew armed opposition, the

admiral feared, and he openly expressed his consternation in his reply to the secretary of the navy: "United States has now actually accomplished a military intervention in affairs of another nation," he radioed. "Hostility exists now in Haiti and has existed for number of years against such action. Serious hostile contacts have only been avoided by prompt and rapid military action which has given United States control before resistance has had time to organize. We now hold capital of country and two other important seaports. Total force at my disposal now one armored cruiser two gunboats one converted yacht and fifteen hundred marines."

This force was already stretched to the limit, the admiral declared. Taking over customshouses in seven additional towns would entail garrisoning each, and the forces to do so were simply not available, nor did Caperton have enough light naval vessels to provide needed support and communications. What was involved was the military occupation of the seacoast of Haiti, a country in which all of the major population centers were coastal. Until adequate resources were available and preparations were made there should be no attempt to implement the customs seizures, Caperton warned. In order to carry them out, he requested a fresh regiment of marines, the marine artillery battalion, and three more gunboats or small cruisers. In the meantime he thought it imperative that the contemplated operations be kept secret; "this secrecy extremely important now pending treaty negotiations." When the treaty was signed and the necessary reenforcements in hand, it would be time enough to reveal the new movement to the Haitians, the admiral thought.[10]

The admiral's call for additional forces came at a time when his military command had just been significantly strengthened. The arrival of 850 men of the First Marine Regiment on August 15 had led to a reorganization of Caperton's forces in Haiti. Colonel Eli K. Cole had been in command of the forces ashore, most of which belonged to his own Second Marine Regiment. The presence of another regiment, however, enabled the organization of a full marine brigade. Cole was outranked by Colonel Littleton W. T. Waller, who came with the new troops to command this brigade, and a general shuffle of commands ensued. Besides his over-all command of the brigade, Colonel Waller was placed in military charge at Port-au-Prince and became second in command of the occupation. After consultation with Waller, Caperton ordered Cole north to Cap-Haïtien with one battalion of his regiment, there to join *Connecticut*'s Captain E. H. Durell. Cole and his troops departed for the Cape on the 16th.[11]

These changes established a command system for the marines that would endure beyond Caperton's tenure in Haiti, with Waller and Cole remaining in their posts throughout 1916. After the frantic improvisation of the first weeks, Caperton welcomed the stability and growing efficiency of his new military organization and increasingly delegated military matters to Waller in the same way in which he had delegated political affairs to Beach. The man who thus began to emerge as a central figure in the Haitian occupation was remarkable in many ways. Almost sixty years old in 1915, he had fought in a dozen obscure corners of the world. After making a notable record for gallantry in the Spanish-American War and the Boxer Rebellion, his career had nearly ended in disgrace in the Philippines during a bitter little campaign waged in 1901 to subdue the island of Samar. Feelings ran high there after the massacre of ' an American army garrison by the Filipinos, leading Waller's superior to forbid the taking of prisoners and to order the execution of all male enemies above the age of ten. Waller privately modified these instructions, but later ordered the summary execution of eleven Filipino prisoners accused of murdering marines. He did so while prostrate with fever after particularly harrowing experiences in the field and was ultimately acquitted by the court-martial which tried him for murder. Nevertheless he gained a reputation for ruthlessness in addition to his proven record as a combat soldier.

A subordinate described Waller as "a little fellow with a fiery mustache and a distinguished bearing," his features marked by an eagle glance and a huge nose. Self-confident and domineering, he was a magnificent horseman who liked to sweep off his hat with a flourish in salute to passing acquaintances. He had become something of a legend in the Marine Corps, the darker chapters of his past merely adding to the drama of his personality. While the marines admired his toughness and courage, civilians smarted under his abrasive and tactless manner, but everyone admitted that he was a highly effective fighting man.[12]

The continued growth of the marines' numbers and the elaboration of their command system did not pass unnoticed by the Haitians, as Captain Beach learned when he attended Dartiguenave's first cabinet meeting on August 15. The group gathered in the president-elect's small, stuffy bedroom, incongruously crowded among the bed and furniture. Dartiguenave had been a widower for years, living simply in a modest Port-au-Prince apartment since he had entered the Haitian Senate in 1910. A mulatto and a devout Catholic, the new chief executive was a big, portly man in middle life. He had been educated as a lawyer and was a native of the Department of the South, which constituted most of Haiti's great southern peninsula. The first president since 1879 to come from Haiti's light-skinned southern elite, he possessed the dignity, culture, and urbanity to which that elite ideally aspired. Sitting apart in the little room, he loomed over his six new cabinet ministers and the one or two other men present.[13]

Beach soon tested the mettle of the new administration. At the proper time, he announced that the battleship *Tennessee* was arriving that morning and that she carried an additional regiment of marines for duty in Haiti. Most of the group received this news without comment, but the minister of foreign affairs, H. Pauléus Sannon, was openly hostile. By what right, he demanded, did Admiral Caperton presume to land troops in Haiti without the permission of the Haitian government? The other ministers instantly shushed their over-bold colleague, but Beach had had his first inkling that the new government might aspire to have a mind of its own. The rest of the meeting went quietly, however, the president deciding to decree a month's postponement of the scheduled adjournment of Congress so that he could secure needed appointments and legislation.[14]

In these same days one complication disappeared: the defeated Rosalvo Bobo passed quietly off the scene. Convinced after Dartiguenave's election that his enemies meant to murder him, Bobo sought refuge in the British Legation. He would abandon his country to its fate, he told callers, and flee abroad to save himself. When Caperton heard that the fallen leader feared for his life, he sent Beach to reassure him. That tireless emissary found Bobo in a small cabin on the British Legation grounds, from which the red-haired doctor emerged disheveled and agitated. Pulling himself together, the Haitian quickly dressed, donning a collar and tie and a Prince Albert coat. "The President of Haiti apologizes for offering you so poor a reception," he told Beach with something of his old style, but he would not listen to the captain's urgings that he return to the comfort of his own home. No one wanted to kill him, Beach insisted; on the contrary, everyone felt kindly toward him. If he wished, however, Bobo could have a marine guard posted at his residence to protect him. And if he felt unable to support the new government, he could do much good for his people by returning to the practice of medicine. But Bobo was adamant; he would leave by the first steamer and asked only for a guard to take him aboard when the time came. To this Beach had to agree, and two days later, on the night of the 15th, the erstwhile revolutionary boarded a French ship for passage to the Dominican Republic. For the next year he drifted about the Caribbean, appearing in Jamaica and Cuba to write letters of bitter protest to Woodrow Wilson and other leading Americans. And for many months Caperton, still afraid of Bobo's influence with the *cacos* of the north, anxiously sought news of the doctor's whereabouts and activities.[15]

All of these developments kept the Americans occupied while the Haitian government debated the draft treaty, an issue which both Davis and Caperton still expected to see resolved fairly quickly. Caperton thought it would help the situation to keep military operations to a minimum and in general to avoid actions which would arouse opposition to the Americans. He would therefore prefer to seize no additional customshouses until the treaty was signed, he again advised the Navy Department. If the Dartiguenave government should resign anyway, then an American military government must replace it, but the consequences of such an act would be serious: "If we establish military government we would be bound not to abandon the situation in Haiti until the affairs of the country are set at rights and the predominant interests of the United States are secure." On the whole, however, the admiral thought that the avoidance of provocation, coupled with some minor concessions on the treaty, would serve to weather the crisis within a week or two.[16]

Such hopes were dashed by the written statement of desired changes which the Haitians submitted to Davis. As the young diplomat reported, "Practically every stipulation of [the] original treaty is either omitted or so changed as to defeat its purpose." Davis told Dartiguenave on August 28 that such sweeping changes were unacceptable and that he would not discuss them, demanding at the same time a response to the original draft terms. Furthermore, it was now decided to proceed at once with the take-over of customshouses. Caperton had already been informed that he would receive none of his requested reenforcements except the marine artillery battalion and that he must carry out his instructions as soon as this final force arrived. Thus he could not long delay in any case, while the prospect of an indefinite deadlock made it appear more necessary to find an interim method of applying the customs revenues to current needs.[17]

By this time the American occupation forces faced widespread unrest in Haiti, while the terms of the draft treaty intensified anti-American feeling. Although every important town had its local committee of safety, many lacked any effective authority. In addition, these local committees were often cool toward the Dartiguenave regime, which was widely regarded as the creature of the American occupation. All this made possible a general breakdown of control, which Caperton attempted to counter through regular coastal patrolling by his gunboats. Early in August he had landed a detachment at Gonaïves for a few days, and on August 17 he ordered one company of marines to St. Marc, which lay some fifty miles up the coast to the northwest of Port-au-Prince, and another to Léogane, about half that distance to the westward. Léogane proved quiet and the marines there withdrew ten days later, but the St. Marc force stayed. On August 20 the admiral directed it to take over and administer the customs-house in order to safeguard the funds from the *cacos* who swarmed the hinterland. All this caused intense excitement among the townspeople, but there was no resistance.[18]

Next the *Nashville* reported that Port-de-Paix, on the north coast, was strongly pro-Bobo and anti-American, while the local authorities were nearly powerless. Since a force of *cacos* was known to be nearby, Caperton spoke to Dartiguenave of the need to occupy this town also. The president made no objection, but told Caperton that if the admiral found it necessary to do so he preferred not to know about it. Irritated by this evasion of formal Haitian approval, Caperton ordered Captain Durell at Cap-Haïtien to send a marine company to secure the threatened town and take control of the customs there. Before the order could be implemented, the *caco* vanguard moved into town on the night of August 23, collecting some money from local merchants and trumpeting defiance to the Americans. On the 24th the *cacos* issued a proclamation of war against the foreign invaders, calling upon all Haitians to unite in a patriotic uprising and drive the interlopers from their shores. When the marines arrived the next day, however, the *cacos* faded into the hills.[19]

At Port-au-Prince the tension grew visibly more acute. On the night of August 14-15 there were two separate incidents of firing on American patrols in the city, leading Caperton the next day to extend the American lines by occupying Pétionville, a hill village a few miles inland. More firing occurred on the night of the 19th and again on the 22nd, while on the latter day a patrol stumbled upon a large cache of arms and ammunition. Hidden in a private house, this arsenal included several machine guns, the most frightening sign yet of serious preparations for a clash. At almost the same time, the Navy Department warned Caperton that it possessed secret but reliable information that the Haitians were prepared for armed resistance and urged the admiral to guard against a surprise attack. Colonel Waller was already taking vigorous precautions, however, including the establishment of a military training school to convert *Washington*'s thousand seamen into temporary soldiers for use in an emergency.[20]

Cap-Haïtien was even more of a storm center, being located in the heart of the *caco* country. Until the arrival of Colonel Cole and his battalion of marines on August 18, the Cape was held by landing parties of seamen from *Nashville* and *Connecticut*, with *Connecticut*'s Captain Durell in command. Before leaving the area, Rosalvo Bobo and Charles Zamor had organized a committee of safety to rule the city in Bobo's name, and the population supported this group. Durell refused to recognize it but could find no other local faction with sufficient strength to install in its place. His solution was to make Commander Olmstead of the *Nashville* acting mayor, with the power of appointment to fill lesser posts. The costs of administration were met by using receipts from the customshouse, which the Americans took over soon after they seized the city. The arrival of Cole's marine battalion made the situation militarily secure at Cap-Haïtien, though Haitian guerrillas sometimes fired into the city at long range from the surrounding hills. Still, neither Durell nor Cole was wholly content until they received a battery of marine field artillery at the end of August.[21]

Haiti's Department of the North was the home base of the *caco* bands, which still roamed freely through the area. In spite of Bobo's instructions to his followers to go to the Cape and disband, virtually none did, to the growing uneasiness of Caperton and his lieutenants. Instead the *cacos* awaited developments, indulging meanwhile in petty looting and sometimes blocking the roads to markets. General Blot's government troops at Cap-Haïtien had been promptly shipped to the capital, disarmed, and discharged, but some thousand other government soldiers who were loyal to General Bourand remained in the vicinity of Oanaminthe, on the Dominican border. These declared themselves ready to obey Bourand's order to go to the Cape and surrender their arms, but claimed that they were surrounded by hostile Boboite troops and unable to fight their way through. There had been small armed clashes between the Bobo and Bourand camps, but so far no major engagements. All through August Durell made repeated efforts to communicate with both sides and particularly to induce the *cacos* to lay down their arms.

On August 10 Admiral Caperton had arranged with the officials of the National Bank of Haiti for the payment at Cap-Haïtien of any *cacos* who turned in their arms. Ordinary soldiers were to get ten *gourdes* and chiefs one hundred. When this proved ineffectual Caperton ordered the rate raised to fifteen *gourdes* per soldier, but still without much success except at St. Marc, where a large *caco* band turned in 512 rifles on August 20. Meanwhile Durell contacted the *cacos* through a local intermediary who ultimately appeared to be acting in his own interests. This worthy insisted that no less than 600,000 *gourdes* must be paid the *cacos* for disarmament, a sum equal to about $120,000. Regarding this sum as out of the question, Durell opened direct negotiations with General Antoine Morenci, a leading *caco* chief and Bobo supporter. On

August 22 the captain met Morenci and other chiefs a few
miles outside Cap-Haïtien for a long parley. While the
meeting was courteous in tone, the result was unpromising.
Rejecting the government's offer of amnesty, the
assembled chieftains declared their fixed enmity to the
Dartiguenave regime; Bobo was the only rightful president,
they insisted. Nor would they sell their rifles as Durell
asked; rather, they announced that they meant to withdraw into the interior, retaining their arms. Ending the
meeting with loud cheers for Rosalvo Bobo, the Haitians
departed, leaving Durell to report that the *caco* threat in
the north was becoming distinctly ominous.[22]

It was against this background that Admiral Caperton
moved to take over most of the remaining customshouses.
With the arrival of the artillery battalion at the end of
August, his total marine strength was just over two
thousand men, with the largest concentration at Port-au-
Prince. From the forces at the capital, single companies
were detached in the next two weeks to occupy Petit-
Goâve, Miragoane, Les Cayes, and Jacmel on the great
southern peninsula, Gonaïves on the Gulf of Gonâve, and
Port-de-Paix on the north coast. The customshouses at Cap-
Haïtien and St. Marc had already been secured. Detachment commanders at each place were ordered to take
charge of local customs receipts and disbursements, under
the general supervision of an administrator of customs at
Port-au-Prince to be appointed by the admiral. The money
collected could be used for the expenses of local government, customs administration, and port services, for public
works projects to provide immediate employment to the
poor, and, at Port-au-Prince only, for the costs of maintaining an efficient constabulary. The appointment of
Navy Paymaster Charles Conard as administrator of customs completed the arrangements by which Admiral
Caperton took control of Haiti's principal public
revenue.[23]

The capstone of this program would be the seizure of
the customs administration in Port-au-Prince, where the

likelihood of active resistance or disorderly protest was highest. As the moment for this move neared, American authorities grew distinctly anxious, a feeling shared in Washington. Left in charge of the Navy Department by the absence of Josephus Daniels, Assistant Secretary Franklin D. Roosevelt wrote his mother on August 29 that he "did not dare leave Washington this Sunday, as the situation in Haiti is ticklish." He had discussed the Haitian situation with the president a few days before, Roosevelt added.[24]

Admiral Caperton found Port-au-Prince politically uneasy on September 1. The Dartiguenave administration was fast losing popularity as the public suspected it of knuckling under to American demands. Further bad feeling arose from the high-handedness of minor officials and police officers, who were widely accused of abuse of authority in fulfilling their duties. A cabinet minister privately reported to Caperton that a coup was rumored and intimated that the government would not be averse to a declaration of martial law by the admiral. The latter decided to take charge of the Port-au-Prince customshouse on the following morning, September 2, and asked Davis to notify the Haitian government, as well as foreign diplomats and consular representatives.[25]

At ten o'clock on the 2nd, United States naval officers entered the customshouse and took control, and for a brief minute it appeared that the much-badgered Dartiguenave would take a stand at last. Rejecting Caperton's request that the customs personnel stay on their jobs, the Haitian president ordered them all to quit in protest. More important, he published a formal proclamation of protest, addressed to the Haitian people. Just at the moment when his government was negotiating with the Americans about their presence on Haitian soil, the president declared, the Americans had seized the capital's customshouse. They had previously seized customshouses in many other towns. Each new seizure had been energetically protested by the government of Haiti, and Dartiguenave solemnly affirmed that his government had no complicity in actions so

opposed to the interests, laws, and sovereignty of the
Haitian people. He expressed his astonishment at such
deeds at a time when he was negotiating in good faith
about proposals presented by the Americans themselves to
settle the very questions involved. "In the presence of this
agonizing situation," the government intended to maintain
the national sovereignty, but the success of its efforts
would depend upon the unity of the entire country for its
own salvation. Right would triumph in the end, the president concluded, over the injustices of which all Haitians
were currently the victims.[26]

As Dartiguenave said, Foreign Minister Sannon had
submitted vigorous notes of protest through diplomatic
channels at each new customs seizure from August 24
through September 2, while Solon Menos, the Haitian
minister in Washington, pushed the issue there as well.
This seemingly united front, however, showed gaping
fissures when Caperton went directly to the national
palace to see the president. In marked contrast to his public stance, Dartiguenave confessed the impotence of his
government and asked Caperton in confidence to institute
martial law. Already considering that step, the admiral
now decided to make the announcement the following
day. His reasons for this decision he listed later: "The
increasing uneasiness at Port-au-Prince; the obvious inability of the existing government to control the situation . . . ;
the frequent publication in newspapers of inflammatory
propaganda against the government and American occupation—all this by men in public life—the open disloyalty of
some government officials to their own administration, all
this made it seem wise that a state of martial law be
proclaimed."[27]

On September 3 Admiral Caperton declared martial
law in Port-au-Prince and its vicinity. This was necessitated,
his proclamation said, because the members of the present
Haitian government, "although loyally attempting to discharge the duties of their respective offices," were unable
to master the problems which faced them. The admiral

Figure 1. Rear Admiral William B. Caperton, USN, who began the Haitian occupation in 1915 and virtually ruled the country for a year thereafter.

Figure 2. Captain Edward L. Beach, Admiral Caperton's chief of staff, as photographed in Port-au-Prince in 1916.

Navy Department, National Archives

Figure 3. U.S.S. *Washington*, Admiral Caperton's flagship and headquarters during the opening phase of the Haitian occupation.

Marine Corps, National Archives

Figure 4. Partial view of Port-au-Prince, Haiti, about 1915-1916.

Marine Corps, National Archives

Figure 5. President Philippe Sudre Dartiguenave, Caperton's choice for president of Haiti, surrounded by marine bodyguards. The two men flanking him are officers in the gendarmerie.

Marine Corps, National Archives

Figure 6. President Dartiguenave of Haiti and the presidential guard, in 1915 or 1916.

Figure 7. Colonel Littleton W. T. Waller, USMC, who commanded the campaign against the *cacos*.

Marine Corps, National Archives

Figure 8. Colonel Waller confers with the *caco* chieftains in October 1915. Colonel Waller is on the extreme right in the front row.

therefore assumed authority in the area, but asked all civil employees to stay at their posts as before. The military government would not interfere in the functions of civil administration or with the courts. Colonel Waller was named as executor of the decree and empowered to make the regulations and appoint the officers needed to enforce it.[28]

As the military occupation steadily extended its hold, Caperton remained dissatisfied with the force levels he had to work with. In his personal correspondence with Admiral Benson, the chief of naval operations, he renewed his arguments for additional ships. The Admiral's low point came on August 17, when the Navy Department asked for the return of *Connecticut* and *Eagle* for other duties. "United States cannot afford hamper me by reduction of my forces if they desire solve Haitien difficulties at this time," he radioed indignantly, and soon had the satisfaction of seeing his superiors retract their request. His mood was further improved by the arrival of a letter from Benson praising "the perfectly splendid manner" in which Caperton had performed so far in Haiti. "I do not believe we have ever had a foreign situation better handled," Benson declared, adding that this view was general in both the Navy and State departments.[29]

Benson continued to radiate confidence and flattery. Concerning the treaty question, we wrote later in August, "I think you can feel assured that there will be no dilly-dallying in this matter by the State Department." Secretary Lansing was able, energetic, and determined, and presumably all would soon come right. As to further ships, however, Benson was not encouraging: with arrival of what was already promised, "you will have everything that the Navy Department can give you, except the main fleet, and it is hoped that nothing will interfere with your being the one to carry this whole matter to a successful conclusion." The wording of this statement seemed to imply that if larger forces were needed, a new commander would accompany them, but Caperton resolutely maintained his position. He had marine detachments scattered along five hundred miles of coast, he replied, and badly needed ships to provide them with quick support and communication. Little *Eagle,* responsible for patrolling the entire north coast of the peninsula, was worn out mechanically and "about on her last legs." The navy tug *Osceola,* which alternated between hauling stores and doubling as a gunboat, was another cripple. Caperton had considered cleaning up the Haitian gunboat *Pacifique* and pressing her into his service, but upon examination her condition proved too bad to make this worth-while. The gunboat *Marietta* had recently joined him, it was true, but she had been sent primarily for service at Santo Domingo and could be used only on a part-time basis in Haiti. He would prefer to do the whole job using only the ships of the cruiser squadron, Caperton wrote, but this was simply impracticable; at the very least, he would have to hold *Connecticut* at Cap-Haïtien for the present, while he badly needed more gunboats. A week later, the gunboat *Sacramento* arrived at Port-au-Prince.[30]

The admiral's problems were the more vexatious because he was forced to cope with them personally, rather than through the medium of Captain Beach. Receiving word that his wife was dying in the United States, the captain had left for home just before the State Department ultimatum was delivered to Dartiguenave on the 22nd. Thus Caperton had temporarily to abandon his favorite posture, that of remaining isolated aboard his flagship while Beach made the face-to-face contacts with the Haitians ashore. For a time he was forced to join Davis at the negotiating sessions and to do his own lobbying with the local big-wigs, a task which he found distasteful and which ended the "splendid isolation" which he had cultivated to enhance his prestige.[31]

On the political front, the admiral continued to press Dartiguenave about the treaty. According to one of the Haitian president's aides, it was Caperton, and Beach while he was there, who kept pressure on the wavering chief executive to accept the American terms. "I saw their comings and goings at the Palace," he later wrote of these two, "never giving respite to the President, striving to emphasize in his eyes the advantages, immense if one believed them, that our country would derive from the treaty: important works to undertake by the aid of American funds graciously put at our disposal by the Government of the United States, systematic development of all our resources, agricultural, mineral, industrial . . . ." Trapped between opposing forces, Dartiguenave came to hope that the completion of an arrangement with the Americans would bring in return economic aid with which to create prosperity in his suffering country.[32]

While Dartiguenave agonized, Davis managed to clarify the principal differences which divided the two sides in the treaty negotiations. With some technical modifications, the Haitians were willing to surrender over-all control of the customs service to the United States, but insisted that its actual administration must remain in Haitian hands. The provision for creating an American financial adviser they rejected altogether as an infringement on the constitutional powers of the minister of finance. The clause allowing either signer to renew the treaty for ten years must be changed so that the agreement of both parties was required for its extension. Rather than the president of the United States directly appointing treaty officials, the president of Haiti should appoint them from a list submitted to him by the American president. Such concessions were essential, the Haitians insisted, in order to make the treaty compatible with the Haitian constitution and, more important, to make it sufficiently acceptable to the public to enable its passage. Davis thought these demands came from a group in the cabinet rather than the president himself and believed that Dartiguenave was personally anxious to reach agreement.[33]

Lansing's summary rejection of the Haitian position left matters deadlocked, but by September 4 they gave promise of moving again. "Government informs me unofficially that our declaration of martial law yesterday afternoon has greatly strengthened its position," Davis reported, "and will facilitate speedy ratification by Chamber of Deputies in case treaty agreement arrived at." The turning point came on September 7, in a long conference between Davis, Dartiguenave, and the Haitian cabinet. The American demanded a definite answer regarding the treaty, and Sannon replied flatly that he could not accept the provision establishing an American financial adviser. He was supported in this position by Antoine Sansaricq, the minister of agriculture and public works. At this point President Dartiguenave, stiffened by Caperton's show of force, crossed his Rubicon and requested the immediate resignation of both ministers. With these two gone, the rest of the cabinet agreed to accept the treaty with whatever modifications could be secured, though the minister of finance, Emile Elie, soon followed Sannon and Sansaricq in resigning. The president asked Davis for a short delay in negotiations to enable him to fill the new cabinet vacancies, to which Davis agreed. It was understood that the new appointees would be favorable to the treaty, and the cabinet thereby solidified in its favor.[34]

This cabinet shake-up was a major victory for the Americans, but it was not without its dangers. Sannon in particular had considerable weight in the capital, while the resignation of half the cabinet dramatized the treaty issue anew. Someone gave Sannon's letter of resignation to the newspapers, and all of Port-au-Prince learned that worthy's strongly stated objections to the treaty. Many readers seized eagerly upon Sannon's argument that in the United States neither the public nor the Congress would support the actions of the Wilson administration if the Haitians remained firm in their opposition. President Dartiguenave responded with a rather discouraged letter to the editors of *Le Matin* defending his own course in regard to the treaty, and speaking gloomily of the current "hour of anguish," the "circumstances afflicting our unfortunate country," and his readiness to bear the insults rained upon him by his enemies. The president's position became so precarious that he called in congressional leaders and threatened to resign if they failed to sustain him. This act had some effect on the congressmen, since even Dartiguenave's enemies hesitated to pull down the government when the probable alternative was outright American rule. The public, however, remained affronted, and the New York *Herald*'s correspondent reported that "the resignation of the three most influential members of the Dartiguenave Cabinet is regarded here as signifying the sentiment among prominent Haytien politicians."[35]

The treaty dispute was also beginning to be reflected in the changed tone of the United States press, heretofore not inclined to criticize the Haitian occupation. In a discussion headed "Strait-Jacketing Haiti," the *Literary Digest* remarked on the appearance of a disapproving editorial minority, and itself took a sardonic stance. "The short and abrupt manner of the Wilson Administration toward the Republic of Haiti" suggested to the *Digest* editors that "small-boy Haiti is evidently going to receive, if not corporal punishment, at least the strictest sort of discipline."[36]

On the day after Sannon's resignation he was replaced as foreign minister by Louis Borno, a man described by an associate as combative, assured, and self-reliant. Borno was one of those Haitians who believed that the only available road to national progress lay through American tutelage. He accepted this principle whole-heartedly and clung to it in the face of adverse public opinion. A man of polish and culture, he was able to work effectively with the Americans and in a later stage of the occupation would ultimately replace Dartiguenave as president of Haiti. Soon after his appointment, Borno called upon Davis to request a delay of several weeks while he familiarized himself with the treaty negotiations. Davis rejected this request and insisted upon the need for speed. As a result, Borno presented a new version of the Haitian demands on September 10, and Davis was gratified to find them much more modest than those Sannon had formulated.[37]

By now the difference between the two sides was narrowing fast. The United States had dropped its demand for a prior Congressional resolution authorizing the treaty. The State Department also proved willing to concede some softening of language, including a new Haitian version of the treaty's preamble, and even to yield marginally on one matter of substance. This largest concession referred to the proposed financial adviser. The American draft had stated that the financial adviser should be attached to the Ministry of Finance and that the finance minister must be pledged to support and implement his proposals. The Haitians wished the adviser merely to be attached to the *minister* of finance, and at least theoretically subordinate to him. The American compromise stated that the financial adviser would be attached to the Ministry of Finance and that the minister would "lend efficient aid" to his "proposals and labors." The resulting ambiguity was to create controversy over the adviser's powers for years after the treaty went into effect. The State Department made it clear that these concessions represented their last word. "The things which the United States consider to be necessary for the rehabilitation of Haiti fall far short of the offers freely made by these Haitians to Admiral Caperton on August 7th 1915," the department's message asserted. The latest terms reflected "a most liberal spirit" on the part of the United States and should "put an end to questions of further amendment and result in an immediate conclusion of the treaty as herein described."[38]

While the Haitians were still dissatisfied with many aspects of the treaty, they recognized that the current version was the best they were likely to get. Louis Borno declared that he was personally willing to sign the treaty as it now stood, and on September 13 he announced that his government was prepared to accept it. The Haitians next wanted assurances as to the implementation of Article I,

however, which read: "The Government of the United
States will, by its good offices, aid the Haitian Government
in the proper and efficient development of its agricultural,
mineral and commercial resources and in the establishment
of the finances of Haiti on a firm and solid basis." They
asked Caperton and Davis for a promise that the United
States would use its "good offices" to obtain for them a
temporary loan of $1,500,000, to be used for the current
operating expenses of the Haitian government. Both
Americans urged the State Department to give the
requested assurance, and they were informed on the 15th
that this was approved. As soon as the treaty was ratified,
the Haitians should send a commission to Washington to
negotiate the loan, as well as to settle old differences with
the National Bank of Haiti and the American railway
company. In the meantime, the State Department would
arrange for the immediate advance to the government of
$100,000 from the National Bank of Haiti.[39]

Reassured on this point, the Haitians asked for further
assurance that the work on the National Railroad would
begin again as soon as the treaty was ratified. Caperton
relayed this new condition, to which the State Department
replied impatiently that it had twice indicated to Davis its
support for this project already. Caperton saw these moves
as designed by Dartiguenave to secure votes for the
ratification of the treaty when it was submitted to
Congress; in effect, as direct inducements to his countrymen, especially those in government. Both Caperton and
the Haitians regarded these assurances as specific and binding. The State Department, it was later to develop,
considered them merely as declarations of policy, subject
to casual and unilateral alteration.[40]

The terms of the treaty being settled, it was next
agreed that the two governments would enter into a *modus
vivendi* which would put the treaty into effect when
signed, without awaiting the exchange of ratifications. The
necessary paper work was completed by September 16. To
forestall disputes as to translation, Davis secured an agree-

ment that the English text would be the only official one, and all seemed ready for signing. At the last moment, Borno presented Davis with a formal letter "interpreting" the treaty articles concerning American customs control and the post of financial adviser. Davis rejected the letter, maintaining that the treaty must be accepted as it stood without interpretations, additions, or reservations, and after a conference at the home of Borno, the Haitians agreed to withdraw their letter. This marked the end of the government's resistance. The treaty was signed the same day, September 16, at eight o'clock in the evening, while the *modus vivendi* was held in abeyance pending an act of the Haitian Congress to authorize it.[41]

The following day witnessed at last the full diplomatic recognition of the Dartiguenave government by the United States. At high noon the *Washington* raised the flag of Haiti to her masthead and fired a twenty-one gun salute, after which Admiral Caperton and his staff went ashore to pay a ceremonial call on the president. Davis's status changed from secretary of legation to chargé d'affaires. The regime had paid the full price demanded by the Americans; now, presumably, it was to receive its rewards.[42]

9
Cacos and Congress

THE *CACO* question came to a head just as the Dartiguenave government formally accepted American treaty terms. United States forces soon found themselves fighting the famed northern mercenaries, in spite of Admiral Caperton's attempts to avert an armed struggle through a combination of bribes, threats, and assurances. His offer to buy each soldier's rifle for fifteen *gourdes* had produced a steady stream of arms, but no really decisive results. Neither had the government's proclamation of amnesty solved the problem, while the reenforcement of Cap-Haïtien at the end of August resulted only in the *cacos* there retiring a few miles into the interior. By the beginning of September the situation in the north was distinctly threatening. *Caco* bands were blocking the movement of the coffee crop to the coast for shipment, preventing the country people from bringing their wares to market towns, and levying tolls on such traffic as they did allow to pass. They continued to claim that Rosalvo Bobo was the rightful president and to spurn the authority of the

159

Dartiguenave administration. Although their public stance toward the Americans was ambiguous, Caperton feared that, if unchecked, they might serve as the nucleus for a general uprising against the occupation.[1]

Late in August the admiral had called in Charles Zamor and General Robin to confer with him about the *caco* problem. His old antagonists from the days of the Revolutionary Committee, the two were influential figures in the politics of the north and had ready access to the *caco* leaders. They quickly agreed to serve as emissaries, proposing that Caperton appoint a commission consisting of themselves and a few others to go into the interior and visit the various *caco* chiefs in their own towns. These commissioners would offer the chiefs new and more favorable terms on which to exchange their weapons for money, the payment to each to vary with his influence and the size of his band. Each chief who agreed to the bargain would get a check drawn on the National Bank of Haiti which he could cash within the American lines after his followers had surrendered their arms and ammunition.

This ingenious scheme was not without its merits, but Caperton regarded the scale of payments as far too high. Zamor and Robin calculated the total cost at about $200,000 in gold, a sum which the admiral thought simply not available. At any rate this was far more than had ever before been paid to *cacos*, and if, as Caperton believed, there were no more than eight thousand *cacos* in all of Haiti, the price per man was out of all proportion to previous rates. Disgustedly, the admiral characterized this as merely another "attempt to bleed the Americans," and suspected that most of the money would go to graft, with the two promoters of the plan figuring prominently in the benefits.[2]

Caperton next looked into the possibility of resuming construction on the national railroad, in the hope that the availability of construction jobs might lure the *cacos* from their bands and diminish their discontent with the current regime. A full-scale resumption of northern railroad building could provide work for up to four thousand men and materially improve the area's economy. At the moment, however, the funds for so expensive a plan were not available from Haiti's revenues. All Caperton could do was to ask that the State Department use its good offices to seek financing, a request that produced no early results. If nothing of the sort could be done, the admiral saw no alternative but to send his forces into the *cacos'* country and bring them to submission. When he reported this conclusion to the Navy Department he suffered another reverse, for a few days later Daniels replied: "unless absolutely necessary to prevent loss of life or property you will take no offensive action against Haytians without first consulting the Navy Department."[3]

This left matters where they had been. At the end of August the number of rifles brought in had reached 400 at Gonaïves and 1,275 at St. Marc. This was a substantial total, but these weapons came almost entirely from individual *cacos* who could not resist a chance at cold cash. The chiefs remained aloof, still commanding considerable forces and controlling the mountainous northern interior. It seemed clear that they meant to hold out for more money than the Americans were willing to pay them to disband. Every Haitian go-between had encouraged the *caco* chieftains to believe that large sums were in prospect, a faith that undoubtedly sprang from the knowledge that they were now dealing with an enormously wealthy United States government rather than a miserably poor Haitian one. The *cacos* simply shared in their way a general Haitian hope that since the Americans had taken responsibility for Haiti's affairs, they would at least bring some of the fabled American wealth into the country. In this hope the *cacos* were to be as disappointed as the rest of their countrymen.[4]

With other courses of action closed, there seemed little to do but send more emissaries to the north. On September 5 the president dispatched his minister of war, Charles Leconte, to Cap-Haïtien to see what he could accomplish, and on the following day Charles Zamor left on a similar errand, armed with credentials and expense money from Admiral Caperton. At this point a new *caco* threat appeared at Gonaïves, across the northern peninsula from Cap-Haïtien, when General Pierre Rameaux appeared outside the town with about 150 men and remained in its vicinity, preventing the entry of food and coffee from the interior. A larger *caco* force was soon reported a short distance inland, and it was rumored that other bands were converging on Gonaïves. Commander Carter of the gunboat *Castine* kept a close watch on the city, while Zamor sought without success to reach Rameaux for a parley when he passed through on his way north. Zamor did manage, however, to arrange with a subordinate *caco* leader for the resumption of food supplies before he left. Even so, the *cacos* continued to levy a toll of fifty cents per person on those who wished to enter or leave Gonaïves, taxed the coffee crop on its way to market, and even ventured to cut off the town's water supply. After this last act, Carter recommended taking action with the forces on hand, consisting of *Castine* and Gonaïves' small marine garrison, but again the Navy Department demurred. Becoming bolder, Rameaux issued a manifesto beginning "En route to Port-au-Prince," that standard opening phrase in the litany of *caco* rebellion, and called upon his countrymen to rise against the Americans.

The first actual fighting occurred on September 18, when Carter sent an armed working party outside of the town to repair the sabotaged water main. A *caco* force fired on the marine party, which unlimbered its machine guns and returned the fire. The Haitians left one dead and several wounded, but returned to attack an American patrol later the same day. Carter responded by putting ashore a landing party from *Castine* and calling for a second marine company to add to the one-company garrison. Two days later four more Haitians died when a *caco* party resisted Carter's attempt to open up the railroad that ran some twenty miles inland from Gonaïves.[5]

The situation took a new turn when Colonel Waller's right-hand man in Haiti, Major Smedley Butler, a marine officer who had served in China, Panama, the Philippines, Nicaragua, and Mexico, arrived on the scene. He had been twice wounded in the Boxer Rebellion and cited for gallantry there, gained the revealing sobriquet of "Old Gimlet Eye" in the Nicaraguan campaign of 1912, and won the Medal of Honor at Vera Cruz in 1914. This redoubtable figure promptly took charge at Gonaïves. With legendary energy, he formed a party of fifty marines and sailors and went after General Rameaux, overtaking him on the 21st at Les Poteaux, a village ten miles inland from Gonaïves on the railroad line. The *caco* leader was accompanied by about five hundred followers, somewhat less than half of whom carried firearms; the rest were armed with machetes, knives, and staves. Backed by his fifty, Butler boldly engaged the Haitians in a parley, pulling Rameaux bodily from his horse to emphasize his demands that the worthy decamp from the area and cease all interference with the local food and water supplies. The chastised *cacos* duly went, while Butler got the railroad running and returned to town. Like everyone else, Admiral Caperton was bemused at the major's unique powers of intimidation. "I could not but commend Butler's success," he recalled, "and often wondered at his methods."[6]

The largest bodies of *cacos* lay far to the north and east, however, and were less easily overawed. Both Zamor and Leconte had initiated talks with their chiefs, but Leconte promptly fell from grace by suggesting what the admiral considered another scheme for excessive payments. This nullified the efforts of Zamor to reach a settlement along more modest lines, but on September 11 Leconte redeemed himself in the eyes of authority by apparently securing an agreement from the *caco* leaders around the Cape to disarm for 60,000 *gourdes,* or $12,000. Encouraged but still skeptical, Caperton decided to send Colonel Waller north to survey the situation. If Leconte's settlement fell through and no other could be arranged, it would be necessary to fight, Caperton was convinced, and the logical man to evaluate conditions in the *caco* country was the one who would be in charge of the fighting. As Waller headed for the Cape, word came from Captain Durell that the principal *caco* chiefs planned a final grand conference within a few days, in which they would determine their position toward the Americans. This would give the colonel an unexpectedly good chance to size up the *cacos* for himself.[7]

The meeting disclosed by Durell took place on September 16 at Quartier Morin, a few miles outside of Cap-Haïtien. Colonels Waller and Cole met the *cacos* in person, taking along only an interpreter and ignoring the warnings of their officers that they would surely be killed. At the *caco* camp they found 136 "generals," the acknowledged leaders of whom were Jean Baptiste Pétion and Antoine Morenci. The *cacos* were eager to state their grievances, charging that the Americans held the rightful president, Rosalvo Bobo, in jail at Port-au-Prince and also that they meant to annex the Môle-Saint-Nicolas to the United States. Waller refuted both charges and demanded that the chieftains disband their forces, which they firmly refused to do. The colonel then announced that he would give them two days to consider his terms, but that in the meantime he meant to reopen the railroad line from Cap-Haïtien to Grande Rivière du Nord, a distance of some fourteen miles. Waller blandly offered them all a ride to the Cape on the first train out, but the chiefs indignantly declared that they controlled the north and that no train would be allowed to pass. On this note the two colonels and their interpreter left unharmed, to return to Cap-Haïtien.[8]

Waller was as good as his word, for on the next day he took a train through to Grande Rivière, though not without difficulties arising from several acts of *caco* sabotage. At the end of the line he again met Morenci and Pétion, but without any new result. When the two *cacos* failed to appear for another meeting scheduled on the following day, the colonel decided to return to the capital and report. Upon his arrival at Port-au-Prince, he had an extended meeting with the admiral in which the two commanders went over the entire *caco* question. The *caco* soldiery were miserably clad and armed, Waller told his superior, deriving their sustenance from petty looting and levies on local commerce. He thought it probable that the chiefs were holding their bands together only with difficulty, while their men were eager for a cash settlement. He had found the chieftains not so much opposed to the Americans as to the Dartiguenave regime, and while they had privately given up hope of seeing Bobo in power, they were not yet ready to come to terms with his rivals, whom they deeply distrusted. Waller had tried to convince them that there would be no treachery, promising that the United States authorities would guarantee the terms of any agreement reached. Treachery was not unknown in Haitian politics, however, and furthermore the *cacos* lacked faith in government promises to pay them. Such promises had always been subject to numerous uncertainties, and Waller thought that the northern chieftains would place more confidence in an agreement based on payment by the Americans rather than the Dartiguenave regime.

A complaint much heard before Waller made his inspection was that local Haitian officials often failed to cooperate with United States forces, sometimes from hostility and sometimes merely from ineffectiveness. Waller corroborated these reports, leading Caperton to declare martial law for all places in Haiti occupied by his troops. This important step gave his officers an authority independent of and superior to the representatives of the Haitian government, marking a further ascendancy of American over Haitian power. The admiral further arranged for the Haitian government to deposit one hundred thousand *gourdes* to his credit at once, with more to be added when necessary. He could now make his own monetary arrangements independently, and at Waller's instance he announced that he would pay fifty thousand *gourdes* for every one thousand serviceable rifles with their attendant ammunition. All previous terms were cancelled in favor of these new and more liberal ones, the *caco* chiefs to have eight days after they were apprised of the offer to take advantage of it. By this time the fighting at Gonaïves had taken place, so General Rameaux and his followers were expressly denied the benefit of these terms or any other.[9]

To the admiral's intense disgust, the *caco* leaders once again decided to hold out for more money. Zamor and Leconte, by now acting together at the Cape, despaired of agreement and asked for a settlement six times larger than the admiral had offered in his latest terms. Although Caperton refused to consider this, the *cacos* naturally waited to determine the success of their move. There did seem to be some decline of tension in the area, however, while food and coffee resumed their normal movement into Cap-Haïtien. At the other trouble spot, Gonaïves, a chastened General Rameaux disclaimed all responsibility for the recent attacks and solemnly denied authorship of his fiery anti-American manifesto, meanwhile innocently inquiring about the possibility of the government naming him minister of war! As a result of his new humility Rameaux was provisionally included in the ranks of those who might receive payment for the surrender of arms, a concession he would ultimately lose as a result of subsequent backsliding. Gonaïves remained quiet, railway operations soon being restored between there and the hill town of Ennery.[10]

On the whole things looked promising, and Caperton was determined not to go beyond his offer of fifty thousand *gourdes* per one thousand rifles. "This will be our upper limit," he wrote to Benson at the Navy Department, "and should they not come across and accept this in a week or eight days, we will then have to take other means of quieting them. . . . One thing I am sure of, is that these *cacos* will not fight, and when we show them that we mean business and propose having our own way about it, they will submit to our ideas and requests." The rank and file were half-starved and unhappy, he believed, while recent experience with Rameaux at Gonaïves had left the admiral with little respect for their leaders; too little, as he soon learned.[11]

As so often happened in Haiti, apparent progress turned suddenly into crisis with the outbreak of fighting at the Cape on a larger scale than had yet taken place. When American patrols left the city on the morning of September 25, they found *caco* outposts awaiting them, and upon Captain Durell's communicating with Morenci and Pétion, the two top *cacos* warned that they would not tolerate such patrolling in the Plaine du Nord. Durell's answer was that the patrols had no hostile intent, and that he meant to continue them. The next morning saw two parties of forty men each leave Cap-Haïtien with orders to push through to their destinations even if attacked. One of these detachments was ambushed a few miles from the town and found itself hard-pressed until Colonel Cole reached the scene with a relieving force. The firing lasted all day, declining in the afternoon into desultory sniping in the brush. The other patrol also ran into a fight, but on a smaller scale. Altogether the marines suffered fourteen wounded on the 26th, while the Haitians left forty dead on the Haut du Cap road and undoubtedly took many more casualties.

On the same day that the fighting took place at the Cape, a fifty-man marine patrol clashed with a *caco* force at Petit Rivière de l'Artibonite, some fifty-odd miles to the southward. In this skirmish the marines lost one man killed and the *cacos* several, so that cumulatively perhaps fifty of the Haitian hill fighters died on the 26th, in addition to what must have been many men wounded. Unless unusually large numbers of *cacos* were engaged in these actions, their loss ratio must have been rather formidable, and this probably goes far to explain the subsequent willingness of all but the most intransigent of their number to come to terms with the Americans.[12]

Admiral Caperton had not expected this sudden and

aggressive resistance to his patrols, but he was determined to continue the patrolling. He had long felt the need to demonstrate his mastery of the *cacos'* home territory and was not averse to seizing the opportunity now presented. The difficulty lay in persuading Secretary Daniels of the necessity to do so, since Daniels had forbidden offensive action. "The sending out of these patrols necessary to insure free entry of food and supplies to Cape Haytien and not considered in nature of offensive operations," Caperton radioed the department hopefully. Privately he wrote Benson that he had tried to avoid armed conflict, declaring that the *cacos* had rejected his attempts at conciliation and must now take the consequences. "They cannot be trusted and need the fear of God to be put into their souls before they will do anything. My instructions and orders have always been, to be careful and not make any offensive moves, and up to the present time I do not believe we have made one such move." Now, however, if the *caco* leaders remained troublesome, "then I fear that I will have to ask the Department for permission to go after them . . . ." This might not be necessary, the admiral hastened to add: "Since our conflict with them on last Sunday [the 26th], their manner, tone, action have been entirely changed for the better."[13]

Caperton's initial response to news of the fighting was to dispatch Waller and Butler to the Cape along with *Eagle* and *Nashville*. While they were still en route, Cole took nearly five hundred men on a reconnaissance in force to Quartier Morin, the former *caco* headquarters. This column, which contained most of Cole's strength, reached its objective with little opposition, only to find Morenci and Pétion gone. These two leaders, however, had left Cole a courteously phrased note asking for an interview. They now seemed cautious, even frightened, and for a time avoided meeting the Americans in spite of their request to do so. They finally came to Quartier Morin to parley on September 29, by which time Waller was present to speak for the Americans. Within a few hours the principals at this meeting reached an agreement which proved to be the turning point of the *caco* crisis.[14]

The terms of settlement were by now well defined. Caperton had already announced what he was willing to pay, while Charles Zamor had explored the other aspects of a settlement with the *caco* leaders during the previous weeks. Caperton and Dartiguenave had agreed upon a common form of Zamor's proposals, and Waller carried all this information with him when he returned to the north. Finding Pétion and Morenci willing to reach agreement on these lines, he put the whole thing into a formal French document and received the adherence of the two leaders and their subordinates.

The bargain struck at Quartier Morin required the Haitian signers to turn in all the arms and ammunition in the possession of their men, and thereafter to go home, disband, and cease to oppose the government. All who did so were guaranteed amnesty, while those still in arms would henceforth be treated as bandits. The terms contained positive as well as negative inducements, beginning with the standing offer of fifty thousand *gourdes* per thousand rifles. In addition, cooperative *cacos* would have a chance to join the new national constabulary which would be created under the Haitian-American convention to replace the old army and police systems, a promise which Waller and Butler kept when they organized the new gendarmerie a few months later. There was also provision for political patronage, of which successful *caco* leaders had always enjoyed a generous share. The agreement specified that the chieftains would send a delegation to Port-au-Prince to confer with the government about "participation in the civil government of Haiti." Since none of them trusted the Dartiguenave regime, Waller agreed that the United States authorities would guarantee the fulfillment of any terms which the *cacos* could secure from the government regarding appointments to office. Beyond this rather vague commitment, Waller promised that the occupation would provide funds for public works in order to create employment for the demobilized troops. Finally, the colonel threw in an offer to treat the many *caco* wounded free of charge at the Cap-Haïtien hospital, although this was not written into the formal agreement.[15]

The next two weeks saw the disbanding of much of the remaining *caco* force in the north. Morenci and Pétion fulfilled their promises faithfully, Morenci's men alone turning in nearly six hundred rifles on October 6. On the same day, Waller arrived at the Cape with some 370 naked and starving survivors of the government force which had been trapped by *cacos* since midsummer at Ouanaminthe on the Dominican border. These men were paid off and disbanded, most of them being sent south to their homes aboard *Nord Alexis,* while marine detachments went to Ouanaminthe and Fort Liberté to secure the northern frontier. By mid-October the north was relatively quiet, and goods and persons moved normally. Some armed bands remained in the hills and some *caco* leaders repudiated the settlement, but in general the *cacos* seemed disheartened, divided, and defensive, and a large portion of them had made peace. As events would prove, only a minority remained to be dealt with.[16]

While Colonel Waller oversaw the taming of the *cacos,* Admiral Caperton's attention remained concentrated largely on affairs at Port-au-Prince, where problems arose over both the financial conditions of the government and the ratification of the treaty by Congress. On September 18 President Dartiguenave convoked the extraordinary session of Congress called for the purpose of ratifying the treaty, and a special committee of the Chamber of Deputies began deliberations on that document. The government expected smooth sailing in the Chamber, but stiff opposition from the Senate. Should the Senate prove irreconcilable, Dartiguenave planned to dissolve the Congress and replace it with a constitutional convention charged with both the modification of the constitution and the ratification of the treaty. The president asked Davis whether the United States would support him in such a move, and the State Department answered Davis's inquiry with a strong affirmative, promising to back Dartiguenave to the limit.[17]

The Chamber of Deputies acted much as expected. Its committee on the treaty submitted a report favorable to ratification on September 28, only one of its members dissenting. On October 6 the Deputies approved the treaty by a vote of seventy-five to six, and another hurdle on the path to ratification had been passed. The deputies were not completely docile, however, for they accompanied their ratification with an "interpretive commentary" which spelled out the Haitian position on certain issues. The voting took place amid what one observer called "moving scenes," and when it was finished a deputy from Gonaïves declared bitterly that the Americans were imposing a protectorate upon Haiti. This man walked out in protest, followed by a scattering of his fellows, but the action was only symbolic; the Chamber had made no real trouble.[18]

In the capital, Caperton noted, it was commonly said that the deputies had done as the president wished because his convoking of an extraordinary session of two months meant six hundred gold dollars in extra pay for each of them. The admiral's cynicism reflected his growing fatigue and irritation at the stresses of Haitian politics, and his letters began to contain outbursts against the people with whom he dealt. "These are the most deceitful, unreliable, graft seekers on earth and I really believe at times that the President's cabinet are all against him but they see that we are here for keeps and that we mean business, so they dare not do much in opposition to his wishes," he wrote Benson.[19] The frustrations of his situation were accentuated by the absence of Captain Beach, who had previously done so much of the negotiating, and by the increasing intervention of the State Department in determining tactics and making decisions for him. In particular, he now faced a crisis in the financial position of the government which was deliberately imposed on him from Washington.

The American take-over of the customshouses in August and September had deprived the government of Haiti of almost all of its regular revenue without making any provision for its replacement. Thus the government found itself financially embarrassed almost at once, and as the weeks passed its position became impossible. An incident in late September added insult to injury. On the 23rd a shipment of 500,000 unsigned *gourde* notes arrived at Port-au-Prince consigned to the government. Under orders from Washington, Caperton seized this currency and held it, thereby not only depriving the government of a possible source of funds but inflicting upon it a considerable humiliation. Sympathizing with the Haitians, the admiral recommended a scheme for issuing the notes through the National Bank in the form of a loan from the bank to the government. The Haitians themselves rejected this plan, however, being unwilling to make any joint arrangement with the hated bank. Dartiguenave instead appealed to Caperton for funds from the customs receipts with which to meet current expenses, and on the 29th Caperton asked his superiors for permission to give the government a regular allowance. This request was refused.[20]

Although it offered no explanation of its course, the State Department presumably intended to keep pressure on the government by refusing it funds until Congress ratified the treaty. Caperton saw matters differently. In his view, the Dartiguenave administration was the principal pro-American force in Haitian politics and to deprive it now of money and prestige would only undermine its usefulness and strengthen the opposition, not to speak of raising questions about the value of cooperating with the Americans. Dartiguenave himself brought things to a head on October 3 by demanding an interview. Davis and Caperton's aide, Lieutenant E. G. Oberlin, went to the palace, where the president told them that he must resign if he did not get money soon. He could not pay the salaries of public employees or carry on government business, he said, while his opponents made capital of his helplessness

and the Congress received the worst possible impression of
American intentions under the treaty. The president's
declaration was reenforced later in the day by the resignation of two members of his cabinet.[21]

Both Davis and Caperton again urged Washington to
provide funds for the needs of the government, while
Caperton set Paymaster Conard, the new director of the
customs, to calculating the current state of his finances.
Conard reported that he had collected $171,000 in
September and retained a balance of $76,000. Reporting
this to the Navy Department, the admiral asked again that
he be allowed to turn over to the government all customs
surpluses left after specified obligations had been met. On
October 5 he at last received authorization to provide
weekly payments to the government out of customs surpluses, but none of the back pay of public officials and
employees was to be paid until after the treaty was ratified, an obvious attempt to keep alive one financial
incentive for ratification. Furthermore, there remained the
question of how much income the government should get,
the State Department preferring a fixed allowance to
giving the Haitians the customs surpluses. Upon inquiry,
the Haitian government put its absolute minimum needs at
$150,000 per month. Caperton gave it some stopgap
money, and on October 13 was authorized to begin a regular weekly allowance of $25,000. While less than their
$150,000 per month minimum request, the Haitians had
little choice but to accept these terms, and the admiral
afterward believed that there was a direct connection
between his order to release the first funds to the government on October 5 and the deputies' ratification of the
treaty on the following day.[22]

This unhappy affair coincided with the growth of friction about another issue, the imposition of press censorship by the American authorities. On September 4, the day
after Caperton declared Port-au-Prince to be under martial
law, Provost-Marshal Alexander S. Williams called in the
city's newspaper editors to confer with him. Williams, a

captain of marines, told the journalists that they would be in the same position as editors in the United States; that is, they could speak freely, but not licentiously. He would not tolerate false or incendiary propaganda against the United States or Haitian governments, indecent or obscene letters, or threats to the public peace, Williams announced. Authors and editors who violated these guidelines would be held personally responsible and punished by a military court. Despite Williams' assertion, this did not seem a true parallel to the practice in the United States, and the capital's newspapermen were left uncertain of their real position.[23]

A new journal, *Haiti Intégrale,* had appeared on the streets of the capital to test the limits of dissent. An early issue of this organ analyzed the terms of the treaty with the United States just signed by the government. The United States, it charged, had first conquered and intimidated Haiti and then imposed terms that were a scandal before the world. The Americans had proven to the civilized world that their diplomacy was that of the dollar and armed force, aimed at violating the sovereignty of the small weak states in the hemisphere which they were pledged to protect. Haiti would become a vassal state; the Americans brought, "not Rights and Progress, but Oppression and Despair."[24]

The author of this thunderbolt was a fiery young Haitian named Elie Guérin, who had already crossed swords with the provost-marshal after failing to submit to him the required copy of each number of his paper. While Guérin ultimately gave Williams a back-file of the paper's two weeks of publications, he continued to defy American censorship. The tone of *Haiti Intégrale* remained incendiary right through the number of September 23, which proved to be its last. On that date, Williams sent for Guérin, who refused to report to the provost-marshal's office. That evening armed marines arrested the editor, his assistant, and the printer who had printed the journal. A military court released the printer with a warning, fined the assistant five hundred *gourdes,* and sentenced Guérin to 130 days in the military jail, spurring one of the established dailies to risk its own prosecution by condemning the entire proceeding in the name of freedom of the press. The net effect was to dampen press opposition to the occupation, the amount and incisiveness of political reporting declining visibly after September.[25]

The imposition of censorship remained thenceforth a significant grievance against the Americans in Haiti. At first sight the charge might seem disingenuous, since Haiti had seldom enjoyed a free press; editors in the past had criticized incumbent governments at their peril. Yet the feeling aroused by American censorship appears to have been genuine, not only because of the felt difference between the exercise of foreign and domestic power, but perhaps as much because it violated another portion of the promise for good which many Haitians had hoped to find in the American presence. Even if censorship harmonized with Haitian realities, it contrasted dismally with American pretensions.

These pretensions were meeting with the expected resistance from the Haitian Senate. With the treaty past the Chamber of Deputies, the Senate remained as the last and most formidable barrier to putting it into force. On October 11 the Navy Department demanded an explanation of the Senate's delay over ratification. Seeking to calm his impatient superiors, Caperton expressed confidence that the government was doing all that it could and would secure favorable results in a few more days. The opposition was admittedly employing stalling tactics, but with patience he thought that these could be overcome. The admiral's optimism was somewhat shaken two days later, when the Senate committee on the treaty recommended that the government reopen negotiations with the United States in order to secure more favorable terms. Davis refused any further discussion of treaty terms, Dartiguenave supported him in this position, and it began to look as though ratification might take longer than had been expected. The cabinet debated tactics to force the committee to make an early report to the Senate, since the government still believed that it could muster enough votes to ratify once the matter could be removed from the clutches of the committee. To make the senators more amenable, the president asked Caperton to authorize enough money from customs receipts to pay their current monthly salaries, a proposal that the admiral at once approved. In another approach the pro-American foreign minister, Louis Borno, wrote a vigorous defense of the treaty for *Le Nouvelliste,* arguing once again that the nation must choose between poverty, famine, and blood or "redemption" with the help of the United States.[26]

Many senators were afraid of a backlash of opinion should they accept the treaty terms, Caperton explained to Benson, and it thus became necessary to create a favorable sentiment. As the admiral saw it, this process was already well under way: "The work of our doctors in connection with the distribution of Red Cross funds, the prompt and efficient manner in which public works have been conducted, the adoption of sanitary measures, the abolition of petty graft formerly collected by local officials, the breaking up of marauding bands"—all of these things tended to put the occupation in a good light. Already they had led to some favorable newspaper comment, one sample of which the admiral enclosed with his letter, while several writers in the local press had criticized the Senate committee's dilatory and obstructive stance.[27]

As October drew to a close President Dartiguenave continued to favor keeping hands off the Senate and allowing time and public opinion to bring around the opposition. Admiral Caperton strongly supported this position, for he saw the advantages of getting the treaty duly ratified after a full and open debate on its merits. Repeatedly he counselled caution and patience in his messages to Washington, where there was a growing demand for some strong, decisive move. Yet the cold mathematics of the situation scarcely justified complacency, for at this time only twelve of the thirty-nine senators were committed to approving the treaty, another twelve being committed to oppose it. This left fifteen uncommitted votes, most of which Caperton counted upon to swing to his side when the time was ripe.[28]

One real improvement in the admiral's situation came with the reappearance of Captain Beach in Port-au-Prince on October 25. The captain had been called home in September by the fatal illness of his wife, who died shortly after he reached her side. He had been detached from the command of *Washington* when he left and would normally have gone on to other duty afterward. Caperton having repeatedly made clear in his reports the importance of Beach's political work, however, the Navy Department found a way to return the captain to Haiti. *Washington* was soon due to return to the United States for overhaul, while *Tennessee* was to come out as her replacement. In an almost unprecedented move, Beach was scheduled to trade commands with *Tennessee*'s captain, so that the admiral would be able to shift his flag to the sister ship while retaining Beach as captain and chief of staff.[29]

Beach promptly threw himself into the treaty struggle, where he once again proved highly effective. The captain's local popularity was attested by a cordial notice in *Le Nouvelliste* extending sympathy for his bereavement and welcoming him back. Yet his return, although warmly welcomed by the admiral, created an incident which threatened for a time to mar the relations between the two men. In an attempt to free Beach from routine shipboard duties, Admiral Benson had directed that he take charge of the work of securing treaty ratification. Benson intended his order to insure that Beach could give Caperton the maximum of help, nothing more. But Caperton, always jealous of his authority, misunderstood this as an order to remove a subordinate from his control, and therefore as a serious slight to himself. "No one knows better than you the friendly and intimate relations between Beach and myself, and the existence of this friendship makes this

situation most embarrassing for both of us," he wrote
Benson. "I cannot believe that this letter was intended by
you as a reflection upon my campaign in Haiti, the
conduct of which I regard as the crowning achievement of
my career and upon which rests my professional reputation." Highly embarrassed, Benson replied with copious
praise for Caperton's work, promising to revoke the
offending order and declaring "how very very sorry I am that
you should have taken the view that you have" of it. Thus
mollified, Caperton let the incident drop and continued to
work with Beach on the closest terms.[30]

In a further change of personnel, Davis, the young
American chargé, was forced to return home by a bad
case of blood-poisoning, and Arthur Bailly-Blanchard was
at last despatched from Washington to resume his regular
post as ambassador. Caperton regretted Davis's departure,
for the younger man had given him the fullest cooperation,
not to say obedience, and at any rate the admiral thought
him an abler diplomat than Bailly-Blanchard. Davis sailed
from Port-au-Prince on November 1, the ambassador arriving on the 10th. In the interval Caperton's aide, Lieutenant
Oberlin, was named acting chargé, so that the final stage of
the campaign for treaty ratification saw the United States
represented entirely by naval officers.[31]

The long-awaited report of the Senate committee on
the treaty appeared on November 5. Of the treaty's sixteen
articles the committee accepted only four as written, reviv-
ing all the issues and arguments that the government had
advanced during the original negotiations. The report concluded that a new convention was necessary, the present
one being wholly unsatisfactory. While the committee's
position was hardly pleasing to Caperton, it was not unexpected, and both he and Dartiguenave still believed that
the full Senate would reject the report and approve the
treaty. Many Haitians reportedly favored ratification in the
belief that it would clear the way for measures to improve
the country's deplorable economic condition. With the
treaty accepted, the Americans would presumably arrange

loans, encourage investment, and make more funds available for public works, a presumption which the admiral not only encouraged but fully shared. Nevertheless, as Caperton reported, "powerful influences are being exercised . . . against ratification."[32]

One of the leaders in the floor fight against the treaty was Senator Lhérisson, long a foe of United States influence in Haiti. Day after day Lhérisson asked sharply pointed questions of Louis Borno, who spoke for the government. Would the treaty terms be acceptable to the National Bank of Haiti? Did they not violate its heretofore sacred contract? Was the economic aid mentioned in the treaty's first article a formal engagement of the United States or merely a statement of intention "in principle"? Would the receiver-general of customs be in practice removable by the president of Haiti and subject to his control? Did not the terms of the treaty violate the nation's constitution? The senator probed mercilessly, but Borno remained steadfast, debating every point and conceding nothing to his opponent.[33]

With the final vote no more than a few days away, Caperton and Dartiguenave brought to bear all the resources at their command to ensure the outcome. A ship was dispatched especially to bring down a pro-treaty senator from the Cape, while lobbying among the uncommitted senators reached a peak of intensity. In Beach's words, "Admiral Caperton came down earnestly upon these fifteen," Beach himself usually acting as the intermediary. The two attempted with some success to recruit influential Haitians to join them in their campaign of persuasion, the former revolutionary, Charles Delva, proving particularly useful in swinging votes.[34]

On the morning of November 11 the admiral received a message from Daniels directing him to meet the president and cabinet as soon as possible, conveying to them as on his own authority some salient points which they in turn should disseminate to others. The first of these was that the United States would remain in control of Haiti even if the treaty failed of approval. The Americans meant to stay and to maintain the Dartiguenave government in power, regardless of what happened. They were, however, very anxious for quick adoption of the treaty, "which was drawn up with the full intention of employing as many Haitians as possible to aid in giving effect to its provisions, so that suffering may be relieved at the earliest possible date." After this implied promise came a threat: should rumors of bribery by the opposition prove to be true, "those who accept or give bribes will be vigorously prosecuted." The admiral was expected, Daniels said, to make all this "sufficiently clear to remove all opposition and to secure immediate ratification."[35]

Caperton at once went ashore and fulfilled his instructions, but this last act was probably unnecessary. The Senate ratified the treaty that same afternoon by a vote of twenty-six to seven, ending a three-month campaign by the admiral and Beach. Weary but satisfied, the two were thankful that they had been able to achieve success through the normal process of congressional ratification, their goal from the start. Caperton received a message of congratulation and praise from the Navy Department which must have further soothed his spirit. The task had indeed been a formidable one.[36]

There is reason to think that it not been accomplished without some bribery on the government side. Colonel Cole later testified that the president told him as much during a conversation in 1917. It had always been customary for the government to pay off the principal politicians for their support, Dartiguenave said, and he had done so himself in 1915 in order to get the treaty ratified. Much later, in 1930, a Port-au-Prince newspaper printed the recollections of a former senator who claimed that he had himself been offered a bribe. According to his story, he was called to the palace just before the Senate voted on the treaty, where in the presence of Dartiguenave an American naval captain offered him five thousand dollars for his vote. When he spurned the offer, both men assaulted him with arguments and warnings, he said. While the amount given for the bribe is too high to seem credible, the story might have been true in its essentials. The Americans and the government were determined to win, and, as the president said, bribery was a normal tool of Haitian politics.[37]

Caperton's efforts to consummate the ratification of the treaty coincided with Waller's final campaign to end the *caco* menace in the north. The fighting in late September had given way to a period of relative quiet, during which a large portion of the *cacos* made their peace with the Americans and the Dartiguenave regime. In mid-October, however, a strong force was reported at Fort Capois, one of the old hill fortresses long used as *caco* strongholds, which lay a few miles east of Grande Rivière du Nord. Marine patrols sent to reconnoiter the area were fired upon in late October, leading Waller to conclude that he must now clean up the very heartland of the *cacos*. Waller and Butler again went north, where Waller instituted a campaign to keep the *cacos* off balance by sending small, fast-moving columns into their central base areas. A sharp three-weeks' campaign followed, with Major Butler taking the principal role in the field.[38]

Fort Capois fell on November 5, the greatest difficulty being to find the place, since it was well-hidden in a roadless jumble of hills. The fort's capture was preceded by a series of skirmishes in which the *cacos* suffered steady losses, and in the days after its fall white flags began to appear throughout the *caco* country. The climax of the campaign came on November 17 with the storming of Fort Rivière, another of the old masonry forts in the area. Here Butler led the attack on the defenders, who represented the boldest and most intransigent of the *cacos* still in arms. Finding a small unguarded entry through the walls of the fortess, the redoubtable major personally led a dash inside which routed the Haitians and ultimately earned Butler a second Medal of Honor. Fifty-one *cacos* died in this action alone, Waller giving the Haitian losses for the entire three weeks as 182 dead. Besides this severe punishment, the *cacos* were shaken by Butler's penetration to the heart of the forbidding hill country in which they had hitherto been secure. No enemy had ever before carried the fighting to their own strongholds, and this impressed them more than any other single factor. With the fall of Fort Rivière, *caco* resistance was at an end.[39]

Already cheered by the successful conclusion of the treaty fight, Caperton was jubilant at Waller's swift suppression of the *cacos*. After the cápture of Fort Rivière he sent the Navy Department a long dispatch detailing recent accomplishments. "The operations against the caco bandits in north Haiti during the last three weeks has [*sic*] resulted in the dispersing of the cacos . . . ," he wrote. "This area is now patrolled throughout by our forces, is now peaceful, and the country people are now busy with their crops." American casualties in these operations, the admiral reported, were an incredible one killed and one wounded. He envisaged a final mop-up period in which more villages would be occupied and any remaining armed bands broken up, but the secretary of the navy at once vetoed this. "Department appreciates excellent work done and gallantry displayed," Daniels radioed. "In view of heavy losses to Haitians in recent engagement Department desires our offensive to be suspended in order to prevent further loss of life. Acknowledge. Daniels."[40]

The admiral received this message with surprise and dismay. He immediately protested Daniels' order: "real intention of the Department is not understood. It is not seen how revolutionary activities and brigandage carried on by armed force can be suppressed without loss of life." His forces must continue to patrol the *caco* country, Caperton insisted, and if they met resistance they must fight. "The suppression of this brigandage and these activities is absolutely essential to peace and security in Haiti. It will be remembered that there is no government authority in these areas at present and that we have disbanded the Haitian army . . . ." Having undertaken the task of suppressing hostile *cacos,* the United States forces stood to lose immeasurable prestige if they stopped short of complete success, he concluded.[41]

Daniels' reply was firm but moderate. "Department strongly impressed with number Haitians killed," he began. "Department feels that a severe lesson has been taught cacos and believes that a proper patrol can be maintained to preserve order and protect innocent persons without further offensive operations. Should these measures prove inadequate inform Department before taking steps that would lead to loss of life on either side except in cases of urgent necessity."[42]

The admiral reluctantly ordered a halt to all further operations except patrolling, but he unburdened himself to Benson in a pained letter. The *cacos* were mere mercenaries and bandits, he insisted, who were feared and hated by the Haitians themselves. "You must not think that the 'offensive operations' have been directed against any part of the Haitian people . . . . What I have done is simply to prevent these detached bands of marauders and murderers from preying upon the peasantry and from killing our troops." Furthermore, the *cacos* were behind every revolution; all classes of Haitians knew that their power must be broken and hoped to see it done. A small *caco* band had recently attacked a village only to be captured by the aroused villagers, who executed the leaders on the spot. The *cacos* were no Haitian patriots, but "people who in the United States would be likened to the band led by Jesse James."[43]

The admiral was loath to leave the campaign against the *cacos* uncompleted, but it soon became apparent that he had achieved almost total success already. Daniels' judgment had therefore been sound; yet the difference between Daniels and Caperton sprang from a natural divergence in their points of view. It was distinctly to the credit of the secretary that he felt responsible for the mounting toll of Haitian dead and sought to halt it, but in granting this it is easy to misunderstand Caperton's position. Expected by the Navy Department to conduct an intervention in Haiti, he had had from the first to master a volatile situation with an absolute minimum of forces. In the early days of the occupation he had commanded only a few hundred troops, but avoided real trouble by moving fast and retaining the initiative. Where another leader might have become cautious and defensive, Caperton used boldness and decision as a substitute for numbers. Later, when Waller took over, the marine colonel showed a similar instinct, which received the admiral's full support. Even under Waller the American forces ashore numbered only two thousand men, while a long-standing contingency plan of the army's for occupying Haiti called for five thousand.

What Daniels failed to understand, as Caperton saw it, was that by sending a small force to do a large job he had created a situation in which an aggressive policy became essential. An overwhelming force might peacefully overawe its opposition but a small one could not. He must crush centers of resistance as fast as they formed, the admiral thought, for any major reverse to American arms could set off a general uprising involving really large-scale bloodshed. In 1918-19, several years after Caperton had left the island, such an uprising did break out in the north, to be suppressed at a cost in Haitian dead of some two thousand, as against the two hundred-odd who fell victim to Caperton's operations. When the well-known difficulties of suppressing a local guerrilla resistance with conventional armed forces are considered, Waller's campaign of 1915 can be seen not only as a model of military efficiency, but also as relatively economical in human life. It was such calculations which shaped Admiral Caperton's thinking; ironically, his very successes helped to persuade Washington that they were remote and unconvincing.

10
Implementing the Treaty

IN THE months following their successes with the *cacos* and the Congress, the occupation commanders labored to implement the terms of the Haitian-American Convention. Although the pace of events slowed markedly from the furious rush of earlier days, serious political problems continued to arise as the Haitian elite became progressively disillusioned with the American occupation and the Dartiguenave government. For a time, however, this trend was countered in the minds of the Americans by their preoccupation with planning the necessary next steps, which fostered a sense of motion and progress. The troubled and dramatic year of 1915 seemed to the Americans in Haiti to end amid significant new beginnings for the country.

On November 29 Arthur Bailly-Blanchard and Louis Borno signed the *modus vivendi* which was to put the treaty into force at once, the Americans once more overcoming strong opposition by a faction of the cabinet. This cleared the way for filling the posts which the treaty created in order to provide for American supervision of Haitian affairs, and Caperton intended to fill them with

naval officers on the spot so that the new American functions could begin promptly. For the three most important
posts he recommended to the Navy Department that Captain Beach be made the financial adviser, Paymaster
Conard the general receiver of customs, and Colonel Waller
the organizer and commander of the national constabulary
provided for in the treaty. All of these men had already
proved themselves effective in closely related jobs, and the
admiral was able to secure approval of their appointment
in advance from the Dartiguenave government. "For the
love of everything good and bad, do not send any politicians down here yet awhile," he privately begged Benson,
fearing that Washington would see the posts as fair game
for patronage appointments. "I would like to say never
send them," he added less hopefully.[1]

One important change resulting from the treaty would
be the creation of an American-led constabulary to replace
both the Haitian Army and the various civil police organi-
zations. The Navy Department had already informed
Caperton that it intended to build this unit around a command structure of United States Marines, who would be
detached solely to that duty. Asked for recommendations,
the admiral consulted Waller and worked out the details,
which he submitted in October. Later considerably
enlarged, this original plan called for a total force of 1530
men, 55 of whom would be officers from the marines. The
junior commissioned ranks were to be filled by marine
sergeants, although the treaty provided for their eventual
replacement by Haitians once the latter were adequately
trained. Caperton was in no hurry to see this happen, hoping that a "reasonable number" of whites would continue
to serve as officers. "Fond as the Haitians were of the
trappings, gold lace and authority which followed in the
wake of military affairs, they could not be depended upon
to make efficient and dependable officers," he wrote later.
"One and all, once clothed with a little brief authority,
they soon overshot the mark."[2]

Beyond these matters lay the more fundamental problem of the wretched state of Haiti's economy. In addition to the other dislocations which it brought, the European war had created a drastic shipping shortage which boosted freight rates to New York from four to twenty dollars per ton and virtually stopped the export of Haitian coffee to its best market in France. The resulting slowdown in trade cut sharply into government revenues, which came almost entirely from export and import taxes, leaving little money for public works. The American firm of Marsh and Berlin held a contract with the Haitian government to reconstruct the streets and sewers of the capital, but the work had lapsed for months for want of funds. Furthermore, both the power and light company and the railroad at Port-au-Prince threatened to cease operations unless the government resumed their agreed monthly payments. The closing of these facilities would cut further into local employment as well as depriving the capital of essential services.

In an attempt to avert this, Admiral Caperton assumed the payments to the railroad and power companies when he took over the customs. At the end of November the Haitian government paid the Central Railroad $58,000 in back interest, Caperton advancing the money at the behest of the State Department, and the admiral later provided money to resume work on the Marsh and Berlin contract as well. After a short time he raised the allowance for this work from $7,000 per month to $11,500, since the money went almost entirely into payroll and thus produced maximum benefits for the people of Port-au-Prince. Later he added over $8,000 per month to be spent on other public works in the area, particularly sanitation and clean-up projects aimed at improving public health. These actions created several thousand jobs, which substantially aided the capital's economy. Even so, enough people were still destitute to require the continuation for many months of the Red Cross relief program and the provision of free meals for the poor.[3]

The cost of these measures pressed heavily on the limited financial resources available, making the admiral all the more anxious to secure the large loan which he had promised the Haitians during the treaty negotiations. Although originally underwriting this promise, the State Department later assumed the position that the loan was virtually contingent upon the resolution of the conflict between the National Bank of Haiti and the government, and perhaps the settlement of other matters as well. Their new plan called for a Haitian commission to come to Washington and negotiate solutions to outstanding issues. Caperton sent this commission off on December 6, but continued to plead for a temporary loan of $1,500,000 to tide the government over until more permanent arrangements should be worked out. If this sum were not available then less must do, but Caperton thought that at least five hundred thousand dollars was necessary soon to save the Haitians from serious embarrassment.[4]

"It certainly was my understanding that the loan of one and a half million would be taken up immediately after the ratification of the treaty by the House of Deputies and the Senate, and later it was said after the modus vivendi was signed," the admiral wrote anxiously to Benson. "Then a message came that the loan would be made after the commission sailed and further, after the commission arrived at home. All of this I cannot understand." In the meantime, the government owed back salaries all over the island, as well as "debts of honor" arising from the treaty fight. Also, it had "made many promises for the education of the country people throughout the land and this brought about the final vote of the Senate." Now the government could not keep its promises, and the opposition was having a field day. "The prestige of the government is on the decrease every day and so is that of our government," the admiral warned; "I am not able to put up much of an excuse to these people when they come to me asking what is the matter and why our government does not keep its faith with them in regard to this loan."[5]

Caperton's efforts seemed for a time to make some headway with the State Department, which promised to expedite the loan once the Haitian commission had done its work. Washington was loath to give the money outright to the Haitian government, however, preferring that its disbursement should be supervised by a naval officer until the appointment under the treaty of the financial adviser. Caperton therefore named Captain Beach as the temporary watchdog of the treasury and secured agreement in writing for this arrangement from Louis Borno and from the National Bank of Haiti, but these efforts proved futile; at the end of December the admiral learned that the Washington negotiations were deadlocked by the National Bank's demand for the restoration of its former powers before it would make any settlement with the Haitians. Nothing more could be done at present, the State Department held, for the National Bank was the only possible source of an unsecured Haitian loan, and to add insult to injury the officials at State blamed the entire credit problem upon the unstable situation in Haiti! Nor did Washington officialdom evince much concern for the Dartiguenave government. The surplus customs receipts held by Caperton, the State Department explained solemnly, were "in the nature of a trust fund as these moneys do not belong to the Haitian government but to the holders of different debts of the Government." Caperton could give Dartiguenave an extra fifty thousand dollars in stopgap funds, but this trifle must go only toward paying the back salaries of government employees, with preference given to the poorer and lower-ranking among them.[6]

Financial frustrations were not the only ones which upset the admiral at this time. After the *modus vivendi* was signed, Caperton desired to turn back to the government several civil functions assumed by the American occupation, particularly those involving local government and public works. Again the State Department vetoed his plans, preferring to keep things as they were until the officials specified under the treaty could take up their duties.

Caperton had already nominated candidates for these posts, but on December 8 he learned that they could not be appointed, at least without some delay. The United States constitution, it developed, forbade American military and naval officers to serve a foreign government unless specifically authorized to do so by Congress. Caperton at once notified the Dartiguenave regime of this new development, offering to seek civilian appointees instead, but the Haitians expressed a strong preference for naval officers and requested special congressional action to sanction their appointment.[7]

Informed of this preference, Washington inquired whether the duties of the treaty officials were presently being performed by Caperton's officers, strongly implying that this should be the case. Caperton answered negatively, however; while his officers performed somewhat similar duties, the current situation was purely one of military control under the occupation. It could not properly be otherwise, the admiral contended, for "no officer should attempt to carry out the duties defined in the treaty until their legal status and their authority and responsibility can be definitely assured by proper appointment." Thus the treaty functions hung in abeyance despite the existence of the *modus vivendi.* The result was another impasse, the proposed resumption of its responsibilities by the Haitian government being blocked indefinitely by the failure to resolve the appointments question.[8]

Although political and financial affairs seemed for the moment to be frozen fast, Admiral Caperton's military circumstances changed appreciably during the winter. The end of the *caco* campaign signified to the Navy Department that some of the forces in Haiti could be spared, and a spate of reassignments occurred in ships and personnel. *Eagle* left in November, while on December 1 *Connecticut* sailed for home after four months' duty at the Cape. During that time her commander, Captain E. H. Durell, had borne the brunt of daily political management at Cap-Haïtien, while her bluejackets had often served ashore in landing parties, at times even joining the marines in inland campaigns against the *cacos*. *Connecticut's* departure left *Washington* as the only heavy naval vessel in Haitian waters. At the end of January *Washington* herself departed, to be briefly replaced as flagship by *Tennessee,* a sister armored cruiser. Captain Beach duly traded commands with *Tennessee's* Captain Benton Decker, as previously arranged, but late in February *Tennessee* unexpectedly left the scene, bearing Beach away for good. Also in February, the gunboats *Marietta* and *Castine* were detached, the latter to Santo Domingo where political trouble was brewing. The dispersal of his ships was accompanied by some shrinkage of the admiral's ground forces as borrowed detachments were returned to their normal stations, so that by the end of February the total forces ashore were down to no more than 1,700 men.[9]

The admiral's personal situation was considerably affected by all these moves. The permanent loss of Beach was of particular significance, and harder to bear because unexpected. *Tennessee* was suddenly assigned to take Secretary of the Treasury William G. MacAdoo on a South American tour, and Beach asked to remain in command for her changed assignment. "I am really sorry that Beach is leaving," Caperton wrote the chief of naval operations, "but as it was his desire to go I did not feel that I should in any way interfere with him. He, as you know has been my . . . go-between, and has saved me many trips to see the President and Minister Borno." The admiral realized that the need to do this himself would cut deeply into his time, but regretted even more the loss of his calculated isolation: "I do not think it very good policy for me to have to visit them personally so often . . . ."[10]

In addition to Beach, the admiral lost most of the rest of his staff by transfers. He personally interceded with Benson for their assignment to desirable new duties in appreciation for "the splendid work which they have done for me." Until they should be replaced, Caperton had only two remaining staff officers to help him carry the burden of work. As a last straw, he did not even have a proper flagship after *Tennessee*'s transfer. The best the department could do for him was the small and ancient *Dolphin,* only conditionally classed as a warship even when she was commissioned back in 1885, and for many years a sort of glorified naval yacht for Washington bigwigs. At first Caperton despaired of fitting his headquarters into her limited spaces, planning for a time to put most of its personnel ashore to live in tents, but with a little squeezing the move was made and proved not so bad in practice. One consolation came in the form of *Dolphin*'s young skipper, Lieutenant-Commander [later Admiral of the Fleet] William D. Leahy, who took over as the admiral's chief of staff. Leahy's unusual ability pleasantly surprised the admiral, though Leahy himself recorded that his inadequate mastery of the French language forced him into a crash study program. Furthermore, the admiral noted that Leahy and his officers were cordial and accommodating, which was more than he could say of "the *Tennessee* crowd."[11]

The departure of Captain Beach coincided with the further rise in status of Colonel Waller and Major Butler of the marines. With Beach gone, Waller became Caperton's principal representative ashore in his capacity as commander of the land forces. While Waller expanded his existing role to include more political duties, it was Butler rather than Waller who organized and commanded the new Haitian gendarmerie, assuming the Haitian rank of major general. Butler began the creation of the new force early in December, aided by a cadre of fellow marines. Marine captains became colonels in the constabulary, first lieutenants became majors, second lieutenants were captains, and marine top sergeants were made lieutenants. Some of these officers learned *Créole,* the language of the common people, and enlistment and training went forward steadily. Recruiting was at first unaccountably slow in spite of the fact that enlisted men received excellent pay by Haitian standards, but this reluctance turned out to stem from popular skepticism as to whether the men would actually get what they were promised. Previous Haitian governments had rarely paid their soldiers in full or on time, frequently failing to pay them at all, or even to feed them. The first payday, when the original recruits received their full pay as promised, created a minor sensation, and afterward enlistment soared, further spurred by reports of good food and living conditions.[12]

Butler was still in the early stages of creating his organization when Waller smashed a minor uprising in the capital. Early on the morning of January 5 small parties of Haitians fired on the marine barracks and the provost-marshal's office. The attackers were soon driven off with one dead and several wounded, but Colonel Waller followed up his victory with vigorous countermeasures. "Sixteen arrests of leaders and bad characters were made on this day by the marines and some arms and ammunition seized," Caperton reported. The admiral believed that the ultimate object of the plot had been to murder Dartiguenave and install a new president, but the presence of the marines and the lack of mass participation made the effort hopeless from the start. Waller's quick and ruthless suppression of the rising and roundup of its leaders sealed his reputation in Haiti as a dangerous man to challenge.[13]

The January outbreak emphasized the desirability of speeding the organization of the gendarmerie, but this in turn led to new and serious frictions with President Dartiguenave. According to the treaty, the gendarmerie was to replace all existing military and police agencies, and in the eyes of the State Department this included the five-hundred-man presidential guard, a ceremonial unit in splendid uniforms manned by socially prominent Haitian youths. Dartiguenave protested its dissolution as a blow to his dignity and a violation of the constitution, which specifically provided for a presidential guard. The State Department replied that both problems could be met by forming a much smaller presidential guard from members of the gendarmerie, and upon that conclusion they stood fast. This did nothing, however, to help extricate the president from the embarrassment of having to dismiss hundreds of scions of influential families from their honorific posts, which also carried salaries. The abolition of the army had previously lopped off some three hundred generals and fifty colonels, not to mention the personnel of the Ministry of War or the junior officers, all of whom lost their income along with their functions. It is no wonder that the president sought at least to limit the carnage.[14]

In addition to military agencies, the creation of the gendarmerie would displace the entire police apparatus of the country. The principal civil law enforcement bodies had been the communal police, who served under the mayor in each town; in addition, the commandants of *arrondissements* were in charge of military police bodies under the Ministry of War, but within the civil administrative districts into which each *département* was divided. Dartiguenave wished to retain the commandants of *arrondissements* in their purely civil capacity, as a link between the new gendarmerie and the existing system of local government. These offices were held by scores of local notables, and their abolition too would create political shock-waves. But the government lost on every count, palace guard, police, and *chefs de arrondissement* as well. The only consolation Caperton could offer the president was the retention of the palace band, a separate organization which could be salvaged by enlisting it as a body into the gendarmerie.

In a rare show of spirit, the long-suffering Dartiguenave struck back by decreeing the immediate dissolution of all police agencies and ordering the gendarmerie to assume its duties on February 1st, much earlier than planned. This gave Butler less than two months altogether to create his organization from scratch and took everyone by surprise. The president probably hoped for more than mere revenge, since a serious failure to keep order on the part of the unprepared gendarmerie might necessitate a restoration of some of the old apparatus. When the president made his announcement, Butler had some 1,500 men available, only partially trained and equipped and concentrated in a few training centers. Through prodigies of effort he got them distributed in the few days that remained to over a hundred local posts throughout the country and formally assumed responsibility for order on the date set. The change-over was not a smooth one, for the new force suffered some embarrassing early setbacks. At St. Michel in the northern interior, the entire local detachment got drunk during a Mardi Gras celebration and was eventually chased into the brush by the inhabitants, thirteen men being court-martialled as a consequence. The gendarmerie suffered other minor mishaps in March and April, but shook down fairly quickly into an effective law-enforcement agency, its strength being raised to more than 2,500 men in the course of the year.[15]

While the gendarmerie dispute was at its height, orders from Washington to change the method of paying government employees had brought on another clash between the Americans and the Dartiguenave regime. The Navy Department wished these employees to be paid directly by the occupation command, bypassing the Haitian government entirely. The unsavory nature of the customary pay procedure provided some justification for this further American seizure of authority. The individual employee normally received no money, merely a certificate of indebtedness from the government. To convert this into cash he had to sell the certificate to a middleman, at a discount often running as high as 30 to 40 percent. This extremely profitable discounting operation was closely controlled by a circle of brokers centered in the government and headed by such high officials as the president of the Senate and the minister of finance. The Americans meant to stop the profiteering off government workers, along with other suspected pay-roll frauds, but Dartiguenave and his cabinet strenuously objected. Such action, they held, was an insult to Haitian honor and a usurpation of government power. While it was indeed both of these things, it was also the heaviest blow yet to the profits and influence of government insiders, and as a recent president of the Senate, Dartiguenave was acutely aware of the importance of the issue.

Early in January, Caperton held a full-scale conference on the matter with Dartiguenave and his cabinet. Accompanied by Beach and Conard, the customs administrator, the admiral labored for an entire day to bring the Haitians into line, and, as he confessed to Benson, "it came near breaking up the whole Government." After hours of fruitless discussion, Caperton and his aides were "taken completely off our feet" by the Haitians' sudden capitulation. They agreed to do whatever the admiral desired, even providing him with complete lists of officials and salaries. It became evident, however, that the incident left the Haitians deeply resentful and the president concerned at his dwindling prestige. The pay-brokers were furious, attempting to attach the salaries of their victims through the courts, but Caperton stopped this with a military order.[16]

Coming one after another in quick succession, these open disputes between Dartiguenave and the Americans inspired rumors that Caperton meant to change presidents. The government's opponents seized on these reports and magnified them, hoping further to undermine Dartiguenave's position. In a campaign of verbal propaganda they suggested that the financial niggardliness of the State Department, the delay in appointing treaty officials, and the steady diminution of the president's authority were additional evidence that the Americans were preparing Dartiguenave for a final blow. The rumors grew so pervasive that Admiral Caperton arranged for an interview with the editor of *Le Matin* in which he could spike them. *Le Matin*'s headlines the next day accurately summed up the admiral's statements: "A Conversation with Admiral Caperton—The governments of the United States and Haiti work in cordial collaboration—To Defeat the Dartiguenave government is to defeat the interests of the country—The government of the United States has faith in President Dartiguenave–Towards a new Haiti."[17]

In February the admiral and Bailly-Blanchard made an inspection tour of the coast towns and the newly pacified north. They were well received everywhere, and Caperton was much encouraged by what he saw. "The people are proud and happy to be at work and to be able to carry on the pursuits of life in a peaceful, safe, and quiet manner," he wrote Benson. "Their demonstrations of appreciation of what the American Occupation is doing for them has greatly encouraged me, and gives me strength to continue the good work." The admiral particularly enjoyed a triumphal entrance into Ouanaminthe, on which occasion he and the minister, accompanied by the bishop of Cap-Haïtien, drove slowly into the town in a Ford car, a rare-enough sight in itself. "As we neared the town . . . , the church bells began to ring, and the people flocked to the main street and greeted us as we passed with cheers and much enthusiasm. You see I was smart enough to have the church along with me." Caperton was impressed to find twelve hundred inhabitants living and working in a town that had been ruined and deserted only a few months earlier.[18]

The admiral was particularly concerned with improving the lot of ordinary Haitians. In his mind, this was to be achieved by the stimulation of the economy through an influx of United States loans and investments, coupled with the achievement of order and political stability through the beneficent tutelage of the United States. He believed all that he had told the Haitians on this score and was therefore intensely frustrated by the lack of progress in Washington toward implementing the treaty, arranging a government loan, and recruiting or encouraging private American investment for the island. "Hurry up matters in Washington and also get the Modus Vivendi in operation," he wrote Benson, "the country needs it." He directed similar pleas to Daniels: "Government and people eagerly awaiting American action on treaty and investment of

American capital." In an appeal to Benson early in March, the admiral once more explained the necessity for a settlement of the stalled issues in order to put the Haitians to work on roads, railroads, irrigation projects: "Their one loud clamor is for work, which means bread and meat to them. They certainly need this help throughout the country, as they are poor beyond all description . . . you would be surprised to see how much we are doing along this line with so little outlay of money. They only want about a gourde a day, which is about 18¢ at present rate of exchange."[19]

In an attempt to improve matters at his end, Caperton conferred with committees of bond-holders and other representatives of the government's creditors, hoping to restore confidence in Haitian credit. He was particularly interested in the state of the internal loans, held by the Haitians themselves, the interest on which was in default. Ultimately the admiral recommended that he be allowed to pay the arrears on the internal loans and to begin regular interest payments on all government debts, domestic and foreign, but, in the absence of the prospective financial adviser, the State Department was reluctant to make any fixed arrangements. Once again the failure to appoint the treaty officials blocked his way.[20]

The total lack of urgency in Washington about filling these positions seems bizarre even today. While Smedley Butler became commandant of the gendarmerie in December, the remaining treaty officials were slow to appear in Haiti. The first financial adviser finally arrived in July 1916, and the general receiver of customs in August, while neither the public engineer nor the sanitary engineer took up their duties until 1917. The delay might be ascribed in part to the slowness of the United States Senate in ratifying the Haitian-American Convention, an action which it took only in May 1916, but the whole purpose of the *modus vivendi* had been to eliminate the effects of this delay, which everyone foresaw. Besides, Congress had moved quickly enough when asked to authorize the use of

marines in the gendarmerie; it was the State Department
which looked the more peculiar, in vigorously pushing
through the *modus vivendi* and then letting its full implementation lapse for so long afterward. The financial
adviser came to Haiti over six months after the *modus
vivendi* was signed, and the sanitary engineer almost two
years after that event.[21]

Nor did the work of the Haitian treaty commission in
Washington go much better. The aims of the commission
were to clarify certain points in the implementation of the
treaty, to settle outstanding differences with the National
Bank of Haiti and other private interests, and, most important to the Haitians, to take advantage of those "good
offices" in securing a loan which the admiral and the State
Department had promised upon ratification of the treaty.
From its very first meeting with State Department representatives, however, the commission found only disillusionment. Frank Polk, counsellor of the department, told
the Haitians that there was no question of an advance from
the United States government and that the only possible
source of a private loan was the National Bank of Haiti.
The Haitians must therefore deal with the bank, Polk said,
driving home his point by ushering in two of the bank's
spokesmen! It was in vain that the Haitians voiced their
distress at falling once more into the bank's clutches. The
bank would do nothing until its former position was
restored, and the State Department would do nothing
except through the bank.

The Haitian commission next sought alternative
sources of credit, entering into negotiations with two
American financial syndicates. By March the Haitians had
secured a loan agreement from a Chicago- and Cincinnati-
based banking group, belying Polk's contention that only
the National Bank of Haiti would put up the money, but
the State Department killed this arrangement by withhold-
ing its approval. Thereafter the talks settled into a grim
endurance contest, the Haitians refusing to include the
bank in any future arrangement, and the State Department

blocking any alternative settlement. It appeared that the "good offices" so long and eagerly awaited meant in practice no more than the restoration of the hated bank at American insistence.

To break the impasse, the State Department put forward a "compromise" under which the National Bank would resume charge of the Haitian Treasury, but under the supervision of the general receiver of customs. This plan left the bank still centrally involved in Haitian government finances, something which the Haitians had vowed to resist to the end, but they finally caved in and accepted the new plan in principle. After much argument over details, including the exact powers and position of the general receiver, the commissioners signed a preliminary financial agreement in May and a final version in July 1916. Ever after this abject surrender, the Haitians continued to wait for their promised loan, while the power of the general receiver would long remain a source of bitter controversy.[22]

More serious than any specific dispute in the early months of 1916 was a massive upsurge of hostility toward Dartiguenave and the Americans on the part of the Haitian elite. Although the great mass of Haitians was poor, illiterate, and politically passive, the educated minority saw politics as, quite literally, its lifeblood. There was comparatively little business activity in Haiti, and much of that was carried on by foreigners. Some members of the Haitian upper class were in theory large landowners, but the peasantry were mostly squatters who paid no rent, so that the rural land claims of the elite had more social than economic significance. In Haiti only the government generated really significant wealth, and almost every influential family expected to share at least part of the time in the government's largess. If one stood well with those in power, this came as a matter of course; if he belonged to an opposing faction, the frequency of revolution was both consolation and cure.

The Haitian ruling caste had reconciled itself to the American presence in the belief that it would bring political stability and an infusion of dollars in place of chaos and wartime depression. The achievement of the first half of this program failed to lead to the second, however; the economy remained depressed and no American dollars appeared. Far worse, instead of bringing more money, the occupation seized control of Haiti's own funds and drastically reduced their distribution to that portion of Haitian society which had long regarded them as indispensable. Those who had accepted the new dispensation in the hope of gaining office found the existing bureaucrats clinging to their posts, except where these were abolished. Since Dartiguenave was a nonparty president, everyone hoped for patronage from him, but of new openings there were none, while the hordes clamoring for appointments were soon joined by the angry victims of the ruthless retrenchment imposed by the Americans.

The customs take-over marked the beginning of a general economy drive, the Haitian personnel of the customs service being sharply cut back. The further total abolition of the army, war ministry, and police was accompanied by selective cuts elsewhere, including diplomatic representation abroad. Besides slashing the government payroll, the occupation had destroyed the most lucrative business in Haiti by putting an end to salary-brokerage. As a final injury, Conard overhauled the enormous pension list, grown huge over the years through the use of pensions for political pay-offs, and through the common practice of collecting several pensions simultaneously. Everywhere incomes long taken for granted suddenly disappeared, for Conard refused to pay more than one pension per recipient and not even that one unless it met strict criteria of legality.[23]

Captain Beach described vividly the results of these policies: "Blow after blow came upon the class who so confidently looked to the government for its financial support. Not only were none of their hopes and wishes gratified, but many of those in office were forced out. In addition, the paralysis of business [due to the war] made matters infinitely worse. The result was a wild howl of rage that constantly increased in volume. And it was directed, not at the Admiral, who had given the orders, but at the President, who with one accord received the blame."[24] It was easy for Americans to be cynical about this reaction, but for most of the people involved the alternatives were few and the hardships real. As to the effects there was no room for doubt: almost all of the Haitians who counted went into opposition.

This opposition soon found a focus in the president's proposal to draft a new national constitution. As critics had charged all along, there were clear contradictions between the terms of the Haitian-American Convention and those of the Haitian constitution, among them the abolition of the army and police and the nature of the powers assigned to various treaty officials. Caperton admitted as much to Benson: "The treaty itself, as you know, violates the Haitian Constitution, that is, makes it necessary for the Haitian Constitution to be changed, in order to make it and the treaty work harmoniously, or together, you might say." In addition, the existing constitution forbade aliens to own property, a provision which threatened to slow the hoped-for arrival of American investment. Neither legitimizing American influence nor opening the door to absentee ownership were apt to be popular causes with congressmen, but Dartiguenave was confident that with American support they could be pushed through.[25]

The president proved overly optimistic. Congress refused to take favorable action on the proposed constitutional changes, its leaders indicating a preference for impeaching Dartiguenave on charges of violating the current constitution. The latter went ahead, nevertheless, with plans to dissolve the legislature and then recall the Chamber of Deputies in the role of a constituent assembly. The dissolution took place early in April, the president simultaneously appointing a twenty-one member Council of State to act as a temporary replacement for the Congress and to draft the desired constitutional changes. These actions created an uproar. The Senate refused to recognize their legality, but when they attempted to meet the next day the senators found themselves locked out of their chambers, which were guarded by marines. The Port-au-Prince newspapers were full of the new developments, and Caperton reported that "It reminds me very much of old times while we were trying to have the convention voted upon."[26]

Acting for the entire body, a committee of Senate leaders protested to Caperton, Waller, and Bailly-Blanchard, but to no avail. Rebuffed by the Americans, the group sought to take its case to the people by starting a new opposition newspaper, but the American press censorship had become so formidable that at first no printer dared defy it. When the paper finally did appear, Caperton ordered it suspended almost at once. Having taken this action, the admiral then attempted to stand apart from the dispute and let the Haitians thrash it out. "Both sides apparently seem to be forcing the occupation to do something and I am determined that they shall not trap me along this line, as I propose to act only when absolutely necessary . . . ," he wrote Benson. He expected some disturbance, he said, but nothing too serious to handle.[27]

Next came the deputies' turn. Though supposedly dissolved to be later transformed into a constituent assembly, the deputies too attempted to meet as usual. Like the Senate before them, they were locked out of their chambers, but the deputies were able to benefit by the Senate's experience; they gathered a quorum, met in the street, and arranged to continue meeting in a rented house. With continuity thus assured, they formed a joint legislative committee including both Senate and Deputy leaders. Dartiguenave now found himself facing a virtually intact and united legislature which defied dissolution and mustered impressive support. Caperton confessed himself somewhat nonplussed by the fact "that the action to date of the Legislative bodies is in full accord with the provisions of the Constitution, and that the action of the President of Haiti, however necessary it may have been, is in direct violation of the Constitution." He saw no alternative to backing the president, but hoped to prevent "having our action appear as a matter of record if it can be avoided."[28]

The next development recalled the recent revolutionary past, as an ad hoc "committee of notables" came forward to play a role analogous to the committees of safety in former days. Headed by ex-President Légitime, the committee offered to help negotiate a compromise between president and Congress. Caperton welcomed the committee's good offices and urged Dartiguenave to cooperate in the search for some middle ground, though the president and Borno were hostile to the attempt. Dartiguenave offered once more to resign, but finally agreed to try secret negotiations. The committee of notables proposed that the president withdraw the decree of dissolution, while the legislators should agree to consider the constitutional revisions. Both sides accepted these terms in principle, but clashed endlessly over details. Conference succeeded conference, impasse followed impasse, for a week and a half. The talks broke down for good on April 29, and Caperton felt obliged to step in at last. Writing in an almost apologetic tone, the admiral notified the legislative leaders on May 2 that he would enforce the president's decree of dissolution.[29]

"I regret exceedingly, with all my heart, that my efforts extending over nearly a month, to bring the opposing elements of your Government into an amicable agreement have failed," he announced. While he accused the legislators of failing to make adequate concessions, his language was mild and civil, though concluding that "there is and has been since April 5 no Senate and no Chamber of Deputies." The admiral was clearly uncomfortable about what had been done. Colonel Waller had opposed the dissolution "bitterly" by his own account, while Caperton himself regarded it as an unconstitutional act. He attempted at length to rationalize his position to Benson, arguing that the constitution had been violated so incessantly of late by all parties in Haiti that it had little remaining weight anyway. This was a queer argument to come from the main agent of Wilson's proclaimed intention to impose constitutionalism on the area, but Caperton coupled it with a sounder one: the Congress had been about to impeach Dartiguenave for constitutional violations forced upon him by the requirements of the occupation, whose leaders could hardly abandon him to his fate.[30]

Rationalize as he would, the admiral had to recognize that the facade of an independent Haitian government had collapsed. For almost a year to come Haiti would have no elected legislative body. It remained official theory that the United States merely exercised a certain limited supervision over the duly elected government of Haiti, but in fact Haiti was ruled by an American military regime which acted, when it pleased, through the president. It was Dartiguenave, not the Americans, who had chosen to dismiss the Congress, but he did so in the certainty that the Americans must enforce his decision, however reluctantly. When this occurred, the Haitian government became a mere rump, largely of American creation, that could not have remained in power for a day without their support. "We had to insure peace and order in the Republic," Caperton wrote afterwards, "and there was no other avenue left open to us."[31]

11

Conclusion

THE FIRST and most formative period of the Haitian occupation came to an end with President Dartiguenave's dissolution of the legislature and with the departure, only a few days later, of Admiral Caperton. Political affairs in the neighboring Dominican Republic had reached a crisis stage in April 1916, and on May 9 *Dolphin* sailed for Santo Domingo City, bearing the admiral and his staff to the scene of new activities.

Caperton remained nominally in charge of Haitian affairs while in Santo Domingo, but in his absence Colonel Waller assumed their direct supervision. Waller still reported to the admiral, of course, but with Caperton four hundred miles away and wholly involved in initiating a new intervention in another country, his Haitian role shrank drastically. Waller and Butler became the real powers in Haiti, while Caperton first quarrelled with them from afar and then left the West Indies for good.

While in Santo Domingo the admiral retained a lively interest in Haiti, and he quickly became uneasy about

Waller's management there. The issue which first opened a breach between the two commanders concerned the powers of Butler's gendarmerie, the exact definition of which was still under negotiation. Waller and Butler wished the gendarmerie to control Haiti's public works, including road building, the telephone and telegraph system, and the postal service, a proposition to which the Dartiguenave regime strongly objected. The president was willing to see these functions supervised by American naval officers acting nominally under the authority of the civil officials of his government, but not to have them effectively removed from Haitian jurisdiction. It was not long before Caperton privately supported him in this position.

The admiral was upset for several reasons: he did not approve of the swollen authority claimed for the gendarmerie, he feared that Waller was further undermining Dartiguenave's position, and he was angry that the proposals in question had been initiated without his knowledge. Waller had recently been in Washington on sick leave, and Caperton believed that the colonel had used the opportunity to lobby at the State Department for measures of his own, bypassing the chain of command. He accused the colonel directly, bringing on an open quarrel. Waller wrote a friend that Caperton was "insane," and complained: "Instead of backing up the men who are working for him, he knifes them when they do well." To Caperton himself Waller denied going behind the admiral's back: "I am quite willing to take my medicine when it is deserved but I wish you would not assume that I always do the wrong thing." The summer weather in the Caribbean produced bad radio communications, he said; perhaps that was why Caperton had remained uninformed. But the colonel insisted that he was only following orders from Washington and that he had kept the admiral fully posted: "You ask me about the reports I make to my headquarters. I make none that you do not see."[1]

Finding the State Department in support of the extra powers for the gendarmerie, Caperton appealed to Benson and the Navy Department. Butler had enough to do to make his force what it should be without taking on extraneous duties, he contended, while the Haitian-American Treaty gave the United States no control over the extra functions at issue. Furthermore, he warned, "Should we ever, in the near future, turn over the Gendarmerie to the Haitiens, think of the power the Director of the Gendarmerie (some Haitien general), would have provided he had the control of all the public utilities in the island under his charge."[2]

Before the matter was settled, the admiral received orders to return to the United States for promotion and new duties. His last chance to affect the decision came when he stopped at Port-au-Prince in mid-July, on the way home. In a stay of only twenty-four hours, Caperton conferred with everyone concerned, giving the most time to the anxious Haitians. As he reported to Benson, Dartiguenave's arguments against the gendarmerie proposals were so similar to his own that he felt the Haitian president might almost have read his official letter on the subject to the Secretary of the Navy. Dartiguenave was discouraged at the prospect before him, telling Caperton: "Admiral, suppose we turn over all of these utilities and various departments to the Gendarmerie and naval officers, we might just as well close up the Government; because there would be no use for us to exist, except as a matter of expense." The president finally said that he would accept a compromise that left the post office and telegraph system free of gendarmerie control, a solution which Caperton privately endorsed and urged on the Navy Department. "Without in any way showing my feelings on the subject I could not but help sympathize with the President . . . ," the admiral reported. The final settlement, reached after Caperton had severed all connection with Haiti, gave the gendarmerie control of all of the utilities except the telephone and telegraph system. This was to be under the treaty engineer, but the gendarmerie was guaranteed unrestricted use of it.[3]

By the time he left, Caperton was less concerned about any one issue than about Waller's general fitness for his political duties. "What I am going to say now I hope you will consider confidential," he wrote Benson. "I am not at all pleased with the manner in which Colonel Waller has been attempting to bring about the signing of this [gendarmerie] agreement . . . . I think he has been very vindictive, showed a lack of consideration, and . . . used intimidation in his dealings with the Haitien Government." When he went to Santo Domingo, Caperton said, relations between the occupation and the Dartiguenave government were cordial, but they had already deteriorated. This was generally known and regretted, even among Haitians not friendly to the occupation. Caperton blamed Waller for the change; though acknowledging Waller's military ability, he thought him tactless and overbearing in political matters. "In conclusion," he wrote, "please do not think I am after anyone's scalp, though I fear some scalping is needed in Haiti."[4]

The admiral's forebodings about the future proved well-founded. Waller became bitterly hostile to Dartiguenave, Borno, and the other leading figures in the Haitian government who had worked most closely with the Americans. Accusing them all of graft and secret obstructionism, he privately called Borno a "crafty rascal" and asserted that "the President is as bad as the rest of them." Admitting to a friend that he had forced changes in the cabinet, he expressed resentment that the government had let that fact leak out "unnecessarily." In a short time the colonel's hostility became so overt as to convince the Dartiguenave regime that Waller sought its overthrow, a suspicion voiced in August by the Haitian minister in Washington. The Haitians attempted a formal protest, but the State Department refused to receive it and procured its withdrawal.[5]

"The American who contributed the most to darkening the first illusions of President Dartiguenave was Colonel Waller," Dartiguenave's aide wrote afterwards. The colonel habitually took a brutal, bullying tone at the palace, writing the most insulting notes to the president himself and continually intervening in the affairs of the civil authorities. According to the same source, Butler was equally overbearing and tactless, a judgment later confirmed by a high United States official in Haiti.[6] Waller's own private statements did little to refute this view of the Waller-Butler imperium. "They are real niggers and no mistake," the colonel wrote to a friend. "There are some very fine looking, well educated polished men here but they are real nigs beneath the surface. What the people of Norfolk and Portsmouth would say if they saw me bowing and scraping to these coons—I do not know—All the same I do not wish to be outdone in formal politeness."[7]

In contrast to this, Admiral Caperton's approach seemed a very model of understanding, and for a time the admiral was remembered rather kindly in Haiti. The same aide of Dartiguenave recorded the president's discouragement at the departure of Caperton and Beach. "How happy had been Dartiguenave to be able to call on these two men in time of difficulty," he proclaimed. The first financial adviser under the treaty terms, who arrived soon after Caperton had left, concurred: "We have used two policies in Haiti, one of force and one of conciliation. Admiral Caperton employed conciliation. He made personal friends of leading Haitians, by associating with them. Colonel Waller, seconded by Colonel . . . Butler, adopted a policy of force."[8]

A leading feature of the new dispensation was the rapid emergence of Butler's gendarmerie as the effective arm of local control in the country. Gendarmerie officers became virtual district bosses throughout the countryside, while Waller's marine regulars continued to garrison the cities and serve as a reserve. The treaty officials who were ostensibly to direct the activities of the Haitian government were a fragmented group lacking a common superior to coordinate their efforts, and even after these agents took up their duties they long wielded less influence than the two marine commanders. Working together, Waller and Butler acted to reduce what little discretion was left the Dartiguenave government, and by the end of 1917 Haiti appeared to be effectively under their control.

Confident of their power, the two officers returned to the constitutional question which in 1916 had almost brought down the Dartiguenave government. A new legislature, elected in January 1917, again received a revised constitution similar to that projected in the previous year, but the new body proved to be no more tractable than its predecessor. In April 1917 the assembly rejected the draft constitution and substituted one of its own which contained anti-American provisions. Again the legislature was dissolved, this time at the instigation of United States officials, not to be recalled or replaced for years to come. The revised constitution was adopted instead by a popular plebiscite held throughout the country under the gendarmerie's control and of doubtful legitimacy. Even the pretense of presidential government had by then broken down, Dartiguenave being a mere pawn of United States power. By 1919 the president himself was hostile to the Americans and would remain so for the balance of his term.

In the meantime, trouble with the *cacos* was brewing once more. In the summer of 1916 Waller and Butler had revived the ancient law of *corvée,* a half-forgotten measure by which the peasantry owed three days' work in each year on the roads of their district. Designed to facilitate military movement in the countryside, this reversion to forced labor was not only unpopular in itself, but it was gravely abused by gendarmerie officers in the remoter country districts. Some victims of this abuse were kept at road building for long periods, receiving no pay and moving ever further from their home districts as the work progressed. In the *caco* country particularly, this soon aroused a spirit of resistance, and marine headquarters ordered the *corvée* abolished in 1918. Local commanders in the *caco* country ignored these orders, however, and by

1919 the *cacos* had risen in full-fledged revolt. Waller and Butler, that formidable duo, had by then left the country, and the gendarmerie was forced to call upon the marine brigade for help. A vigorous year-long campaign ensued, and by the time it was over, some two thousand Haitians had been killed and the *cacos* defeated once more.[9]

Although armed resistance ended, the fighting had caught the attention of the American public, and the Haitian occupation came under serious attack in the United States. As usual, criticism began with the press. Atrocity stories began to creep into American newspapers, while the *Union Patriotique d'Haiti* at last found a forum for its cause. A national magazine, *The Nation,* took up the *Union*'s charges in 1920, running a long series of articles on the iniquity of American actions in Haiti and the Dominican Republic.[10] Seeking issues for the presidential campaign of 1920, the Republican party seized on the Caribbean record of the Wilson administration as a flagrant contradiction of Wilson's idealistic pronouncements about international behavior. The Republicans promised to investigate these matters, though lack of time prevented their doing so until after the election.

The war-weariness and disillusionment of the postwar period fed an antiimperialist trend, and in 1921 the Senate began a year-long investigation of the Haitian and Dominican interventions. A select committee dominated by Republicans and chaired by Senator Medill McCormick of Illinois conducted the inquiry. The senators heard testimony in Washington, Port-au-Prince, Santo Domingo, and elsewhere, sitting from the summer of 1921 to that of 1922. As is usual in such cases, the Senate Committee published its hearings, recommended that affairs be conducted better in Haiti, and disbanded, leaving the Haitian occupation to run on until 1934.[11]

These hearings had, however, evoked candid and revealing testimony from the marine officers who had staffed the occupation. Colonels Cole and Waller and Major Butler, all generals by 1921, voiced confidence that intervention in Haiti had been not only necessary but beneficial. Asked why the United States had needed to interfere there, Cole replied:

Well, in the first place, it is at our front door. . . . the islands of the Caribbean guard the entrance to a considerable part of the United States and the Panama Canal, absolutely. We can not afford to have any foreign country obtain additional power and influence in that part of the world . . . . I think there was danger of that. . . . France had $150,000,000 worth of francs invested in Haiti in the loans, and she had other sums there. Germany had large sums invested in Haiti, and . . . I believed that the European situation was the one thing that prevented active operations in Haiti by either one or two European nations.[12]

Furthermore, Cole declared, the intervention had also been necessary "unless you wanted to allow what I think to be almost the richest part of the globe to become an African jungle." Asked about United States objectives within Haiti, he replied that "it had a moral duty to clean that place up and establish decency down there, because it did not exist." Once the intervention had begun, "there was not anything else to be done but to stay there and save Haiti."[13]

Smedley Butler agreed that the occupation had exercised an essential and beneficial tutelage. The Americans had never forgotten that the country did not belong to them, he averred; they had always felt themselves to be "trustees of a huge estate that belonged to minors." "My object down there was to do what they wanted, not to make out of Haiti an America, but . . . a first-class black man's country . . . . The average Haitian who gets a little money goes to France, and brings back some conception of a French palace and builds it, and destroys Haiti. What we wanted was clean little towns, with tidy thatch-roofed dwellings. That is what the country can afford, and that is what it ought to have, and then there would never be any temptation to anybody to grab it either."[14]

Littleton Waller expressed a parallel view. Asked about the material effects of the occupation, he replied: "Uplifting in every direction. That was our attitude toward them." And Cole declared unhesitatingly that he had kept the interests of the Haitians more at heart than had the members of the Haitian Assembly.[15] The marine commanders were without exception unapologetic and sure of the rightness of their actions.

As principal initiator of the intervention, Admiral Caperton was a major witness and a prime target. Called out of retirement, he testified for over a week in October of 1921. The admiral did not appear to advantage in his sessions before the committee. In contrast to the confident, straightforward answers of Waller, Butler, and Cole, Caperton's responses were dilatory and evasive. Pleading lack of memory, he brought along masses of relevant orders and correspondence, refusing to answer questions until he had shuffled through them at length and then often merely reading some extract from the official record. He made few spontaneous statements and ultimately wore down the senators with his time-consuming tactics. Despairing of getting what they wished from him, the committee allowed him to complete his testimony by filing a collection of papers with them.[16]

Neither was the admiral very convincing when he did attempt direct answers. Asked why he had first intervened in Haiti, he testified that he had done so "for the protection of foreigners and foreign property." Upon Senator McCormick's demand for instances of foreigners killed in Haiti then or previously, Caperton had to confess lamely that he knew of none, though later in the day he recovered himself sufficiently to argue that this was only because United States warships had always appeared to protect foreign lives at times of stress. What the committee most wanted to know, however, was by whose decision the United States had initiated a long-term intervention in Haiti. This put the admiral in an embarrassing position, for he himself had made almost all of the early decisions, the authorities in Washington merely ratifying them after the event. Understandably unwilling to say that he, personally, had been solely responsible for the intervention, Caperton could point to no official orders upon which his most significant actions were based. Lacking an answer, he merely stalled: "I think the answer to that question would be found somewhere in my notes. I can not just put my hand on it now."[17]

The somewhat shabby pathos in the spectacle of a twisting, badgered old man was overborne by the weight of charges hurled at the occupation by the *Union Patriotique* while the hearings progressed. The *Union* rightly insisted that the bloody events surrounding the fall of Guillaume Sam were not the real reason for the occupation, but merely the occasion for it. They further charged, with less justice, that the Wilson administration acted throughout as a tool of the National City Bank of New York and its capacity of stockholder in the National Bank of Haiti and that the chief purpose of the intervention was to serve American financial interests. That these interests were narrowly construed was demonstrated, the Haitians said, by the unaccountable failure to pay anything on foreign bond issues for years after the United States took control. As a result American actions benefited no one but the bank, which was alleged to be no coincidence. "Thus the principal object of the treaty, which was to place Haitian finances on a solid basis, has not been fulfilled, nor has the financial aid which was promised by the United States been effectively given."[18]

This interpretation grossly oversimplified the motives for American intervention in Haiti, while Caperton had fought hard to make good the very fiscal omissions now charged against the occupation. Nevertheless, the known imtimacy of Roger Farnham with State Department officials seemed to support the Haitian statements, as did the solicitude of Secretary of State Bryan for American economic interests in Haiti before the intervention and the favoritism shown throughout to the National Bank of Haiti by the State Department, which regarded it as a useful tool for controlling the Haitians. The cry of "economic imperialism" rang out in the American press, with the Haitian intervention pictured as a leading example.[19]

More valid were complaints that the United States had forced a treaty upon the helpless Haitians and then refused to abide by its terms, that it had extended its authority over Haiti by the arbitrary use of force and threats, and that the marines and gendarmerie constituted a "military autocracy" under United States control. Finally, the undeniable appearance of American racism in the wake of the Haitian occupation went far to discredit the entire enterprise.[20]

An otherwise friendly American journalist who visited the country in 1917 found in the introduction of racism the principal flaw in the record of the occupation: "thoughtful Haitians are now beginning to realize that the Americans will make them feel the question of color, will bring back the inequality and subordination which they have dreaded and have not known in their native island for more than a hundred years." Attitudes had further hardened with the appearance in the capital of American wives, come to live with husbands in the marines or the civil administration. At an official reception the journalist found white Americans dancing freely with Haitian women, but no Haitians attempting to dance with American women. A few years later, another visitor found such social fraternization almost ended, the American Club virtually closed to Haitians, and the color line sharply drawn by United States officers and their families.[21]

Caperton had conscientiously avoided such overt racism, never exhibiting the open contempt which would so poison Waller's official relations with the Haitians. In spite of the admiral's preferred posture of splendid isolation aboard his flagship, he maintained close personal relations with a number of prominent Haitians and periodically sampled the social life of the capital. He regularly sought advice from Francois Légitime, the elderly former president. As he told Benson: "When I became discouraged, I usually went to see the old man, and through an interpreter, frequently his good looking Daughter, I managed to get a great deal of consolation and encouragement." He was also a leading figure at some of the larger social functions. "He was a tireless dancer, like all sailors [one Haitian recalled]; one found him, after a waltz, with the buttons of his uniform remaining imprinted on the breast of his partner, so tightly did he hold her in his arms." The admiral's enthusiasm for the dance, in fact, laid him open to local criticism: "Unkind observers claimed that he therebye reheated his blood, chilled by the years, in the warmth of the young bodies which he found in abundance in the *salons* of our worldly circles."[22]

While Admiral Caperton was an unabashed exponent of the "firm hand" school of handling Caribbean peoples, he kept in mind the need for what he called "kind consideration" in conjunction with firmness. In this connection, the role of Captain Beach was of considerable importance. Beach was remarkably free from the racial prejudices of his time; a sensitive and intelligent observer, he radiated a genuine liking for the Haitian elite with whom he dealt. He regularly defended Haiti from the calumnies and sensationalism of his contemporaries, depicting the upper class as cultured and refined, the peasants as kindly and hospitable. While gaining a shrewd understanding of Haitian politics, the captain never saw any incongruity in the spectacle of a black ruling class and had little patience with the preconceptions of American travelers. "With some acquaintance with distinguished men in his own and foreign countries, a visitor to Haiti will not find representative Haitians inferior to them in culture, intelligence, dignity, or personal habits of thought and conduct," he later wrote. "This is here mentioned for the benefit of any Americans who may intend to visit Haiti and who have thought otherwise," he added pointedly.[23]

As Caperton's closest collaborator and most trusted adviser in Haiti, Captain Beach was a significant influence for understanding. He kept the admiral accurately informed of the Haitian point of view and helped him to understand it. Although Beach fully supported the intervention and shared the belief that it would help Haiti, his paternalism was largely free of racial overtones: he thought the Haitians needed outside help, not because they were inferior but because they were victims of history. When one realized, he wrote, "the odds against which Haitians won their independence, and how, for more than a century they have maintained it, struggling, in spite of every discouragement, against indifference, contempt, hostility, and at certain times, brutality of great powers; how, in spite of internal disorders, they have ever clung to and maintained for their educated class a high standard of education, culture, and conduct; one may justly say, from the large view, that the history of Haiti has been Heroic."[24]

If Caperton was free from Waller's outward discourtesy, he was far from attaining the open-minded detachment of Beach. The admiral fully shared the prevailing racism of his day and nation, at the same time that he respected some Haitians individually and harbored humanitarian sentiments toward the Haitian people generally. Not only their race but their history made him see the Haitians as essentially different from himself. In his narrative of his activities there, Caperton continually referred to the savagery of Haiti's independence movement, when the French were exterminated or driven out: "The planters they sawed in two, roasted or skinned alive and on some occasions drank their blood mixed with rum." He never lost the suspicion that savagery still lurked just beneath the surface, "in a country where within the memory of this generation Vaudoux rites had supposedly been held; where cannibalism in its most terrifying forms possibly existed, where children were presumably drugged into unconsciousness, buried, disinterred and revived in order to appease the appetites of the barbarous Vaudoux worshippers, who clamored for human flesh."[25]

Most often, however, the admiral's prejudice manifested itself in a kind of private amusement at Haitian vagaries. Of the *caco* General Rameaux, he wrote: "How childishly foolish and how like an infant of nature was this man. And how like many others who had preceded him down the pages of history in his own land, where comic opera occasions grew up like mushrooms, overnight, with a rapidity startling and withal amusing."[26] The tendency to make the Haitians comic recurs often in the admiral's prose and is the most obtrusive evidence of his feelings.

Sometimes a harsher feeling showed itself, as in Caperton's comment that male Haitians were "notoriously lazy" and that "work generally offered no inducement to the males in that Republic." Sometimes, too, irritation and frustration soured the admiral's outlook. Late in his career there he wrote: "I still keep in excellent shape and spirits as long as these devils do not try to rub it in too much."[27] Yet Admiral Caperton's unquestionable racial bias was less virulent than that of the average white American of his day. He was, in the last analysis, ambivalent; if he could not shake off his prejudice, neither did he surrender entirely to it.

The principal marine officers took a different stance, professing great fondness for ordinary Haitians but intense dislike for their leaders. As Smedley Butler said, the entire Haitian people was divided into two classes, one which wore shoes and one which did not. The latter class, comprising "ninety-five per cent of the people of Haiti" he described as "the most kindly, generous, hospitable, pleasure-loving people" that he had ever known. On the other hand: "Those that wear shoes I took as a joke. Without a sense of humor you could not live in Haiti among those people, among the shoe class." The common people, left to themselves, would harm no one, but they were corrupted by the elite. "When the other one per cent that wears vici kid shoes with long pointed toes and celluloid collars, stirs them up and incites them with liquor and voodoo stuff, they are capable of the most horrible atrocities."[28]

Cole spoke similarly. "The Haitian politician I never had much use for," he declared, though he "rather liked" the *caco* chiefs, whom he thought "more sincere." The elite may have been discontented with the occupation, Cole said, "But we had absolutely the respect and confidence . . . of 95 per cent of the country people of Haiti." Waller, too, spoke of the contentment of the rural peasantry under the occupation, even those working on the marines' road-building program![29] All three marine officers painted the same picture of a likable, contented peasantry and a selfish and obstructive elite.

These statements, while they may have expressed honestly held views, also reflected their authors' expectations about black people. The poor and illiterate Haitian peasantry, socially submerged and used to taking orders, "knew their place." They harmonized with the conditioning of these Americans and could therefore be seen as likable and "sincere." The Haitian elite was another matter. Men like Butler and Waller simply could not relate to black men of culture and social standing. Such a phenomenon violated their conditioning; it was offensive to them. Upper class Haitian society appeared to such men as a kind of parody or charade, made the more hateful because it was also the prime source of opposition to United States activities in Haiti. Their preference for the common people, therefore, was not merely democratic but racist.

It is nevertheless true that the Haitian occupation cannot be charged with pandering to the local elite or "selling out" the common people to their interests. Such a charge has been leveled at the United States occupations of Cuba and the Philippines following the Spanish-American War; American authorities co-opted the local leaderships, the argument runs, at the price of strengthening an unjust status quo, favoring large landowners, and the like. In Haiti the opposite was true, for virtually every important change

Conclusion   221

imposed by the occupation damaged and alienated the traditional upper class.

In large part this grew out of the overwhelmingly political nature of the Haitian elite's interests. It was not land, or trade, that had supported the position of the upper class so much as the bounties of government: offices, bribes, pensions, payroll brokerage, and other perquisites. United States authorities in Washington and Haiti were collectively unwilling to trust the Haitians with continued control of the government or possession of its bureaucratic machinery. When they seized power for the United States, they ejected many incumbents of the previous political system as a matter of course. Furthermore, the values of the Progressive era exalted honest, efficient, and economical government, and the military officers of the occupation saw these as the chief attributes of good administration. Their attacks on bribery and corruption, sinecures and multiple pension-holding, were therefore direct expressions of their ideas of what government should be. While the Haitian victims naturally tended to see malice in this assault on their privileges, the privileges at stake were, in the American mind, naked abuses verging upon crime. If the racism of many occupation officers made them readier to suppress the elite, the political norms of the elite reenforced the prevailing American biases.

During the first year of the occupation, much of the money saved by curbing the costs and abuses of government went into public works programs designed to provide jobs for workers or otherwise benefit the masses. Thus the occupation not only cut the total sum of government expenditures in Haiti, but attempted to shift much of the remainder from the service of the elite to that of the workers. Admiral Caperton in particular had urged a large public works program, both to minimize the sufferings of the poor during a period of economic depression and to lay an infrastructure for the country's future economic growth. In addition, he had hoped that such a program would serve to make the occupation more popular with the people and thus strengthen its political position. In this latter calculation, Caperton failed to give due weight to the elite's virtual monopoly of politics, and the resulting futility of bidding for the support of the poor. In any case, early occupation policy was unquestionably more socially conscious than that of preceding Haitian regimes, at least in its concern for the health and welfare of the common people, though actual results were always limited by lack of funds.

One might therefore conclude that the Haitian elite's vehement opposition to the occupation, while clothed in the rhetoric of patriotism, was merely a self-serving struggle to regain their lost boodle. It is certainly true that they received the intervention originally with mixed emotions and a readiness to benefit by new developments, whereas the roar of patriotic defiance rose loudly only after their interests had been damaged. Yet it is equally true that Haitians of all classes had treasured their independence and disliked alien white rule. Furthermore, the elite had been frightened by the bloody upheavals of July 1915 and appreciated the physical security which the intervention brought them; it was only natural that their acquiescence should fade with their fears. Thus interest, emotion, and ideals interacted in the Haitian ruling class just as it did among the new occupation overlords.

Simple stereotypes, therefore, are of little value in understanding the Haitian events of 1915 and thereafter. Many of the charges hurled by each side at the other were true, while on neither side was principle totally lacking. Since it was the United States, however, which had intruded itself into the affairs of another nation, the question is ultimately not one of the relative merits of the occupation and its Haitian opponents, but whether the occupation should ever have existed at all.

Even when tested against the Wilson administration's stated purposes, the intervention was hardly an unqualified success. It is true that some objectives were met: the occupation did impose political stability and effectively ended whatever possibility there may have been of European influence or incursion in Haiti. That Washington officialdom greatly exaggerated the dangers from Europe is evident in hindsight, however, and the Haitian intervention seems to have contributed little to the security of the United States. Nor was there much progress toward the Wilsonian aims of teaching democracy and constitutionalism, or improving the lot of the people. The assumption that the Haitians could simply be coerced into orderly elective democracy seemed in Washington to be validated when Caperton successfully brought off the presidential election of Sudre Dartiguenave, but Caperton almost certainly knew better at the time and his superiors at home quickly became wiser. The admiral put his own faith in a period of tutelage, while the State Department lost interest in any broader goals whatever in Haiti once order had been imposed. With President Wilson's attention wholly occupied elsewhere, the admiral found little Washington support for schemes of Haitian progress.

While the admiral was in frequent disagreement with his superiors over the nature of occupation policy, he too favored a thorough-going United States control of Haitian affairs. It was nevertheless true that Caperton intended the Haitian government to retain distinctly more status and functions than it was ultimately allowed. He had not willed that the occupation should take over the customs service, that public utilities should fall to the gendarmerie, and the other encroachments that eventually reduced the Dartiguenave regime to a figurehead. Rather, he envisioned a situation conforming more precisely to the terms of the treaty, which he took very seriously. This implied a regime staffed by Haitians, formally under Haitian jurisdiction, but supervised at the top by a limited number of Americans wielding ultimate authority. On the other hand, he believed that the United States must keep military forces in Haiti indefinitely to protect the new status quo. The policy followed earlier in Cuba seemed roughly to fit his model: a fairly long but temporary military occupation followed by a permanent protectorate relationship, leaving the Haitians autonomous but under United States tutelage and controls.

Beyond this, Caperton had believed that the United States would actively aid Haitian economic development, and he was deeply disappointed that the State Department viewed this function so casually. Washington never did do much to stimulate loans and investment in Haiti, while the costs of what was done there came almost wholly out of Haitian government revenues. The United States government wanted stability and security in the Caribbean, and having attained this it showed little further interest in those for whose fate it had assumed responsibility. This attitude stemmed in part from the legal theory of the occupation, which held that the Haitian government continued in its autonomous authority and thereby denied that the United States was in fact responsible for Haiti's internal affairs. An area officially under the American flag would have had undeniable claims upon the nation, but no such claims accompanied a mere treaty relationship. So long as it denied the existence of its de facto rule over the Haitians, the administration was debarred from asking Congress for the means to help them, though it may not have done so in any case. It was an attitude which the admiral did not share. Caperton may have been far too optimistic about what could be accomplished in Haiti, as one critic charged,[30] but he did intend that the intervention should usher in direct attempts to improve living conditions there.

Instead of Caperton's hoped-for improvements, the first year of the Haitian occupation witnessed the mutual disillusionment of occupied and occupiers, the progressive abandonment of the more constructive occupation goals, the decline of real Haitian participation in government, and the emergence of a military autocracy as a central mechanism of power. Perhaps little else could be expected from an enterprise based so largely on force and lacking the consent of the governed. Haitian realities also went far to account for failure, and the sum of defeat was rounded out by the absence of enlightened vision or practical understanding among the Washington officialdom. Nor was Admiral Caperton blameless, whatever his hopes and goals, for he had freely interlarded his diplomacy with misrepresentation and intimidation. Yet it is difficult to see how he could otherwise have fulfilled his mission without added bloodshed, and it is worth noting that he differed from his civilian superiors chiefly in believing more literally than they in the promises to the Haitians which they had jointly made.

Epilogue

THE FUROR over the Haitian occupation, and the United States Senate inquiry which resulted, culminated in 1922 with a general reconsideration of the United States presence in Haiti. Both Haitians and Americans found the status quo unsatisfactory. President Dartiguenave, locked in a struggle with the American financial adviser for retention of at least some fiscal discretion, took heart from events in the United States and demanded a literal adherence to the 1915 treaty. In his view this entailed an end to the marine occupation and a closer integration of the treaty services into the Haitian government, as well as a greatly enhanced role for the latter. In a forceful written presentation, he appealed directly to newly inaugurated President Warren G. Harding to restructure Haitian-American relations along these lines.

The State Department, on the other hand, wished to consolidate the intervention under a more effective structure rather than relax its grasp. Arguing that United States withdrawal inevitably meant renewed anarchy in Haiti, its

227

policy-makers advised Harding to centralize control of the occupation in a ranking marine officer, who would act as the personal representative of the president of the United States and supervise and coordinate the work of the treaty officials. It was this advice which Harding ultimately accepted. Early in 1922 he promoted the current commander of the marine brigade at Port-au-Prince, Colonel John H. Russell, to the rank of brigadier general and named him United States high commissioner to Haiti. Once again, the civil authorities in Washington had chosen to work through their military command in Haiti in preference to a conventional civil bureaucracy.

At almost the same time, Philippe Sudre Dartiguenave left the presidential palace in Port-au-Prince. When his term expired in 1922, Dartiguenave was on bad terms with United States authorities while lacking Haitian support as well. Since there was no Haitian Congress after its dissolution in 1917, the presidential succession was decided by the appointed council of state. Dartiguenave had hoped to secure reelection from this body, but found that his prospects were hopeless and withdrew his candidacy. The council chose Louis Borno, who had formerly been a prominent member of Dartiguenave's cabinet. After serving as foreign minister he had become minister of finance, until forced out by the Americans during the early stages of the showdown with the financial adviser.

Borno was regarded in 1922 as anti-American, but once in power he soon developed an effective working relationship with General Russell. The long-awaited government loan finally reached fruition during Borno's first year in office, while the objectionable financial adviser gave way to a new and more acceptable man. Having proved himself no puppet, Borno was able to cooperate closely with Russell in what became a kind of dual autocracy. From 1922 to 1929 Haiti was reasonably stable and quiet, while Borno's reelection in 1926 once more occurred without the benefit of an elected legislative branch. This tidy and durable arrangement began to crumble, however, with the approaching end of Borno's second term.

In the winter of 1929-30 economic depression joined with political frustration to arouse the Haitian political elite once again. Its widespread demands for the restoration of an elected congress to choose the new president marked the beginning of a campaign against the occupation more vigorous than anything since 1920-21. President Herbert Hoover, never happy with his inherited military occupations, became concerned at student strikes and public demonstrations in Haiti, especially after one clash provoked a shooting affray with the marines in Aux Cayes. In December 1929 Hoover appointed a commission to study the Haitian situation and make recommendations for an eventual United States withdrawal. After due deliberation, the commission urged a "Haitianization" of the treaty services such as Dartiguenave had previously demanded, along with the replacement of General Russell by a civilian diplomat and the gradual abandonment of United States controls. In 1930 the Hoover administration began the implementation of these measures by recalling Russell, holding congressional elections to reconstitute the Haitian congress for the first time since 1917, and acquiescing in the election of Stenio Vincent to replace Borno in the presidency. Once embarked upon this road there was no turning back. The Haitian intervention ended in 1934, after nineteen years of substantial United States control. The record of United States activities in that period was interesting and significant; yet it was instructive to note how many things in Haiti, after it all was ended, had remained unchanged.

Admiral Caperton had proved himself in Haiti to be an energetic and decisive commander who fully grasped the relationship between force and politics. Having gained the confidence of both the Navy and the State departments, he went on to exercise his special talents in a number of other countries, beginning with the Dominican Republic. When he left Port-au-Prince in May of 1916, it was to take charge of a military intervention at Santo Domingo which had already been initiated by the United States minister at that capital. The stability which Washington had attempted to impose upon the Dominicans had broken down, and naval forces had landed to restore order. When a revolutionary force defied the United States authorities, Caperton called in marine reenforcements which by mid-summer had seized control of most of the country. Yet the Dominicans' universal hostility toward the intervention made it impossible to erect a submissive new government like that in Haiti, and while the admiral was easily able to quell armed opposition, his diplomatic colleague remained unable to reestablish civil government on United States terms. The upshot, after Caperton had left the country, was the installation of a United States military government in which there was no Dominican participation whatever.

In the meantime Admiral Caperton had left the Caribbean entirely, to become commander-in-chief of the Pacific Fleet. He was not yet finished with Caribbean politics, however, for in the autumn of 1916 the admiral sailed to Nicaragua to assist the United States minister in "supervising" a presidential election there. This task included the removal from contention of the front-running candidate, an operation which Caperton had already essayed in Haiti and which he once more performed successfully in this new setting. Although disappointed by the failure of his more constructive policies in Haiti, and impressed with the depth of Dominican hatred of *Yanqui* control, Admiral Caperton nevertheless continued to find disorder and instability repellent in themselves and shared as well the Wilsonian belief that they constituted the principal obstacle to any sort of progress in the Caribbean. His Nicaraguan manipulations, therefore, found him still confident that United States tutelage was both necessary and beneficial.

Soon after the United States declared war against Germany in 1917, Caperton took a squadron to Brazil on a two-year mission which quickly became more diplomatic than military and sought to solidify the influence of the United States in the entire region. Few, if any, of his contemporaries had practiced naval diplomacy over such a wide range of applications, and when he retired in 1919 the admiral sought vainly to persuade his superiors to reorganize the navy in such a way as to maximize its diplomatic functions. The failure of this campaign marked the end of Caperton's active career, and he was quickly forgotten in his retirement. When he returned to the limelight in 1921, during the Senate hearings on Haiti and the Dominican Republic, the admiral already appeared as a fading figure from the past. He died at the age of eighty-six in December 1941, just two weeks after the Japanese attack on Pearl Harbor. One wonders what he would have thought of the new and expanded uses of United States military and naval diplomacy which were to characterize the coming era.

Notes

A Note on Sources

Index

Notes

CHAPTER 1: INTRODUCING HAITI AND THE CRUISER SQUADRON

1 The orders are quoted in full in William B. Caperton, "History of U.S. Naval Operations Under Command of Rear Admiral W. B. Caperton, USN, Commencing January 5, 1915, Ending April 30, 1919." This 400-page typescript is to be found in the Naval Records Collection of the Office of Naval Records and Library, Subject File ZN (Personnel), 1911-1927, Record Group 45, National Archives, Washington, D.C. It will be cited hereafter as Caperton, "History of Flag Career."

2 Bradley A. Fiske, *From Midshipman to Rear Admiral* (New York, 1919), pp. 550-51.

3 For the composition and deployment of the Cruiser Squadron, see Caperton to Commander in Chief Atlantic Fleet, March 3, 1915, in Area File C, Record Group 45, National Archives.

4 The Latin American policies of the Wilson administration are summarized in Arthur S. Link, *Wilson: The Struggle for Neutrality, 1914-1915* (Princeton, N.J., 1960), especially chapters 14 and 15. See also Rayford Logan, *Haiti and the Dominican Republic* (New York, 1968), pp. 117-23; and Lansing to Wilson, October 28, 1914, in Records of the Department of State relating to the Internal Affairs of Haiti, 1910-1929, Record Group 59, National Archives, cited hereafter as Decimal Files, Haiti, Internal.

5 See Harold P. Davis, *Black Democracy: The Story of Haiti* (New York, 1936); James G. Leyburn, *The Haitian People* (New Haven, Conn., 1941); and Robert I. Rotberg, *Haiti: The Politics of Squalor* (Boston, 1971), for varying approaches to these matters.

6 Logan, *Haiti and the Dominican Republic,* pp. 102-17; Ludwell Lee Montague, *Haiti and the United States, 1714-1938* (New York, 1966), pp. 81-208; Dana G. Munro, *The United States and the Caribbean Area* (Boston, 1934), pp. 147-53.

7 Samuel Guy Inman, *Through Santo Domingo and Haiti, a cruise with the Marines* (New York, 1919), p. 59.

8 This is a major conclusion of Leyburn, *The Haitian People,* still a classic in the literature about Haiti.

9 In addition to previous citations, this section summarizes data from Arthur C. Millspaugh, *Haiti Under American Control, 1915-1930* (Boston, 1931), pp. 3-24; Montague, *Haiti and the United States,* pp. 9-27; and Inman, *Through Santo Domingo and Haiti,* pp. 57-75.

10 "Tennessean Center of Eyes," *Nashville Banner,* October 9, 1915.

11 B. Danache, *Le Président Dartiguenave et Les Américains* (Port-au-Prince, 1950), p. 45. Translation mine.

12 For basic biographical data, see *Who's Who, 1914-15;* and *National Cyclopaedia of American Biography,* vol. 36 (New York, 1950), pp. 30-31.

CHAPTER 2: REVOLUTION IN HAITI

1 Caperton, "History of Flag Career," pp. 2-3; Caperton to SecNavy, Report of Operations from 10 January to 27 January 1915, and Bryan to AmLegation, Port-au-Prince, January 16, 1915, in Decimal Files, Haiti, Internal.

2 Livingston to SecState, January 18, 1915, Blanchard to SecState, January 18, 1915, and Caperton's Report of Operations dated 27 January 1915, in Decimal Files, Haiti, Internal.

3 Caperton's Report of Operations dated 27 January 1915, ibid.; the admiral's attitudes are made abundantly clear in Caperton, "History of Flag Career," pp. 2-4. The quotation is from p. 3.

4 Caperton's Report of Operations dated 27 January 1915, and Livingston to SecState, January 27, 1915, in Decimal Files, Haiti, Internal; Caperton, "History of Flag Career," pp. 3-4; Harold P. Davis, *Black Democracy: The Story of Haiti* (New York, 1936), p. 155.

5 Caperton's Report of Operations dated 27 January 1915, in Decimal Files, Haiti, Internal. See also Robert Rotberg, *Haiti: The Politics of Squalor* (Boston, 1971), p. 107; and Caperton's testimony in U.S., Congress, Senate, *Inquiry into the occupation and administration of Haiti and Santo Domingo. Hearings before a select committee on Haiti and Santo Domingo, pursuant to Senate Resolution 112,* 67th Cong., 1st and 2d sess., 2 vols. (Washington, D.C., 1922), pp. 288-89. Cited hereafter as Senate Inquiry, *Hearings.*

6 This description of the revolutionary process follows Captain Edward L. Beach, U.S.N., "Admiral Caperton in Haiti," pp. 29-36. This is a typescript of more than 200 pages now filed in Record Group 45, National Archives, Washington, D.C., under Subject File ZWA-7, "Haiti." Cited hereafter as Beach, "Caperton in Haiti." For a brief discussion of *cacos*, see Davis, *Black Democracy*, pp. 304-5.

7 Livingston to SecState, December 19, 1914, in Decimal Files, Haiti, Internal.

8 Caperton, "History of Flag Career," pp. 4-5; Beach, "Caperton in Haiti," pp. 80-81, 85. The quotations are from Caperton, p. 5.

9 Beach, "Caperton in Haiti," pp. 81-82.

10 Ibid., p. 84.

11 Caperton's Report of Operations dated 27 January 1915, in Decimal Files, Haiti, Internal.

12 Caperton, "History of Flag Career," p. 6.

13 Caperton's Report of Operations dated 27 January 1915, in Decimal Files, Haiti, Internal.

14 Ibid.; James A. Padgett, "Diplomats to Haiti and Their Diplomacy," *Journal of Negro History* 25 (July 1940): 309-10. The description of Port-au-Prince is based upon old photographs and accounts plus my own visit.

15 Beach, "Caperton in Haiti," p. 86; Davis, *Black Democracy*, p. 306.

16 Beach, "Caperton in Haiti," pp. 51-53; Hans Schmidt, *The United States Occupation of Haiti, 1915-1934* (New Brunswick, N.J., 1971), pp. 38-41; Rayford Logan, *Haiti and the Dominican Republic* (New York, 1968), pp. 115-16.

17 Dana G. Munro, *The United States and the Caribbean Area* (Boston, 1934), pp. 150-53; Paul Douglas, "The American Occupation of Haiti," *Political Science Quarterly* 42 (1927): 229-30, 233-35; Schmidt, *The United States Occupation of Haiti*, pp. 37-38.

18 Douglas, "The American Occupation of Haiti," pp. 236-39; Schmidt, *The United States Occupation of Haiti*, pp. 50-52.

19 Arthur S. Link, *Wilson: The Struggle for Neutrality, 1914-1915* (Princeton, N.J., 1960), pp. 518-19.

20 Ibid., p. 521.

21 Ibid., pp. 521-25; Blanchard to SecState, August 10, 1914, in Decimal Files, Haiti, Internal.

22 Blanchard to SecState, December 16, 1914, and Commanding Officer, U.S.S. *Hancock*, to Navy Dept., December 19, 1914, in Decimal Files, Haiti, Internal.

23 Bryan to AmLegation, Port-au-Prince, December, 19, 1914, in Decimal Files, Haiti, Internal; Link, *Wilson,* pp. 526-27.

24 Wilson to Bryan, January 13, 1915, in Decimal Files, Haiti, Internal. See also Link, *Wilson,* pp. 528-29.

25 Caperton's Report of Operations dated 27 January 1915, in Decimal Files, Haiti, Internal.

26 Caperton to SecNavy, 28 January 1915, Daniels to Caperton, 28 January 1915, and Lansing to SecNavy, January 29, 1915, in Decimal Files, Haiti, Internal.

27 Caperton, "History of Flag Career," pp. 6-7.

28 Ibid., pp. 7-9.

29 Ibid., p. 8; Caperton to SecNavy, 9 February 1915, in Decimal Files, Haiti, Internal; Caperton's testimony, in Senate Inquiry, *Hearings,* p. 293.

30 Caperton to SecNavy, 10 February 1915, in Decimal Files, Haiti, Internal.

31 Caperton, "History of Flag Career," pp. 6-8.

32 Ibid., pp. 8-10.

33 Ibid., pp. 10-11; Davis, *Black Democracy,* pp. 155-56, 306-7.

34 Caperton, "History of Flag Career," p. 11; Commanding Officer, U.S.S. *Des Moines,* to SecNavy, Report of Operations from 24 January to 21 February 1915, in Decimal Files, Haiti, Internal; and Caperton to SecNavy, 18 February 1915, ibid.

35 Commanding Officer, U.S.S. *Des Moines,* to SecNavy, 21 February 1915, and Caperton to SecNavy, 19 February 1915, in Decimal Files, Haiti, Internal.

36 Caperton, "History of Flag Career," pp. 11-12; Senate Inquiry, *Hearings,* pp. 298-99.

37 Caperton, "History of Flag Career," pp. 12-13; Senate Inquiry, *Hearings,* p. 299; Caperton to SecNavy, Report of Operations from 23 February to 9 March 1915, in Decimal Files, Haiti, Internal.

38 Bryan to AmLegation, Port-au-Prince, February 20, 1915, Blanchard to SecState, February 25, 1915, and Bryan to AmLegation, Port-au-Prince, February 27, 1915, in Decimal Files, Haiti, Internal. See also Link, *Wilson,* p. 529.

39 Link, *Wilson,* pp. 529-32; Fuller to SecState, May 22, June 4, 1915, in Records of the State Department relating to Political Relations between the United States and Haiti, 1910-1929, Record Group 59, National Archives, cited hereafter as Decimal Files, Haiti, U.S. Relations; "Brief of Mr. Fuller's report of conditions in Haiti," Memorandum, Department of

State, Division of Latin American Affairs, dated June 22, 1915, in Decimal Files, Haiti, Internal.

40 Caperton to SecNavy, 9 March 1915, in Decimal Files, Haiti, Internal; Caperton, "History of Flag Career," p. 32.

CHAPTER 3: THE FALL OF GUILLAUME SAM

1 Caperton, "History of Flag Career," p. 34; SecNavy to Caperton, June 22, 1915, in Decimal Files, Haiti, Internal.
2 Caperton, "History of Flag Career," pp. 34-35.
3 Ibid., p. 35.
4 Ibid., pp. 35, 40-41. See also Blanchard to SecState, April 6, 1915, in Decimal Files, Haiti, Internal.
5 Arthur S. Link, *Wilson: The Struggle for Neutrality* (Princeton, N.J., 1960), pp. 531-32.
6 Ibid., pp. 532-33; Caperton, "History of Flag Career," pp. 34-35, 38.
7 Caperton, "History of Flag Career," p. 36; Caperton to SecNavy, July 3, 1915, in Decimal Files, Haiti, Internal.
8 Caperton, "History of Flag Career," pp. 36-37; Caperton to SecNavy, July 3, 1915, in Decimal Files, Haiti, Internal.
9 Copies of the letter are in Box 161, Area File C, Record Group 45, National Archives, Washington, D.C. All are dated 2 July 1915.
10 Beach, "Caperton in Haiti," pp. 91-93.
11 Ibid., pp. 93-95.
12 Caperton, "History of Flag Career," pp. 34, 37-38.
13 Ibid., p. 37; Caperton to SecNavy, July 4, 1915, in Decimal Files, Haiti, Internal.
14 Caperton, "History of Flag Career," p. 39.
15 Ibid., pp. 39-40; Caperton to SecNavy, July 10, 1915, in Decimal Files, Haiti, Internal.
16 Caperton, "History of Flag Career," pp. 41-43.
17 Admiral William S. Benson to Caperton, July 23, 1915, in Caperton Papers, Library of Congress, Washington, D.C.
18 Caperton, "History of Flag Career," pp. 44-45.
19 Caperton's testimony, in Senate Inquiry, *Hearings*, p. 306.
20 Memorandum of R. B. Davis, Jr., to SecState, submitted January 12, 1916, printed in U.S., State Department, *Papers Relating to the Foreign Relations of the United States, 1916*

(Washington, D.C., 1925), pp. 311-20, cited hereafter as Davis, "Memorandum"; Harold P. Davis, *Black Democracy: The Story of Haiti* (New York, 1936), pp. 161-65. The *gourde,* which had fluctuated wildly, was exchanged at about ten to the dollar when the intervention began, but was eventually stabilized at five to the dollar, or 20¢ U.S.

21 Davis, *Black Democracy,* pp. 161-65; Beach, "Caperton in Haiti," pp. 98-100.
22 Beach, "Caperton in Haiti," pp. 99-100; Davis, "Memorandum"; *Le Matin,* Port-au-Prince, July 28, 1915.
23 Davis, "Memorandum"; Caperton, "History of Flag Career," pp. 45, 46.
24 Davis, "Memorandum"; see also *Le Matin,* July 28, 1915, and *Le Nouvelliste,* Port-au-Prince, July 29, 1915.
25 Davis, "Memorandum"; Beach, "Caperton in Haiti," pp. 99-100.
26 Davis, "Memorandum"; Caperton, "History of Flag Career," p. 46.
27 Davis, "Memorandum."
28 Ibid.; Caperton, "History of Flag Career," p. 46. See also Davis, *Black Democracy,* pp. 167-68.
29 Davis, "Memorandum."
30 Ibid.; Caperton's testimony, in Senate Inquiry, *Hearings,* p. 308; Caperton, "History of Flag Career," pp. 45, 47.
31 Caperton, "History of Flag Career," p. 47; Beach, "Caperton in Haiti," p. 103.
32 Beach, "Caperton in Haiti," pp. 102-4.
33 Ibid., pp. 103-5; Caperton, "History of Flag Career," pp. 47-48.

CHAPTER 4: FIRST DAYS OF THE HAITIAN INTERVENTION

1 Caperton, "History of Flag Career," p. 48; New York *Herald,* July 30, 1915.
2 Beach, "Caperton in Haiti," pp. 106-8. Caperton fails to mention these concerns in his official memoirs; see Caperton, "History of Flag Career," p. 48.
3 Lansing to AmLegation, Port-au-Prince, July 28, 1915, in Decimal Files, Haiti, Internal; Caperton, "History of Flag Career," p. 48.

4 Caperton to SecNavy, July 29, 1915, in Box 161, Area File C, Record Group 45, National Archives, Washington, D.C.; Caperton, "History of Flag Career," p. 49.
5 Beach, "Caperton in Haiti," pp. 108-9; Lansing to AmLegation, Port-au-Prince, July 28, 1915, in Decimal Files, Haiti, Internal; James A. Padgett, "Diplomats to Haiti and Their Diplomacy," *Journal of Negro History* 25 (July 1940): 315.
6 Beach, "Caperton in Haiti," pp. 109-11.
7 Ibid.; Caperton, "History of Flag Career," p. 49; *Le Matin,* Port-au-Prince, July 29, 1915.
8 Caperton to SecNavy, July 29, 1915, in Box 161, Area File C, RG 45, National Archives; Caperton to SecNavy, August 3, 1915, in Decimal Files, Haiti, Internal.
9 Caperton to SecNavy, July 30, 1915, in Box 161, Area File C, RG 45, National Archives; New York *Herald,* July 31, 1915; Caperton, "History of Flag Career," p. 50; Hans Schmidt, *The United States Occupation of Haiti, 1915-1934* (New Brunswick, N.J., 1971), p. 67.
10 New York *Herald,* July 31, 1915.
11 Caperton to SecNavy, July 30, 1915, in Box 161, Area File C, RG 45, National Archives. Two messages are covered by this citation, sent at different times on the 30th.
12 Daniels to Caperton, July 30, 1915, ibid. Again, this covers two messages received the same day.
13 Caperton to SecNavy, July 30, 1915, ibid.; Caperton, "History of Flag Career," p. 53; *Le Nouvelliste,* Port-au-Prince, July 30, 1915.
14 *Le Nouvelliste,* July 29 and July 30, 1915.
15 *Le Matin,* July 31, 1915; *Le Nouvelliste,* July 31, 1915.
16 New York *Herald,* August 3, 1915.
17 Caperton, "History of Flag Career," pp. 51, 53, 56.
18 Beach, "Caperton in Haiti," p. 131.
19 Davis to SecState, July 31, 1915, in Decimal Files, Haiti, Internal; Caperton to SecNavy, July 30, 1915, in Box 161, Area File C, RG 45, National Archives; *Le Nouvelliste,* July 30, 1915.
20 Caperton to SecNavy, July 31, 1915, in Decimal Files, Haiti, Internal.
21 Caperton, "History of Flag Career," pp. 51, 54; Lansing to SecNavy, July 30, 1915, and Caperton to SecNavy, July 31, 1915, in Decimal Files, Haiti, Internal. For an incident with the troops see *Le Nouvelliste,* August 2, 1915.

22 Caperton to SecNavy, August 1, 1915, in Box 161, Area File C, RG 45, National Archives; Caperton, "History of Flag Career," p. 54.

23 Caperton, "History of Flag Career," pp. 51, 52.

24 Ibid., pp. 54-55; Beach, "Caperton in Haiti," p. 122.

25 Beach, "Caperton in Haiti," pp. 122-23, 113.

26 Ibid., p. 124; Caperton, "History of Flag Career," p. 55; Le Matin, August 2, 1915.

27 Caperton, "History of Flag Career," pp. 51, 54; Caperton to SecNavy, August 1, 1915, and Daniels to Caperton, August 2, 1915, in Box 161, Area File C, RG 45, National Archives.

28 Caperton to SecNavy, August 2, 1915, in Box 161, Area File C, RG 45, National Archives; Caperton, "History of Flag Career," p. 55; Beach, "Caperton in Haiti," p. 116; Le Matin, August 3, 1915.

29 Caperton, "History of Flag Career," p. 58; Caperton to SecNavy, August 3, 1915, in Decimal Files, Haiti, Internal.

30 Beach, "Caperton in Haiti," pp. 111, 116, 118; Caperton to SecNavy, July 30, 1915, in Box 161, Area File C, RG 45, National Archives.

31 Beach, "Caperton in Haiti," pp. 118-20.

32 Caperton, "History of Flag Career," p. 59.

33 Ibid., pp. 59, 62; Cole's testimony, in Senate Inquiry, Hearings, p. 671; Le Matin, August 5 and 6, 1915.

34 Delva to Caperton, August 5, 1915, in Box 161, Area File C, RG 45, National Archives.

35 Beach, "Caperton in Haiti," pp. 131-33; Caperton to SecNavy, August 3, 1915, in Decimal Files, Haiti, Internal.

36 Caperton, "History of Flag Career," pp. 59, 61; Caperton to SecNavy, August 5, 1915, in Decimal Files, Haiti, Internal.

37 Beach, "Caperton in Haiti," pp. 111-12, 132; Caperton to SecNavy, August 2, 1915, in Decimal Files, Haiti, Internal; Caperton, "History of Flag Career," p. 59.

CHAPTER 5: TIGHTENING THE GRIP

1 Beach, "Caperton in Haiti," p. 112.

2 Ibid., pp. 133-34.

3 Ibid., pp. 136-38; *Le Nouvelliste,* August 2, 4, 1915; *Le Matin,* August 3, 1915. The other declared candidates included General Edmond Défly and Horace Pauléus Sannon.

4 Caperton to SecNavy, August 5, 1915, in Decimal Files, Haiti, Internal. See also Caperton's testimony, in Senate Inquiry, *Hearings,* pp. 363-64.

5 Caperton, "History of Flag Career," p. 64.

6 Ibid., pp. 57-58, 69-70. Coffey's report of the mission is reproduced verbatim on pp. 69-73.

7 Ibid., pp. 57-58, 70-71.

8 Ibid., p. 71.

9 Ibid., pp. 57, 59-60, 63, 71-73; *Le Matin* and *Le Nouvelliste,* August 4, 1915.

10 Caperton, "History of Flag Career," pp. 60-61, 71-72.

11 Ibid., pp. 60-61; Caperton to SecNavy, August 4, 1915, in Box 161, Area File C, Record Group 45, National Archives, Washington, D.C.; New York *Herald,* August 5, 1915.

12 Caperton, "History of Flag Career," pp. 61-64, 72.

13 Ibid., pp. 62, 64, 73; Caperton to SecNavy, August 4, 1915, in Box 161, Area File C, RG 45, National Archives.

14 Beach, "Caperton in Haiti," pp. 118-20; Caperton, "History of Flag Career," pp. 66-67.

15 Caperton to SecNavy, August 7, 1915, in Decimal Files, Haiti, Internal; New York *Herald,* August 7, 1915.

16 New York *Herald,* August 7, 1915. In "History of Flag Career," p. 66, Caperton minimizes these events.

17 Beach, "Caperton in Haiti," p. 129. For Caperton's opinion of Bobo see Caperton, "History of Flag Career," p. 76. Elsewhere Caperton frequently suggested that Bobo was mentally unbalanced.

18 Caperton, "History of Flag Career," p. 64.

19 Ibid., pp. 64-65; Beach, "Caperton in Haiti," pp. 128-29, 140.

20 Beach, "Caperton in Haiti," pp. 140-42.

21 Ibid., pp. 143-44; Caperton, "History of Flag Career," p. 65.

22 Beach, "Caperton in Haiti," p. 144; Caperton, "History of Flag Career," pp. 64-66; New York *Herald* and *Le Nouvelliste,* August 7, 1915. Caperton claimed that Bobo's reception was merely due to his throwing quantities of coins to the crowd.

23 Caperton, "History of Flag Career," pp. 66, 68.

24 Ibid., pp. 67-68; *Le Nouvelliste,* August 7, 1915.

25 New York *Herald* and New York *Tribune,* August 8, 1915.
26 New York *Herald,* August 8, 1915.
27 *Le Matin,* August 7, 1915.
28 Caperton to SecNavy, August 8, 1915, in Decimal Files, Haiti, Internal. This message was actually sent on the night of August 7, but dated as of its reception in Washington the following morning; similarly, messages were frequently received in Haiti the next day after the date on the file copy, which is that on which they were submitted for transmitting.

CHAPTER 6: ELECTION OF A PRESIDENT

1 Benson to Caperton, August 7 and 8, 1915, in Decimal Files, Haiti, Internal.
2 Caperton, "History of Flag Career," p. 78; *Le Matin* printed the text of this proclamation in both English and French on August 9, 1915.
3 Caperton to SecNavy, August 8, 1915, in Decimal Files, Haiti, Internal; Beach, "Caperton in Haiti," p. 145.
4 Beach, "Caperton in Haiti," pp. 145-47; Caperton, "History of Flag Career," pp. 76-77.
5 Beach, "Caperton in Haiti," pp. 125-27; Caperton, "History of Flag Career," p. 75.
6 Beach, "Caperton in Haiti," p. 127; New York *Sun,* August 11, 1915; Caperton, "History of Flag Career," pp. 75, 78-79.
7 Caperton to SecNavy, August 7, 1915, in Decimal Files, Haiti, Internal.
8 Livingston to SecState, August 6, 1915, ibid.; Beach, "Caperton in Haiti," pp. 147-48; Caperton's testimony, in Senate Inquiry, *Hearings,* pp. 319-21.
9 Caperton to SecNavy, August 3 and 10, 1915, in Decimal Files, Haiti, Internal; Caperton, "History of Flag Career," p. 80.
10 B. Danache, *Le Président Dartiguenave et Les Américains* (Port-au-Prince, 1950), pp. 35-36.
11 Caperton, "History of Flag Career," p. 80; Caperton to SecNavy, August 10, 1915, in Decimal Files, Haiti, Internal.
12 Caperton, "History of Flag Career," pp. 82-83.

13 Lansing to AmLegation Port-au-Prince, August 10, 1915, in Decimal Files, Haiti, Internal.

14 Lansing to Wilson, August 9, 1915, ibid.

15 Beach, "Caperton in Haiti," p. 150; Caperton, "History of Flag Career," pp. 82-83; New York *Herald*, August 11, 1915.

16 Beach, "Caperton in Haiti," pp. 149-50; Caperton, "History of Flag Career," pp. 83-84; *Le Nouvelliste*, August 11, 1915; Dantès Bellegard, *Histoire du Peuple Haitien, 1492-1952* (Port-au-Prince, 1953), p. 254.

17 Caperton, "History of Flag Career," p. 84; Beach, "Caperton in Haiti," pp. 116-17.

18 Beach, "Caperton in Haiti," pp. 151-52; Caperton, "History of Flag Career," p. 84.

19 Beach, "Caperton in Haiti," pp. 154-55; Caperton, "History of Flag Career," p. 84.

20 Davis to SecState, August 12, 1915, in Decimal Files, Haiti, Internal; Beach, "Caperton in Haiti," pp. 155-57. *Le Matin*, which on August 12 reported the meeting and printed Lansing's message in full, mentioned no disorders or demonstrations of protest in its account.

21 Caperton, "History of Flag Career," p. 87; Beach, "Caperton in Haiti," p. 158; New York *Herald*, August 13, 1915. The *Herald's* headline was: "Hayti Chooses President Under American Guns."

22 Beach, "Caperton in Haiti," pp. 158-62; Caperton, "History of Flag Career," pp. 87-88; Davis to SecState, August 12, 1915, in Decimal Files, Haiti, Internal.

23 Beach, "Caperton in Haiti," p. 163; Caperton, "History of Flag Career," p. 88; New York *Herald*, August 18, 1915.

24 "Restoring a Republic," *World's Work* 30 (October 1915): 634.

25 "The Fractious Black Republic," *Outlook* 110 (August 11, 1915): 832; New York *Sun*, August 11, 1915.

26 Josephus Daniels, "The Problem of Haiti," *Saturday Evening Post*, July 12, 1930, p. 34; Beach, "Caperton in Haiti," pp. 134-35; Caperton's testimony, in Senate Inquiry, *Hearings*, p. 317; Caperton, "History of Flag Career," p. 88.

27 This point is made in Ludwell Lee Montague, *Haiti and the United States, 1714-1938* (New York, 1966), pp. 213-14.

28 Daniels, "The Problem of Haiti," p. 34.

CHAPTER 7: PUBLIC OPINION AND GOVERNMENT POLICY

1 Caperton to SecNavy, August 2 and August 7, 1915; quotation
   is from same to same, August 5, 1915, all in Decimal Files,
   Haiti, Internal.
2 Caperton to SecNavy, August 2, 1915, ibid.
3 Beach, "Caperton in Haiti," p. 130. See also Ludwell Lee
   Montague, *Haiti and the United States, 1714-1938* (New York,
   1966), pp. 193-95, 212.
4 New York *Herald,* July 31, 1915; for *Le Nouvelliste,* the July
   29 and August 7, 1915, issues contain typical expressions; *Le
   Matin,* August 14, 1915, reports the birth of the *Union Patriotique.*
5 *Le Matin,* August 25, 1915. See also the issues of August 23
   and 24, 1915, for a sample exchange of views.
6 *La Plume,* August 25, 1915. Translation mine.
7 Ibid., August 28, 1915.
8 Carl Kelsey, "The American Intervention in Haiti and the
   Dominican Republic," *Annals of the American Academy of
   Political and Social Science* 100 (March 1922): 136-37.
9 *Le Nouvelliste,* October 19, 1915.
10 "The Fractious Black Republic," *Outlook* 110 (August 11,
    1915): 832; "Our Call of Duty in Haiti," *Literary Digest* 51
    (August 14, 1915): 288; New York *Herald,* July 28, August 8,
    1915; John W. Blassingame, "The Press and American Inter-
    vention in Haiti and the Dominican Republic, 1904-1920,"
    Caribbean Studies 9 (July 1969): 30.
11 *Literary Digest* 51 (August 14, 1915): 288.
12 The Minneapolis *Journal* editorial was reprinted in the Phila-
    delphia *Press,* August 9, 1915; for voodooism, etc., see
    Blassingame, "The Press and American Intervention," pp. 29-
    30; "Restoring a Republic," *World's Work* 30 (October 1915):
    633.
13 Blassingame found that forty-nine out of the sixty-nine jour-
    nals he studied consistently supported United States interven-
    tion in Haiti and the Dominican Republic in the period 1904-
    19, almost all of them on similar grounds. See Blassingame,
    "The Press and American Intervention," p. 37.
14 Arthur S. Link, *Wilson: The Struggle for Neutrality, 1914-
    1915* (Princeton, N.J., 1960), pp. 497-99.
15 "Brief of Mr. Fuller's report of the conditions in Hayti
    together with his recommendations," Department of State,

Division of Latin-American Affairs, Memorandum, June 22, 1915, and Wilson to Bryan, July 2, 1915, in Decimal Files, Haiti, Internal.

16 "Memorandum submitted to Boaz W. Long . . . by Arthur Bailly-Blanchard," dated July 31, 1915, in Decimal Files, Haiti, Internal.

17 "Notes and Recommendations on the Political Situation in Haiti," typed on the letterhead of the Division of Latin-American Affairs and signed "BWL." The memorandum is undated, but internal evidence places it with certainty in the first week of August 1915. In Decimal Files, Haiti, Internal.

18 Lansing to Wilson, August 2, 1915, in Decimal Files, Haiti, Internal.

19 U.S., State Department, *The Lansing Papers, 1914-1920,* 2 vols. (Washington, D.C., 1940), 2: 463-65, a supplement to the department's *Foreign Relations of the United States* series.

20 Ibid., pp. 466-67, 470. See also Hans Schmidt, *The United States Occupation of Haiti, 1915-1934* (New Brunswick, N.J., 1971), pp. 55-58.

21 Fort to Wilson, July 30, 1915, in Decimal Files, Haiti, Internal.

22 Lansing to Wilson, August 3, 1915, ibid.

23 Wilson to Lansing, August 4, 1915, ibid.

24 New York *Herald,* July 31, August 3, 1915; New York *Sun,* August 3, 1915; New York *Tribune,* August 8, 1915.

25 Lansing to Wilson, August 9, and Wilson to Lansing, August 9, 1915, in Decimal Files, Haiti, Internal. See also Caperton, "History of Flag Career," pp. 73-74; and Schmidt, *The United States Occupation of Haiti,* pp. 56-57.

26 Lansing to Wilson, August 13, 1915, in Decimal Files, Haiti, Internal. Wilson's handwritten, undated reply is attached.

CHAPTER 8: THE SIGNING OF THE TREATY

1 Lansing to AmLegation Port-au-Prince, August 14, 1915, in Decimal Files, Haiti, Internal.

2 Caperton, "History of Flag Career," pp. 102-3; Beach, "Caperton in Haiti," p. 166; Davis to SecState, August 23, 1915, in Decimal Files, Haiti, U.S. Relations; New York *Herald,* August 25, 1915.

3 New York *Herald,* August 25, 1915. For an example of more moderate Haitian newspaper opposition, see *Le Nouvelliste,* September 7, 1915.

4 Lansing to AmLegation Port-au-Prince, August 24, 1915, in Decimal Files, Haiti, U.S. Relations; Caperton, "History of Flag Career," pp. 104, 110.

5 Caperton's Report of Operations dated August 27, 1915, in Decimal Files, Haiti, Internal.

6 Davis to SecState, October 25, 1915, in Decimal Files, Haiti, U.S. Relations; Caperton to SecNavy, August 25, 1915, in Decimal Files, Haiti, Internal. See also Caperton's Report of Operations dated August 27, 1915, in Decimal Files, Haiti, Internal.

7 Lansing to AmLegation Port-au-Prince, August 18, 1915, in Decimal Files, Haiti, U.S. Relations; Caperton, "History of Flag Career," pp. 89-90, 92; Beach, "Caperton in Haiti," p. 171; Philadelphia *Press,* August 15, 1915.

8 Caperton, "History of Flag Career," pp. 89, 91-92, 96; Beach, "Caperton in Haiti," pp. 173-74; *Le Matin,* August 17, September 14, 1915.

9 Lansing to AmLegation Port-au-Prince, August 18, 1915, in Decimal Files, Haiti, U.S. Relations; Caperton, "History of Flag Career," p. 99.

10 Caperton to SecNavy, August 19, 1915, in Decimal Files, Haiti, Internal.

11 Caperton, "History of Flag Career," pp. 93-94; James H. McCrocklin, *Garde d'Haiti, 1915-1934: Twenty years of organization and training by the United States Marine Corps* (Annapolis, Md., 1956), pp. 22, 28.

12 Beach, "Caperton in Haiti," p. 171; Joseph L. Schott, *The Ordeal of Samar* (Indianapolis, 1964), especially pp. 68-69, 71-76, 139-45.

13 Beach, "Caperton in Haiti," pp. 164-65; Ludwell Lee Montague, *Haiti and the United States, 1714-1938* (New York, 1966), pp. 213-14; B. Danache, *Le Président Dartiguenave et Les Américains* (Port-au-Prince, 1950), pp. 38-42.

14 Beach, "Caperton in Haiti," pp. 164-65; Caperton, "History of Flag Career," p. 92.

15 Caperton, "History of Flag Career," pp. 89, 92; Beach, "Caperton in Haiti," pp. 169-70.

16 Caperton to SecNavy, August 25, 1915, in Decimal Files, Haiti, Internal. See also Caperton's Report of Operations dated August 27, 1915, ibid.

17 Davis to SecState, August 28, 1915, in Decimal Files, Haiti, U.S. Relations; Caperton's Report of Operations dated August 27, 1915, in Decimal Files, Haiti, Internal; Caperton, "History of Flag Career," p. 117. See also the statement attributed to Davis in *La Plume,* September 4, 1915.

18 Caperton, "History of Flag Career," pp. 63, 68, 78-79, 95-96, 101, 117.

19 Ibid., pp. 107-8, 110; Caperton's Report of Operations dated August 27, 1915, in Decimal Files, Haiti, Internal.

20 Caperton, "History of Flag Career," pp. 92, 101, 103; Caperton to Captain Durell, August 25, 1915, in Box 161, Area File C, Record Group 45, National Archives, Washington, D.C.

21 Caperton, "History of Flag Career," pp. 67, 74, 81, 85-86; New York *Herald,* August 31, 1915.

22 Caperton, "History of Flag Career," pp. 81, 82, 85-86, 97, 101-3, 105, 116.

23 Ibid., pp. 111-15, 120-21, 124; McCrocklin, *Garde d'Haiti,* p. 29. Paymaster Charles Morris acted as administrator of customs from August 23 to September 1, 1915, after which Conard held the post.

24 Elliot Roosevelt, ed., *F. D. R.: His Personal Letters,* vol. 2, *1905-1928* (New York, 1948), p. 290. See also p. 288.

25 Caperton, "History of Flag Career," pp. 123-25; Caperton to SecNavy, September 1, 1915, in Decimal Files, Haiti, Internal.

26 *La Plume,* September 4, 1915; the president's proclamation is printed in the government gazette, *Le Moniteur,* September 4, 1915.

27 *Le Moniteur,* September 4, 1915; Caperton, "History of Flag Career," pp. 125-26.

28 Caperton to SecNavy, September 3, 1915, in Box 161, Area File C, RG 45, National Archives. The proclamation of martial law was printed in parallel columns of English and French in *Le Matin,* September 4, 1915.

29 Caperton, "History of Flag Career," p. 98; Caperton to SecNavy, August 17, 1915, in Decimal Files, Haiti, Internal; Benson to Caperton, August 14, 1915, in Caperton Papers, Library of Congress, Washington, D.C.

30 Benson to Caperton, August 25, 1915, and Caperton to Benson, August 31, 1915, in Caperton Papers, Library of Congress; Caperton, "History of Flag Career," p. 132.

31 Caperton, "History of Flag Career," p. 98; Edward L. Beach, Jr., to the author, July 9, 1971.

32 Danache, *Le Président Dartiguenave et Les Américains,* p. 46.
33 Davis to SecState, August 30, 1915, in Decimal Files, Haiti, U.S. Relations.
34 Davis to SecState, September 4 and September 11, 1915, ibid. See also the New York *Herald,* September 9, 1915; and Caperton, "History of Flag Career," p. 133.
35 *Le Matin,* September 10, 11, 1915; Danache, *Le Président Dartiguenave et Les Américains,* p. 49; New York *Herald,* September 9, 1915.
36 *Literary Digest* 51 (August 14, 1915): 456.
37 Danache, *Le Président Dartiguenave et Les Américains,* p. 47; Beach, "Caperton in Haiti," p. 168.
38 Lansing to AmLegation Port-au-Prince, September 12, 1915, in Decimal Files, Haiti, U.S. Relations; copies of the American and Haitian treaty drafts, with written notations, can be found in the file at this point.
39 Caperton to SecNavy, September 14, 1915, and Lansing to AmLegation Port-au-Prince, September 15, 1915, ibid.
40 Caperton to SecNavy, September 15, 1915, and attached memo, in Decimal Files, Haiti, Internal; Danache, *Le Président Dartiguenave et Les Américains,* p. 50.
41 Davis to SecState, October 25, 1915, in Decimal Files, Haiti, U.S. Relations; Caperton, "History of Flag Career," pp. 144-45.
42 Caperton, "History of Flag Career," p. 146.

CHAPTER 9: *CACOS* AND CONGRESS

1 Caperton's Report of Operations dated August 28, 1915, in Decimal Files, Haiti, Internal; New York *Herald,* September 7, 14, 1915.
2 Caperton's Report of Operations dated August 28, 1915, in Decimal Files, Haiti, Internal.
3 Caperton, "History of Flag Career," p. 119; Daniels to Caperton, September 5, 1915, in Decimal Files, Haiti, Internal.
4 Caperton, "History of Flag Career," p. 118.
5 Ibid., pp. 129-37, 141, 147-48, 150, 155-56.
6 Ibid., p. 157; James H. McCrocklin, *Garde d'Haiti, 1915-1934: Twenty years of organization and training by the United*

States Marine Corps (Annapolis, Md., 1956), pp. 29-30. For a popularized account of Butler's career see Lowell Thomas, *Old Gimlet Eye: The Adventures of Smedley D. Butler as told to Lowell Thomas* (New York, 1933).

7 Caperton, "History of Flag Career," pp. 138-40, 141, 143.

8 Ibid., p. 147; Waller's testimony, in Senate Inquiry, *Hearings,* pp. 609-10.

9 Caperton, "History of Flag Career," pp. 152-56.

10 Ibid., pp. 159-60.

11 Caperton to Benson, September 24, 1915, in Caperton Papers, Library of Congress, Washington, D.C.

12 Caperton, "History of Flag Career," pp. 163-64; Cole's testimony, in Senate Inquiry, *Hearings,* p. 678.

13 Caperton to SecNavy, September 26, 1915, in Decimal Files, Haiti, Internal; Caperton to Benson, September 29, 1915, in Caperton Papers, Library of Congress.

14 Caperton, "History of Flag Career," pp. 164-65, 166, 167.

15 Ibid., pp. 169-70; Waller's testimony, in Senate Inquiry, *Hearings,* pp. 611-12.

16 Caperton, "History of Flag Career," pp. 177, 181, 185, 189; New York *Herald,* October 7, 1915. In paying off the *cacos,* Morenci and Pétion received 15,000 *gourdes* each, while Charles Zamor got 3,200 *gourdes* for his work, according to Caperton's Operations Report dated December 6, 1915, in Decimal Files, Haiti, Internal. Accused of selling out to the Americans, Zamor justified himself in a letter printed in *Le Nouvelliste,* October 14, 1915.

17 Caperton, "History of Flag Career," p. 148; Davis to SecState, September 25, 1915, and Acting SecState to AmLegation Port-au-Prince, September 27, 1915, in Decimal Files, Haiti, U.S. Relations.

18 Caperton, "History of Flag Career," pp. 169, 180; Davis to SecState, October 6, 1915, in Decimal Files, Haiti, U.S. Relations; Dantès Bellegard, *Histoire du Peuple Haitien 1492-1952* (Port-au-Prince, 1953), p. 257.

19 Caperton to Benson, September 24, 1915, in Caperton Papers, Library of Congress.

20 Caperton, "History of Flag Career," pp. 156, 160-61, 165-66, 171, 175-76.

21 Ibid., pp. 176-77.

22 Ibid., pp. 178, 180, 185, 189.

23 *Le Matin,* September 4, 1915.
24 *Haiti Intégrale,* September 18, 1915.
25 Ibid.; *Le Nouvelliste,* September 25, 1915.
26 Caperton, "History of Flag Career," pp. 188, 190, 192; *Le Nouvelliste,* October 21, 1915.
27 Caperton to Benson, October 26, 1915, in Caperton Papers, Library of Congress; Caperton, "History of Flag Career," pp. 196-97.
28 Caperton, "History of Flag Career," pp. 196, 199; Beach, "Caperton in Haiti," p. 184.
29 Caperton, "History of Flag Career," p. 198; Edward L. Beach, Jr., to the author, July 9, 1971.
30 *Le Nouvelliste,* October 26, 1915; Caperton to Benson, November 1, 1915, and Benson to Caperton, November 9, 1915, in Caperton Papers, Library of Congress.
31 Davis to SecState, October 26, 1915, in Decimal Files, Haiti, U.S. Relations; New York *Herald,* November 2, 1915; Caperton, "History of Flag Career," pp. 200, 203, 212.
32 Caperton, "History of Flag Career," pp. 206, 211; Caperton's Reports of Operations dated November 6 and November 19, 1915, in Decimal Files, Haiti, Internal.
33 *Le Nouvelliste,* November 12, 1915; Caperton, "History of Flag Career," p. 211.
34 Caperton, "History of Flag Career," p. 211; Beach, "Caperton in Haiti," p. 185; Oberlin to SecState, November 8, 1915, in Decimal Files, Haiti, U.S. Relations.
35 Daniels to Caperton, November 10, 1915, in Decimal Files, Haiti, Internal.
36 Caperton, "History of Flag Career," p. 213; Daniels to Caperton, November 12, 1915, in Decimal Files, Haiti, Internal.
37 Cole's testimony, in Senate Inquiry, *Hearings,* p. 700; Alcius Beauharnais Jean-Francois, "An essay of anecdotes on the Haitian-American Convention," *La Presse,* July 11, 1930.
38 Caperton, "History of Flag Career," p. 190; Waller's testimony, in Senate Inquiry, *Hearings,* pp. 613-14.
39 Caperton, "History of Flag Career," pp. 197-98, 203, 206, 212, 216; Waller's testimony, in Senate Inquiry, *Hearings,* p. 614; Cole's testimony, ibid., pp. 680-81.
40 Caperton's Report of Operations dated November 19, 1915, in Decimal Files, Haiti, Internal; Daniels to Caperton, November 19, 1915, ibid.

41 Caperton's Report of Operations dated November 19, 1915, in Decimal Files, Haiti, Internal. See also Caperton, "History of Flag Career," p. 218.
42 Daniels to Caperton, November 20, 1915, in Decimal Files, Haiti, Internal.
43 Caperton to Benson, November 21, 1915, in Caperton Papers, Library of Congress.

CHAPTER 10: IMPLEMENTING THE TREATY

1 Caperton, "History of Flag Career," pp. 224-25; Caperton to Benson, December 6, 1916, in Caperton Papers, Library of Congress, Washington, D.C.
2 Caperton, "History of Flag Career," pp. 173, 188.
3 Ibid., pp. 217, 223; Beach, "Caperton in Haiti," pp. 171-73.
4 Caperton, "History of Flag Career," pp. 226-27; Caperton to SecNavy, December 6, 1915, and Caperton's Report of Operations dated January 6, 1916, in Decimal Files, Haiti, Internal.
5 Caperton to Benson, December 6, 1915, in Caperton Papers, Library of Congress.
6 Caperton, "History of Flag Career," pp. 227-28, 229-30, 233-34; Caperton's Report of Operations dated January 6, 1916, and Daniels to Caperton, December 30, 1915, in Decimal Files, Haiti, Internal.
7 Caperton, "History of Flag Career," pp. 231, 233; Caperton's Report of Operations dated December 17, 1915, and Daniels to Caperton, December 8, 1915, in Decimal Files, Haiti, Internal.
8 Caperton's Report of Operations dated December 16, 1915, in Decimal Files, Haiti, Internal.
9 Caperton, "History of Flag Career," pp. 210, 225, 240, 242, 243.
10 Ibid., p. 242; Caperton to Benson, February 23, 1916, in Caperton Papers, Library of Congress.
11 Caperton to Benson, February 23, April 5, March 2, 1916, in Caperton Papers, Library of Congress; William D. Leahy, "Diary," 1: 211, from a typescript copy seen at Manuscripts Division, Library of Congress.
12 Lowell Thomas, *Old Gimlet Eye: The Adventures of Smedley D. Butler as told to Lowell Thomas* (New York, 1933), pp.

209-10; James H. McCrocklin, *Garde d'Haiti: Twenty years of organization and training by the United States Marine Corps* (Annapolis, Md., 1956), p. 61; Hans Schmidt, *The United States Occupation of Haiti 1915-1934* (New Brunswick, N.J., 1971), pp. 86-89.

13 Caperton, "History of Flag Career," pp. 235-36; Caperton's Report of Operations dated January 6, 1916, in Decimal Files, Haiti, Internal. See also *Le Nouvelliste,* January 5, 1916, and *Le Matin,* January 8, 1916.

14 Lansing to AmLegation Port-au-Prince, January 8, 1916, in Decimal Files, Haiti, Internal; Caperton, "History of Flag Career," p. 237.

15 Caperton, "History of Flag Career," pp. 239, 240, 245; McCrocklin, *Garde d'Haiti,* pp. 55-56, 66-68. See also Schmidt, *The United States Occupation of Haiti,* pp. 89-91.

16 Caperton, "History of Flag Career," pp. 236, 237, 238, 242-43; Waller's testimony, in Senate Inquiry, *Hearings,* p. 620; Caperton to Benson, January 5, 1916, in Caperton Papers, Library of Congress.

17 Beach, "Caperton in Haiti," p. 193; *Le Matin,* February 9, 1916 (translation mine).

18 Caperton to Benson, February 23 and March 2, 1916, in Caperton Papers, Library of Congress.

19 Caperton to Benson, February 5 and March 2, 1916, ibid.; Caperton to SecNavy, February 6, 1916, in Decimal Files, Haiti, Internal. The *gourde* was soon permanently stabilized at 20¢ United States currency.

20 Caperton, "History of Flag Career," pp. 243-45; Caperton to Benson, March 2, 1916, in Caperton Papers, Library of Congress.

21 See Harold P. Davis, *Black Democracy: The Story of Haiti* (New York, 1936), pp. 194-201.

22 This account is based on the Report of the Haitian Commission to Washington dated July 10, 1916, which is found in pp. 82-156 of the "Rapport de M. Louis Borno, Secrétaire d'état des relations extérieures, a S. E. Monsieur Le Président de la Republique d'Haiti," printed in *Négociations Diverses, Réclamations et Litiges Diplomatiques, 1916* (Port-au-Prince, 1918).

23 Beach, "Caperton in Haiti," pp. 178-80, 190-92; Leahy, "Diary," 1: 211; Caperton, "History of Flag Career," p. 241.

24 Beach, "Caperton in Haiti," p. 192.
25 Caperton to Benson, March 27, 1916, in Caperton Papers, Library of Congress.
26 Caperton to Benson, April 5, 7, 1916, ibid.; Caperton, "History of Flag Career," p. 246. See also Davis, *Black Democracy,* pp. 201-15.
27 Caperton, "History of Flag Career," pp. 246, 248; New York *Herald,* April 11, 1916; Caperton to Benson, April 7, 1916, in Caperton Papers, Library of Congress.
28 Caperton, "History of Flag Career," p. 247; Caperton to Benson, April 17, 1916, in Caperton Papers, Library of Congress.
29 Caperton, "History of Flag Career," pp. 247-50; Caperton's Reports of Operations dated April 27 and May 5, 1916, in Decimal Files, Haiti, Internal.
30 Caperton, "History of Flag Career," pp. 250-51; Waller's testimony, in Senate Inquiry, *Hearings,* p. 623.
31 Caperton, "History of Flag Career," p. 251.

CHAPTER 11: CONCLUSION

1 Caperton, "History of Flag Career," pp. 253-54; Caperton to Benson, June 26, July 20, 1916, in Caperton Papers, Library of Congress, Washington, D.C.; Waller's comments about Caperton are printed in Hans Schmidt, *The United States Occupation of Haiti, 1915-1934* (New Brunswick, N.J., 1971), p. 79; Waller to Caperton, June 25, 1916, in Caperton Papers, Library of Congress.
2 Caperton to Benson, June 26, 1916, in Caperton Papers, Library of Congress.
3 Caperton to Benson, July 20, 1916, ibid.; Lansing to AmLegation Port-au-Prince, August 25, 1916, in Decimal Files, Haiti, U.S. Relations.
4 Caperton to Benson, July 20, 1916, in Caperton Papers, Library of Congress.
5 Waller to Caperton, June 25, 1916, ibid.; Waller to Wright, May 19, 1916, in Decimal Files, Haiti, Internal; Stabler to SecState, August 16, 1916, in Decimal Files, Haiti, U.S. Relations.

6 B. Danache, *Le Président Dartiguenave et Les Américains* (Port-au-Prince, 1950), pp. 53-59 (translation mine); Schmidt, *The United States Occupation of Haiti,* p. 81.

7 Quoted in Schmidt, *The United States Occupation of Haiti,* p. 79.

8 Danache, *Le Président Dartiguenave et Les Américains,* p. 51 (translation mine); the financial adviser is quoted in Schmidt, *The United States Occupation of Haiti,* p. 78.

9 For an overview of these events see Schmidt, *The United States Occupation of Haiti,* pp. 89-91, 96-107; and Ludwell Lee Montague, *Haiti and the United States, 1714-1938* (New York, 1966), pp. 225-37.

10 Beginning in July 1920, *The Nation* ran almost weekly commentary on the Haitian occupation. For good examples see the issues of July 10 and 17, August 28, September 4, 11, and 25, and December 1, 1920.

11 Senate Inquiry, *Hearings.* The printed hearings total 1842 pages.

12 Ibid., p. 692.

13 Ibid., pp. 674, 692.

14 Ibid., pp. 516, 518.

15 Ibid., pp. 631, 727.

16 Caperton's testimony appears, ibid., pp. 285-421.

17 See ibid., pp. 297, 310, 314.

18 "Memoir on the Political, Economic, and Financial Conditions Existing in the Republic of Haiti under the American Occupation by the Delegates to the United States of the Union Patriotique d'Haiti," in Senate Inquiry, *Hearings,* pp. 5-33 (the "Memoir" was previously printed in full in *The Nation* on May 25, 1921). See *Hearings,* pp. 21-23.

19 See Herbert J. Seligman, "The Conquest of Haiti," *Nation* 3 (July 10, 1920): 35-36; James Weldon Johnson, "Self-Determining Haiti," *Nation* 3, pt. 1 (August 28, 1920): 236-38, pt. 3 (September 11, 1920): 295-97; and Paul H. Douglas, "The American Occupation of Haiti," *Political Science Quarterly* 42 (1927): 228-58.

20 See "Memoir," in Senate Inquiry, *Hearings,* especially pp. 7-15.

21 George Marvin, "Healthy Haiti," *World's Work* 34 (May 1917): 51; Carl Kelsey, "The American Intervention in Haiti

and the Dominican Republic," *Annals of the American Academy of Political and Social Science* 100 (March 1922): 142.

22 Caperton to Benson, October 30, 1916, in Caperton Papers, Library of Congress; Danache, *Le Président Dartiguenave et les Américains*, p. 45 (translation mine).

23 See Beach, "Caperton in Haiti," pp. 218-19.

24 Ibid., pp. 220-21.

25 See Caperton, "History of Flag Career," pp. 2-3.

26 Ibid., p. 160.

27 Ibid., p. 206; Caperton to Benson, February 5, 1916, in Caperton Papers, Library of Congress.

28 Butler's testimony, in Senate Inquiry, *Hearings*, p. 517.

29 Senate Inquiry, *Hearings*, pp. 680, 704, 627.

30 See Arthur C. Millspaugh, *Haiti Under American Control, 1915-1930* (Boston, 1931), p. 63.

A Note on Sources

ARCHIVAL MATERIALS

The largest body of archival materials used for this work was drawn from the Navy Department and State Department records in the National Archives of the United States, Washington, D.C. Record Group 45, Naval Records Collection of the Office of Naval Records and Library, was especially valuable, the greatest concentration of relevant material appearing in Subject Files ZN (Personnel), 1911-1927, and WA-7 (Attaches' Reports), 1911-1927, and Area File C, Caribbean. Particularly useful was a long typescript narrative by Admiral Caperton entitled "History of U.S. Naval Operations Under Command of Rear Admiral W. B. Caperton, USN, Commencing January 5, 1915, Ending April 30, 1919." This account, running to 401 types pages plus another 91 pages of appended documents, is in Subject File ZN (Personnel), 1911-1927. It is essentially a digest of the admiral's operations reports, but contains added commentary and personal interpretations which do not appear in official reports. An invaluable supplement to Caperton's account is Captain Edward L. Beach, "Admiral Caperton in Haiti," a typescript account of more than 200 pages now filed in Record Group 45 under Subject File ZWA-7, "Haiti." Beach, who was Caperton's chief of staff and closest adviser in Haiti, provides a surprisingly frank "inside" view of events and proves to be a sensitive observer of Haitian society.

An indispensable bloc of State Department records are the so-called Decimal Files, held in Record Group 59 of the National Archives' State Department Branch. Used for this study were the Records of the Department of State relating to the Internal Affairs of Haiti, 1910-1929, and the Records of the Department of State relating to Political Relations between the United States and Haiti (1910-1929). These files are comprehensive, integrating naval reports with diplomatic materials.

The Manuscripts Division of the Library of Congress in Washington, D.C. provided a small but significant collection of William B. Caperton's papers, the most important portion of which was a file of personal letters from Caperton to Admiral William S. Benson, chief of naval operations, written during the period covered by this work. Caperton used this correspondence mainly to tell Benson things which could not be said in official reports, and it is therefore valuable. A small number of Caperton items is also held by the Naval History Division, Navy Department, Washington, D.C.

PRINTED MATERIALS

A massive published documentary source is U.S., Congress, Senate, *Inquiry into the occupation and administration of Haiti and Santo Domingo. Hearings before a select committee on Haiti and Santo Domingo, pursuant to Senate Resolution 112,* 67th Cong., 1st and 2d sess., 2 vols. (Washington, D.C.: Government Printing Office, 1922). Also useful for diplomatic data and background was the State Department's documentary series, *Papers Relating to the Foreign Relations of the United States,* particularly the annual sets for 1915 and 1916 and a special supplement, *The Lansing Papers, 1914-1920,* 2 vols. (Washington, D.C.: Government Printing Office, 1940).

Thanks to the courtesy of the Frères de l'Instruction Chrétienne in Port-au-Prince, which maintains a fine library of printed Haitian materials, I was enabled to read the daily press of the capital during the period described. Daily newspapers included *Le Matin, Le Nouvelliste,* and *La Plume,* as well as the short-lived *Haiti Intégrale.* Also useful were *La Moniteur,* the official government gazette, and some printed government reports, particularly: "Rapport de M. Louis Borno, Secrétaire d'état des relations extérieures, a S. E. Monsieur Le Président de la Republique d'Haiti," over 200 pages of relevant commentary and documents printed in *Négociations Diverses, Réclamations et Litiges Diplomatiques, 1916* (Port-au-Prince: Imprimerie Nationale, 1918).

Among American newspapers of Caperton's time, the New York *Herald* showed by far the most thorough and consistent coverage of Latin American affairs. Also used were the New York *Sun* and *Tribune,* the Philadelphia *Press* and *Public Ledger,* and the Baltimore *Sun.* The Nashville *Banner* and *Tennessean,* both of which reported on Admiral Caperton as a local celebrity, are best for personal notes, obituaries, and the like. Surveys of contemporary editorial opinion appeared from time to time in the *Literary Digest.*

Of the copious contemporary comment in the United States on the Haitian occupation, the following are useful and representative samples. Most general is Carl Kelsey, "The American Intervention in Haiti and the Dominican Republic," *Annals of the American Academy of Political and Social Science* 100 (March 1922): 110-99. In the *Literary Digest* see "Our Call of Duty in Haiti," 51 (August 14, 1915): 288; "Straight-Jacketing Haiti," 51 (September 4, 1915): 456; "Our Twenty Years in Haiti," 52 (March 11, 1916): 628. In the *Nation* see Herbert J. Seligman, "The Conquest of Haiti," 3 (July 10, 1920): 35-36; James Weldon Johnson, "Self-Determining Haiti," 3 (August 28, September 4, 11, and 25, 1920): 236-38, 265-67, 295-97, 345-47; Senator Medill McCormack, "Our Failure in Haiti," 3 (December 1, 1920): 615-16; and short, unsigned editorials almost weekly throughout the year 1920. In the *North American Review* see W. P. Livingston, "A Caribbean Derelict," 195 (1912): 261-65. In the *Outlook* see "The Fractious Black Republic," 110 (August 11, 1915): 832-33; "The Island of Haiti," 111 (September 1, 1915): 6; and Booker T. Washington, "Haiti and the United States," 111 (November 17, 1915): 681. In the *Political Science Quarterly* see Paul H. Douglas, "The American Occupation of Haiti," 42 (1927): 228-58, 368-96. In the *Saturday Evening Post* see Josephus Daniels, "The Problem of Haiti," July 12, 1930, pp. 30-36. In *World's Work* see George Marvin, "Helping Haiti," 30 (September 1915): 524-29; "Restoring a Republic," 30 (October 1915): 633-34; George Marvin, "Healthy Haiti," 34 (May 1917): 33-51.

Contemporary first-hand reporting is also found in Samuel Guy Inman, *Through Santo Domingo and Haiti, a cruise with the Marines* (New York, 1919); and Emily Balch Greene, *Occupied Haiti* (New York, 1927).

Helpful biographical or memoir material can be found in James A. Padgett, "Diplomats to Haiti and Their Diplomacy," *Journal of Negro History* 25 (July 1940): 265-330; Joseph L. Schott, *The Ordeal of Samar* (Indianapolis, 1964), a book about L. W. T. Waller's campaign and court-martial in the Philippines; Lowell Thomas, *Old Gimlet Eye: The Adventures of Smedley D. Butler as told to Lowell Thomas* (New York, 1933), a highly popularized and anecdotal memoir which must be used cautiously; and Faustin Wirkus and Taney Dudley, *The White King of La Gonave* (New York, 1931), the story of a former marine. John Houston Craige, *Cannibal Cousins* (New York, 1934), is a curious blend of fact, experience, and sensationalism.

From the Haitian side, B. Danache, *Le Président Dartiguenave et Les Américains* (Port-au-Prince, 1950), contains the views and recollections of a former aide of the president whom Caperton placed in office. Also useful for the Haitian point of view are Dantès Bellegarde, *Histoire du Peuple Haitien, 1492-1952* (Port-au-Prince, 1953), and the same author's *La République d'Haiti et les Etats-Unis devant la justice internationale* (Paris, 1924), *L'Occupation Américaine d'Haiti: ses conséquences morales et economiques* (Port-au-Prince, 1929), and *Un Haitien Parle* (Port-au-Prince, 1934). Other relevant Haitian works include Louis R. E. Gation, *Aspects de l'économie et des finances d'Haiti* (Port-au-Prince, 1944); Joseph Jolibois, *La Doctrine de Monroe* (Port-au-Prince, 1932); Jean-Price Mars, *La Vocation de l'élite* (Port-au-Prince, 1919); and Hogar Nicolas, *L'Occupation Américaine d'Haiti, La Revanche de L'Histoire* (Madrid, ca. 1955).

The classic study of Haitian society is James G. Leyburn, *The Haitian People* (New Haven, Conn., 1941). Much additional information can be found in Robert I. Rotberg, *Haiti: The Politics of Squalor* (Boston, 1971), while Harold P. Davis, *Black Democracy: The Story of Haiti* (New York, 1936), and Rayford Logan, *Haiti and the Dominican Republic* (New York, 1968), are also useful. An excellent account of the entire Haitian occupation is Hans Schmidt, *The United States Occupation of Haiti, 1915-1934* (New Brunswick, N.J., 1971). Arthur C. Millspaugh, *Haiti Under American Control, 1915-1930* (Boston, 1931), is an earlier evaluation, while Ludwell Lee Montague, *Haiti and the United States, 1714-1938,* reprint ed. (New York, 1966), provides a diplomatic overview. A useful and thorough survey of its subject is John W. Blassingame, "The Press and American Intervention in Haiti and the Dominican Republic, 1904-1920," *Caribbean Studies* 9 (July 1969): 27-43. Information about the marines in Haiti can be found in James H. McCrocklin, *Garde d'Haiti, 1915-1934: Twenty years of organization and training by the United States Marine Corps* (Annapolis, Md., 1956).

Arthur S. Link provides a mine of information about the Wilson administration and the State Department in his *Wilson: The New Freedom* (Princeton, N.J., 1956), and *Wilson: The Struggle for Neutrality, 1914-1917* (Princeton, N.J., 1960). The volumes of this series are virtually essential for any serious student of the Wilson years.

For general information about the navy, its ships, and its immediate past, John D. Alden, *The American Steel Navy: A*

Photographic History of the U.S. Navy from the Introduction of the Steel Hull in 1883 to the Cruise of the Great White Fleet, 1907-1909 (Annapolis, Md., 1972), proved especially valuable. Also useful was Peter Dagget Karsten, *The Naval Aristocracy: The Golden Age of Annapolis and the Emergence of Modern American Navalism* (New York, 1972). A number of biographies and memoirs helped to flesh out the author's picture of the naval life of the period, including Damon E. Cummings, *Admiral Richard Wainwright and the United States Fleet* (Washington, D.C., 1962); Robley D. Evans, *A Sailor's Log* (New York, 1908), and *An Admiral's Log* (New York, 1911); Bradley A. Fiske, *From Midshipman to Rear Admiral* (New York, 1919); and Elting E. Morison, *Admiral Sims and the New American Navy* (Boston, 1942). The *Army and Navy Journal* regularly detailed the organization and location of the navy's ships up to 1917, while its seagoing commanders were surveyed in "The War Chiefs of the Navy," *World's Work* 30 (August 1915): 409-27. Finally, a provocative study of military-civilian relations in national policy-making is Richard D. Challener, *Admirals, Generals, and American Foreign Policy, 1898-1914* (Princeton, N.J., 1973).

Miscellaneous sources include the following: Josephus Daniels, *The Wilson Era: Years of Peace, 1910-1917* (Chapel Hill, N.C., 1944); Clyde H. Metcalf, *A History of the United States Marine Corps* (New York, 1939); Elliot Roosevelt, ed., *F. D. R.: His Personal Letters*, vol. 2, *1905-1928* (New York, 1948); "Wards of the United States: Notes on What Our Country is Doing for Santo Domingo, Nicaragua, and Haiti," *National Geographic* 30 (August 1916): 143-77; and Rubin Francis Weston, *Racism in U.S. Imperialism: the Influence of Racial Assumptions on American Foreign Policy, 1893-1946* (Columbia, S.C., 1972).

Index

265

COMPOSED BY THE BLUE RIDGE GROUP, LTD.,
EAST FLAT ROCK, NORTH CAROLINA
MANUFACTURED BY THOMSON-SHORE, INC., DEXTER, MICHIGAN
TEXT IS SET IN PRESS ROMAN, DISPLAY LINES IN TIMES ROMAN

Library of Congress Cataloging in Publication Data
Healy, David F
Gunboat diplomacy in the Wilson era.
Includes bibliographical references and index.
1. United States—Foreign relations—Haiti.
2. Haiti—Foreign relations—United States.
3. Haiti—History—American occupation, 1915-1934.
4. United States—Foreign relations—1913-1921.
I. Title.
E183.8.H2H42   327.73'07294   75-32074
ISBN 0-299-06980-X